MORE GIRLS WHO ROCKED the WORLD

HEROINES FROM ADA LOVELACE TO MISTY COPELAND

MICHELLE ROEHM McCANN

ALADDIN
New York London Toronto Sydney New Delhi

BEYOND WORDS
Hillsboro, Oregon

ALADDIN
An imprint of Simon & Schuster
Children's Publishing Division
1230 Avenue of the Americas
New York, NY 10020

BEYOND WORDS
20827 N.W. Cornell Road, Suite 500
Hillsboro, Oregon 97124-9808
503-531-8700 / 503-531-8773 fax
www.beyondword.com

Managing Editor: Lindsay S. Easterbrooks-Brown
Editor: Emmalisa Sparrow Wood
Copyeditor: Jen Weaver-Neist
Proofreader: Ashley Van Winkle
Interior and cover design: Devon Smith
Composition: William H. Brunson Typography Services
The text of this book was set in Adobe Garamond Pro.
The illustrations for this book were rendered in Adobe Illustrator.

For information about special discounts for bulk purchases, please contact
Simon & Schuster Special Sales at 1-866-506-1949 or business@simonandschuster.com.

The Simon & Schuster Speakers Bureau can bring authors to your live event.
For more information or to book an event contact the Simon & Schuster Speakers Bureau at
1-866-248-3049 or visit our website at www.simonspeakers.com.

Manufactured in the United States of America 0917 FFG

10 9 8 7 6 5 4 3 2 1

Library of Congress Cataloging-in-Publication Data
Names: McCann, Michelle Roehm, 1968- author.
    Title: More girls who rocked the world : heroines from Ada Lovelace to Misty
    Copeland / Michelle Roehm McCann.
        Description: New York : Aladdin ; Hillsboro, Oregon : Beyond Words, 2017. |
        Includes bibliographical references. | Audience: Ages 8-12. | Audience:
        Grades 3 to 7.
    Identifiers: LCCN 2017006516 | ISBN 9781582706405 (hardback) |
    ISBN 9781582706412 (paperback) | ISBN 9781481496889 (eBook)
    Subjects: LCSH: Girls—Biography—Juvenile literature. | Women
    heroes—Biography—Juvenile literature. | Heroes—Biography—Juvenile
    literature. | BISAC: JUVENILE NONFICTION / Biography & Autobiography /
    Women. | JUVENILE NONFICTION / Girls & Women. | JUVENILE NONFICTION /
    History / General.
    Classification: LCC CT3207 .M35 2017 | DDC 920.72—dc23

LC record available at https://lccn.loc.gov/2017006516

For my daughter, Fiona,
who is one of the bravest, kindest,
funnest girls I know. You've got a Big Spirit, girl!
And you inspire me and make me proud every day.
And for my niece Lucy, who brings me great joy
and laughter always. You will both rock the world
in your own unique ways—I'm sure of it!

We cannot all succeed when half of us are held back. We call upon our sisters around the world to be brave—to embrace the strength within themselves and realize their full potential.

—MALALA YOUSAFZAI

CONTENTS

In the profiles in this book, passages of literary narrative based on factual events were imagined by the author in an attempt to draw the reader into the life and perspective of the profiled girl.

Note from the Author

I wrote this book during a very challenging time in my life. We were caring for a beloved family member who was dying. During those dark months, I found great comfort in reading about these girls and women who struggled—who had to fight just to survive, to be heard, and to follow their dreams. Life felt hard, but I also felt like I wasn't alone. As I was writing, I felt surrounded by friends who were there with me at the computer, holding me up, giving me some of their strength.

I was terrified at first by the prospect of finding forty-five *more* girls to write about. *Was it even possible?* Of course it was possible! History and our current world are *full* of amazing girls and women doing amazing things. It's been a while since I wrote the last *Girls Who Rocked the World*, and a lot has changed since then. We've seen the Arab Spring (a series of antigovernment protests in the Middle East and North Africa that took place from late December 2010 into early 2011), and the women and girls of Afghanistan fighting back against the Taliban. We've seen the rise of social media and a whole slew of girls making their voices heard there, as well as starting businesses and stepping into what used to be adults-only territory (magazine publishing, fashion design, mogul-hood!). And there have been some amazing new sports stars who've broken all kinds of records. To my surprise and glee, I found way more girls than I could use! Guess I'll have to write another sequel.

The biggest challenge this time around was finding women and girls from ancient history, especially nonwhite women. The reason, of course, is that white men wrote history, so history is full of white men. Women? Girls? Not so much. Even famous women like Cleopatra have very little recorded about them, and their childhoods even less. For some of the ancient women I included, I had to fill in the blanks a bit. The good news is that I was able to include tons of amazing nonwhite girls who are making history *right now*. White men are no longer the only ones writing the history books these days.

My favorite part of writing this book was uncovering more incredible stuff about the girls and women I thought I already knew, like politician Hillary Clinton, tennis stars Venus and Serena Williams, and writer Beverly Cleary. Four-year-old Hillary punched a neighborhood bully! Venus and Serena started playing tennis in Compton, outside Los Angeles, as gangs fought around them and even threatened them! Beverly Cleary was a reluctant reader when she was a girl, but one special teacher recognized and nurtured her phenomenal talent! I grew to love these women even more after digging into their childhoods and discovering the hurdles they overcame.

I was also thrilled to learn about new girls I had never even heard of. Rock climber Ashima Shiraishi is the best female climber in the world, and she's only sixteen! Nepalese author Jhamak Ghimire writes award-winning poetry with her toes! Soccer star Nadia Nadim began honing her foot skills in Afghanistan, where it was illegal for girls to even play soccer. Adventurer Sarah McNair-Landry dogsledded to the North and South Poles as a teenager. These girls and many more were glorious surprises to me. After writing each chapter, I would call a girlfriend and say, "Do you want to know who my new favorite person is? You won't believe this!"

And I found just as much inspiration from the girls who answered the question "How will you rock the world?" Girls just like you are already thinking about the impact they want to make. Girls from Texas and Oklahoma to Illinois to Alaska and Oregon. Girls like Wendy below, and *all* the girls featured in the book. They're all going to rock the world!

You girls out there reading this, I hope these stories will fire you up as they fired me up. I hope these stories show that you don't have to wait until you're a grown-up to go after your dream, to begin changing the world. Why wait? You might as well start now. And it doesn't have to be something huge. Hillary Clinton started out running for middle school president. And she lost! Mindy Kaling started out watching a lot of TV and imitating skits with her BFF. Bethany Mota and Tavi Gevinson started out making videos in their bedrooms.

It doesn't have to be hard. It doesn't have to be earth-shattering. It starts with you having a passion for something.

Ask yourself, *What do I love? What makes me happy? What interests me?* Then ask, *What small step can I take toward doing that thing?* That's what all the girls in these pages did. They started taking steps toward their dream while they were still girls—just like you!

Like the Nike slogan says, JUST DO IT!

HOW WILL YOU ROCK THE WORLD?

I will rock the world by becoming a doctor. I will help people all over the world. I will also help research treatments on how to actually end diseases. I want to travel the world. I want to help everyone from young to old. I want to help people with their situations, big or small.

WENDY MUNOZ ☼ AGE 15

Esther

492 BC–C. 460 BC ◎ QUEEN ◎ PERSIAN EMPIRE (OR MIDDLE EAST)

*And who knows whether you have not attained royalty
for such a time as this?*

—ESTHER 4:14

Esther stood outside the door to the king's courtyard. Her hands were shaking and her feet felt rooted to the floor. Where would she find the courage to enter? Inside was her husband, King Ahasuerus. But she wasn't allowed to see him unless he asked for her, and he hadn't asked for her in weeks. The punishment for breaking this law? Death.

But she *had* to see the king. The king's prime minister, Haman, had ordered the killing of every Jew in the Persian Empire. Thousands of people would soon be massacred if she didn't convince the king to stop it. There wasn't much time left to save them.

But she was terrified. How could she, a mere girl, change the king's mind about this genocide? What would she say? And if he became angry, would the king have her killed or just banish her, as he had done with his last wife?

1

Fourteen-year-old Esther took a deep breath. She knew she was the only hope left for her family, her people—she had to do it. She *would* convince the king to spare the Jews.

"And if I perish, I perish," she resolved, pushing open the palace door.[1]

The story of Esther has been told for millennia. It was written in the Bible, in the appropriately named book of Esther. Scholars aren't totally sure if Esther was real or not, but King Ahasuerus was real, and the persecution of Jews throughout history was certainly real. Real or not, this is Esther's story.

Over two thousand years ago, the Persian Empire stretched from India to Ethiopia. At that time, it was the largest kingdom in the world. Esther and her family were from the Jewish tribes of Judah and Benjamin, whose people had been conquered by the Babylonians and exiled from their homeland in Jerusalem. Then the Persians conquered the Babylonians, and some of the exiled Jews returned to Jerusalem. But Esther's people decided to stay in Persia, the land of their exile. They weren't treated badly by the ruling Persians, but they weren't exactly equals either.

The Persian leader at the time was King Ahasuerus, a vain and foolish man. When his queen, Vashti, refused one of his orders, he banished her. With no queen to boss around, Ahasuerus went looking for a new one. He held a kingdom-wide beauty contest to find his new bride.

In the nearby city of Shushan lived fourteen-year-old Esther. Her parents died when she was very young, so her cousin Mordecai raised her as his own daughter. When the king's soldiers came to town

"Esther" was her Persian name. Her Jewish name, Haddassah, is also the name for myrtle, a common tree in Persia.

Jewish exiles who returned to Jerusalem from Persia brought the myrtle tree back with them, and it is now a symbol for the nation of Israel.[2]

----

looking for beauties, Mordecai hid Esther—he knew how the king had treated his last wife and feared Esther would be in danger because she was a Jew. But Esther's beauty was well-known and the soldiers found her anyway, taking her to the palace to join the king's harem.

One by one, each woman was paraded before the king. He rejected them all. But Esther must have been quite a looker, because when it was her turn, King Ahasuerus proclaimed her the most beautiful woman in the kingdom. Esther became the new queen of the Persian Empire.

Mordecai missed his cousin dearly, so he spent most of his time hanging around the palace, hoping to see her. One day, he overheard two servants plotting to poison the king, and he sent an urgent message to Esther. Just as her husband was about to drink the poison, Esther rushed to stop him. The king was saved! Esther was praised and the servants were hanged.

Around this same time, King Ahasuerus named Haman his prime minister. Haman was not a nice guy. When he walked down the street, every Persian had to bow down before him. But Mordecai wouldn't bow. When he explained that he was a Jew and Jews don't bow down to humans, only to God, Haman was enraged. He decided he would have Mordecai and *all* the Jews in the kingdom killed for this insult. He cast lots (called *purim*) to choose the day to kill the Jews (the casting of lots, or cleromancy, was like rolling dice to reveal the will of God).

The thoughtless king agreed to Haman's scheme; he wasn't paying much attention. When Mordecai sent a message to Esther about Haman's plan and begged her to intervene, she was terrified. She knew the risk she would have to take. The king hadn't called for her in weeks—perhaps she was falling out of favor—and he was reckless and unpredictable.

Esther fasted and prayed for three days before making her decision. On the third day, she gathered her courage and entered the king's courtyard. To her surprise, the king wasn't angry with her. "What is it you wish, Queen Esther?" he asked.[3] Instead of pleading for her people right away, she invited the king and his prime minister to a banquet she had prepared.

After wining and dining with Esther, the king asked again, "What is it you wish, Queen Esther?" Again, she postponed asking and invited them to a final banquet the next day.

Purim is celebrated by millions of Jews around the world on the 14th day of Adar (in the early spring). To celebrate the holiday, Jews follow four special *mitzvahs*, or commands:

1. Go to synagogue to hear the reading of the book of Esther (also called the *Megillah*). Whenever you hear Haman's name, twirl noisemakers or stamp your feet to banish his evil name.

2. To celebrate Esther's sacrifice, give to the needy.

3. To celebrate friendship and community, send gifts of food to friends.

4. Feast with friends and family. (Other Purim customs involve drinking wine, and wearing masks and costumes.)[6]

That night, Haman decided to build a gallows to hang Mordecai the next day. In a truly miraculous coincidence, the king had trouble sleeping that night and asked his servants to read to him from the royal diary. They read about Mordecai saving the king's life—he had forgotten all about that!

The next morning, Haman came to tell the king of his plan to hang Mordecai, but before he could, the king asked him, "What should be done to a man I wish to honor?"[4] Thinking the king was talking about him, Haman enthusiastically suggested he dress the man in royal clothing, sit him on the king's horse, and then lead him through the streets in celebration.

King Ahasuerus loved this idea and ordered Haman to find Mordecai and make it happen! Thus, instead of leading Mordecai to the gallows, Haman led him through the streets of Shushan on the king's horse. Everyone in town knew the story and witnessed Haman's humiliation.

At Esther's final banquet, the king asked one more time, "What is it you wish?" This time she was ready: "I would like you to save my life and the life of my people."[5] She confessed to the king that she was Jewish and that Haman had ordered death to all of Persia's Jews, including her and Mordecai.

Furious that his prime minister had tried to make a fool of him, he ordered that Haman be hanged from the very gallows he had built to hang Mordecai. The next day it was done and the Jews of Persia rejoiced. Disaster averted, thanks to brave Esther!

King Ahasuerus remained a vain and foolish man, but he made Mordecai his new prime minister. Together, Mordecai and Queen Esther ruled the Persian Empire; for more than two thousand years since, Jews have celebrated Esther's courage and how she saved the Jewish people. This is the meaning behind the holiday Purim. Today, Esther is a feminist icon in the Jewish faith.

HOW WILL YOU ROCK THE WORLD?

I will rock the world by recycling in my neighborhood and picking up trash from the parks. Be clean and go green! Do not leave trash around; instead, pick it up. If you don't, there will be more pollution on the earth, which harms the earth.

DULCE ALVARADO ☼ AGE 16

CleopatRa

69–30 BC ◦ QUEEN ◦ EGYPT

No one in the modern world controls the wealth or territory that Cleopatra did.

—STACY SCHIFF, AUTHOR OF *CLEOPATRA: A LIFE*

Julius Caesar paced the palace floor. What should he do? He didn't trust Egypt's King Ptolemy XIII. The young king had just brought him Pompey's severed head as some kind of peace offering. Pompey was his rival, yes, but that is not how Romans treated their enemies—by stabbing them in the back when they weren't looking. It was a cowardly, treacherous deed.

No, Caesar didn't trust the king at all. And the queen, Cleopatra, was in exile, banished by her young husband and his scheming advisors. Caesar needed the Egyptians and their great wealth to bankroll the military plans of Rome, but whom in Egypt could he trust to be his ally?

His worries were interrupted by a knock on the door. A servant entered carrying a large sack over his shoulder, and before Caesar could protest, the leather strap was loosened and the sack unrolled at his feet.

Out stepped a young woman. Caesar could not believe his eyes!

"I am Cleopatra. I have come to speak with you about Egypt."

Caesar was amazed. Somehow this girl had sneaked past all the king's troops stationed at Egypt's border, into the heavily guarded city of Alexandria, and past all the palace sentries. If she had been caught, she would have been executed on the spot for her treachery. Cleopatra had risked her life on this daring plan to meet with him.

Caesar was pleased. This was the kind of courageous and clever leader he could work with!

—~~~—

Cleopatra's roller-coaster life began in 69 BC, when she was born to King Ptolemy XII. Her ancestors came from Greece, descended from Alexander the Great, and had ruled Egypt for more than 250 years. The Egyptian empire had been the greatest in the world, but by the time of Cleopatra's birth, it was fading. Rome loomed large, and the Ptolemies were only in power because Rome allowed it. Cleopatra wanted to change that—she wanted her family's former lands back to bring Egypt back to its former glory. And she wanted to be in charge.

When Cleopatra was eighteen, her father died. Following Egyptian custom, she became queen, but to do it, she had to marry her ten-year-old brother, Ptolemy XIII, and share power with him! Cleopatra had little interest in co-ruling and took immediate control. From the start, her power was under threat, and two years after Cleopatra became queen, the king's advisors staged a coup, banishing her from Alexandria. She

> "Cleopatra" was a Greek name meaning "her father's glory." And before her father's death, Cleopatra did rule jointly with him for a time.
>
> —~~~—

had to flee for her life across the desert into Syria, roughing it in a tent in the harsh desert while she recruited an army of mercenaries to help her fight her way back to the throne.

During Cleopatra's power struggle, similar struggles were happening in Rome. Two great generals, Julius Caesar and Pompey, fought for control of the Roman Republic. Eventually, their civil war brought them to the shores of Egypt. Pompey arrived first and asked for help from King Ptolemy in exchange for all the help he'd given his father. But Ptolemy's advisors decided it was wiser to kill him than to try to pick the winning side. They sent a boat to bring Pompey to the king, but as soon as it set sail, they stabbed the unsuspecting general to death. Then they put Pompey's severed head in a basket and sent it to Caesar to show their allegiance.

Caesar was not impressed. On the contrary, the murder made him suspicious of King Ptolemy. At nearly the same moment, Cleopatra hatched her brilliant plan to sneak in to Alexandria to meet Caesar. She knew her only hope was to get the power of Rome behind her. But it was 150 miles back to the city, and King Ptolemy's soldiers were at Egypt's eastern border looking for her. She would be killed on sight.

The trip took eight days. Cleopatra and her trusted friend Apollodorus paddled a small boat along the coast. At sundown on the last day, they slipped unseen into Alexandria's harbor and pulled ashore. Apollodorus then rolled up Cleopatra in a large bag (probably the kind used to transport rolls of papyrus) and slung her over his shoulder. Thus disguised, he walked through the city, past the palace guards, and right into Caesar's private rooms.[2]

Was it Cleopatra's beauty that charmed Caesar at that surprise meeting? Probably not. Writings about the queen describe her as ordinary looking; it was her brains and personality that made her irresistible. The ancient historian Plutarch wrote, "Interaction with [Cleopatra] was captivating, and her appearance, along with her persuasiveness in discussion and her character that accompanied all interaction, was stimulating."[3]

Cleopatra and Caesar were immediately smitten with each other. The queen was the answer to Caesar's prayers—a brilliant coleader with a fortune to finance his military dreams. And to Cleopatra, Caesar was more experienced with women than her preteen brother, and it didn't hurt that the military could protect her position in Egypt.[4] Together, they would be a power couple the likes of which the world had never seen.

The two became lovers, and Caesar used his army to defeat her brother, who drowned while trying to escape the battlefield. Caesar made Cleopatra queen of Egypt once again. And once again, due to Egyptian custom, she had to marry her other little brother, twelve-year-old Ptolemy XIV. No matter—Cleopatra and Caesar enjoyed several years together until, finally, a reluctant Caesar was pulled back to business in Rome. Soon after Caesar left, Cleopatra gave birth to his one and only son, whom she called Caesarion ("Little Caesar").

Cleopatra and Caesar couldn't stay apart for long, and a few months later he sent for her. But from the start, Romans hated Cleopatra. For one, Caesar already had a wife! And it was illegal to marry a foreigner or to have multiple wives. Also, Romans didn't believe women should have power, and Cleopatra had as much power as Caesar. Finally, life in Rome was simple and modest. Cleopatra was used to living like a god, and in Rome, Caesar set her up in style.

Romans were horrified.

Public opinion of Caesar plummeted and rumors swirled: he planned to make himself king; Cleopatra would be queen; they would move the capital to Alexandria. When Caesar began sitting on a golden throne and commissioned a golden statue of Cleopatra as a goddess, Romans had had enough. On March 15, 44 BC—the Ides (middle) of March—Caesar's former friends and colleagues attacked him on the senate steps. More than sixty noblemen stabbed Caesar to death (twenty-three times!).[5]

> While in Egypt, Cleopatra and Caesar took a famous cruise up the Nile. They traveled in the luxe royal barge, along with a fleet of 400 boats! They visited the pyramids, the Sphinx, and other treasures. Servants and the Egyptians on shore treated both as living gods. For Cleopatra, it was a brilliant way to advertise her newly restored power. And pregnant with Caesar's child, she was the embodiment of Isis, the Egyptian fertility goddess, with her conquering warrior by her side.[6]

Caesar's murder shocked Rome, but Cleopatra was surely terrified. Her protector was dead and she was next. She packed up her family and fled to Egypt, her position in the world once again shaky. Back in Alexandria, someone poisoned Cleopatra's brother-husband (most likely Cleopatra herself, because he was old enough to threaten her leadership) and she named baby Caesarion her co-ruler.[7]

In Rome, Caesar's second-in-command, Mark Antony (who wasn't involved in the murder), became head of state. But his position was also shaky. Caesar's great-nephew Octavian and another powerful general, Marcus Lepidus, both wanted the job. The three Roman powers came to a compromise: they caught and killed Caesar's assassins, then divided up the Roman Empire between them. Lepidus would rule Africa, Octavian the west, and Antony the east. Of course, ruling the east meant dealing with Cleopatra.

Antony headed east to secure his territories. In what is now Turkey, he sent a message asking Cleopatra to meet him there. He wanted to secure her support for his war against the Parthians. Cleopatra ignored the summons. Antony called her again, and again she ignored him; the queen would not be commanded. Then one afternoon, Antony noticed a crowd gathering along the river. Everyone in town was watching Cleopatra's remarkable arrival. She sailed in on the royal barge—the golden ship with purple sails and oars made of silver—paddling in time to music. Cleopatra reclined beneath a golden canopy, dressed as Venus, and being fanned by boys dressed as Cupid. She certainly knew how to make a first impression.

Just as she had with Caesar, Cleopatra charmed Antony. And as with Caesar, her relationship was as much about politics as it might have been about love. Antony needed Egypt's wealth to secure his position in Rome, and Cleopatra needed land and protection. It was a match made in heaven.

Antony was a handsome, fun-loving man and Cleopatra was ready for some fun (and to finish what she had started with Caesar). Instead of continuing his tour of the eastern territories, Antony followed Cleopatra back to Alexandria, where the two fell in love. They spent the winter of 41–40 BC together, enjoying all the city had to offer. By day, they toured the sights and went to parties; by night, they feasted and drank. Egyptians nicknamed Antony "the new Dionysus," for the Greek god of wine.[8]

Over the next ten years, they had three children together. Antony held on to his power—he made a political union with Octavian by marrying his sister—while Cleopatra ruled Egypt. But in 37 BC, things shifted. Antony and Cleopatra married, which was illegal in Rome. In what was called the Donations of Alexandria, Antony held a lavish ceremony where he named Cleopatra and Caesarion as co-rulers of much of Rome's eastern provinces. He also gave Roman territories to their three younger children. He dubbed Cleopatra the "Queen of Kings." With Egypt's former lands and glory restored and her own power secured, Cleopatra had realized her childhood dream.

> Cleopatra and Antony enjoyed practical jokes. One of their favorite pranks was disguising themselves as beggars and running through the streets of Alexandria, knocking on doors and racing away.[9]

But the good times didn't last. Romans were shocked by Antony's actions and by how much power he'd given Cleopatra. Octavian, whose sister had been humiliated, finally had an excuse to turn against his rival. He whipped up old anti-Cleopatra hatred— she was a temptress who had bewitched Antony—and declared war on her.

In 31 BC, at the battle of Actium, Octavian defeated Egypt's fleet of ships. Antony and Cleopatra fled back to Alexandria to defend Egypt, and the events that followed are right out of Shakespeare's *Romeo and Juliet*. When Octavian attacked Alexandria, Antony received a message that Cleopatra had died in battle. He was so distraught at the news that he threw himself on his sword. As he lay dying, Antony got word that Cleopatra was not actually dead but hiding in the tomb she'd built for herself. Slaves carried Antony to her and he died in her arms.

Cleopatra knew that if Octavian took the city and captured her, she would be taken back to Rome as his prisoner. There, she would be led through the streets as the people heckled and taunted her. It was a humiliation she could never allow. Instead, she killed herself using the bite of a snake, the poisonous asp.[10] She and Antony died together.

Why do we remember Cleopatra's name thousands of years after her death? Not just because she was queen of Egypt—there have been countless queens we don't remember. Her name lives on because she was one of the most powerful leaders in the world during a time when women had no power. She refused to accept what the men in her life would allow her and instead took what she wanted. She ruled the wealthiest kingdom in the world for twenty-two years and managed to make allies and lovers of not one but two of the most powerful men in history. While she's remembered in pop culture as a beautiful temptress, historians agree that her power lay in her personality. She was brilliant, charming, courageous, and ambitious. She was the Queen of Kings.

HOW WILL YOU ROCK THE WORLD?

I will follow my path of destiny to learn what I need to do.

GRACE ELLERS ☀ AGE 13

Grace O'Malley

1530–1603 ✤ PIRATE ✤ IRELAND

A notorious woman in all the coasts of Ireland.

—LORD DEPUTY SIR HENRY SIDNEY SPEAKING ABOUT O'MALLEY

Gráinne stood in her room, a pair of rough scissors clutched tightly in her hand. Her father, the Ní Mháille clan leader, was sailing to Spain in a few days time and Gráinne desperately wanted to go with him. Her mother wanted her to stay home, to learn the work of women: sewing, cooking, entertaining visitors, and running the castle.

But young Gráinne had no interest in any of that. She loved the sea. Fiercely. She loved everything to do with the sea: the ships and trading and traveling. Just like her father. And that is where she wanted to spend her life, not at home in the castle.

"The sea is no place for a young girl," argued her mother.

"Your long hair would get caught in the lines," argued her father.

Well, Gráinne had an answer for their arguments. *Snip, snip, snip*—off it came. All of it. Her long locks lay strewn about her feet, and Gráinne rubbed her fuzzy head with satisfaction.

That evening at dinner, her parents froze when Gráinne walked into the room with her head shaved and boys' clothing in place of her usual wardrobe.

"Now will you take me?" she asked her father. He gave no answer, just sat staring at her. *Will they get angry?* Gráinne worried. *Will they lock me in my room?*

But to her surprise, her parents burst out laughing.

"Aren't you a headstrong one?" said her mother, wiping tears from her eyes.

"From now on, we shall call you Gráinne Mhaol," said her chuckling father.

But Gráinne didn't care if they nicknamed her Gráinne the Bald. They could call her whatever they liked, so long as they let her go to sea.

And they did.

~~~

This story of how Grace O'Malley got her name has been told for nearly five hundred years. It is the stuff of legends, but there is surely some truth in it, for Grace spent the rest of her life at sea. And no matter who tried to stop her—even the queen of England—no one could keep her from it.

Grace O'Malley was born on the northern coast of Ireland. Her name, Gráinne Ní Mháille, would be anglicized to Granuaile Ó Máille and later to Grace O'Malley.[1] In that part of Ireland, her ancestors had made their living fishing for salmon, lobster, and herring. Her father, a successful, wealthy man, was chosen as the chief of the area, and Grace was born at his castle on Clare Island.

As a young girl, Grace sailed with her father up and down the coast of Ireland, and as far away as Spain and Portugal. She learned how to sail and navigate, how to command and defend a ship, and how to fight like a pirate. Grace was a natural.

Fights at sea were common back then. If another clan's ship sailed into their waters, Grace and her father would demand payment for "safe passage" or take their entire cargo. And when they were sailing in someone else's waters, they had to defend their ships and cargo from other raiders. Back then, most seamen were what we now consider pirates.[2]

At sixteen, Grace was married off (like all girls in Ireland at that time); fortunately, it was a good match, to Donal O'Flaherty, of another seafaring clan. Grace was soon in charge of Donal's entire fleet of ships. Donal was a fighter, like his wife, and was eventually killed in a brawl. When his family denied her a "widow's portion" of his property, she took her men off to Clare Island, her childhood home, and began attacking ships and plundering islands all around her. She was building a kingdom (or "queendom") of her own.

Soon she controlled most of Clew Bay, the area around Clare Island, which included five castles and numerous islands. But she desperately wanted Rockfleet Castle because of its safe, commanding position deep inside Clew Bay. So she married its owner, Richard Burke, and that was that. She had a new husband, her favorite castle, *and* a new fleet of ships to command.

Like Grace's first husband, Richard was a hothead. In the 1500s, England was trying to take over Ireland, and when Richard started a rebellion against the English invaders, Grace fought alongside him. In the end, the English troops outnumbered them, and Grace was captured and thrown into prison, where she languished for a year and a half. The justice finally agreed to free her so long as she promised to quit pirating. Of course she promised (she wanted to get out of prison, right?), but she must have had her fingers crossed when she did.

Even as a young girl, Grace wasn't afraid of the pirate life. Once, on the way home from Spain, Grace's fleet was attacked by English pirates. Young Grace hid up in the rigging, as her father had instructed her. But when she saw him attacked by a knife-wielding pirate, she couldn't stay put. With a banshee wail, she pounced on the attacker and saved her father. Then she and the crew battled until all the English pirates were in chains.[3]

Grace didn't stay out of trouble for long. Richard had died while she was in prison, so when she returned to Clew Bay, she took over his castle, lands, and fleet of ships. Soon, Queen Elizabeth I sent a tyrant, Sir Richard Bingham, to conquer the Irish in Grace's area. Sir Bingham hanged or killed anyone who fought English rule. Grace spent years battling him as he tried to destroy the "Pirate Queen." He wrecked much of her fleet and took over much of her territory, until he finally went too far. In 1593, Sir Bingham put Grace's son in prison for treason. It was the last straw. Grace decided to demand justice from Sir Bingham's boss—the queen of England!

> Even childbirth didn't slow Grace down. The day after she gave birth to her first son, Owen, while at sea, Turkish pirates attacked her ship. Grace, who was recovering in her galley, leaped into battle and fought the Turks off.[6]

Grace's followers begged her not to go. Queen Elizabeth was no fan of the Irish, whose rebellion was a thorn in her side. And no Irish chieftain had been brave enough to set foot on English soil . . . until Grace. When the Pirate Queen met with the queen of England, she explained that Sir Bingham's cruelty made the Irish want to rebel even more. Grace promised that if the queen got rid of him, she would pledge allegiance to her; she would stop supporting the Irish rebellion.[4]

Legend says that right about then, Grace sneezed. When the queen handed her a fancy lace handkerchief, Grace blew her nose in it and then tossed it into the fire (as was Irish custom). Everyone in court gasped with shock at this great insult and all were sure the queen would order Grace's head cut off. When the queen demanded to know why she'd done it, Grace explained that in Ireland, they value cleanliness too much to put a dirty hankie in their pocket.

To everyone's surprise, Queen Elizabeth burst out laughing. And then she agreed to Grace's demands.[5]

In time, both queens went back on their promises (of course): Queen Elizabeth returned Sir Bingham to Ireland and Grace rejoined the rebellion. But five hundred years later, Irish children are still hearing this and other heroic tales of their fearless Pirate Queen.

ROCK ON!

OLA OREKUNRIN

As a Nigerian foster child living in England, Ola Orekunrin began medical school while in her teens and graduated at twenty-one, becoming one of the youngest doctors in the United Kingdom. While Ola was still in school, her twelve-year-old sister got gravely ill on a family visit to Nigeria. The local hospital couldn't help, so Ola's family searched for an air ambulance to fly her to a hospital that could. They found none in the whole country, and Ola's sister died. Already passionate about improving healthcare in Africa, Ola learned how to fly helicopters and then founded Flying Doctors Nigeria, the first air ambulance service in West Africa. In its first three years, Flying Doctors transported more than five hundred patients to hospitals for lifesaving care.

Naya Nuki

1788–? ⚜ SURVIVOR ⚜ UNITED STATES

We drew near to the camp, and just as we approached it, a woman made her way through the crowd toward Sacagawea; and recognizing each other, they embraced with most tender affection.

—MERIWETHER LEWIS DESCRIBING THE SURPRISE REUNION OF NAYA NUKI AND SACAGAWEA

Naya Nuki heard it first: the pounding of horse hooves. She and her best friend, Sacagawea, turned to see a scout race past them, shouting, "Attack! Attack!"

"They're coming!" yelled Sacagawea, her eyes wide with fear. The girls dropped the berries and roots they were collecting and searched frantically for hiding places. Naya Nuki splashed across a stream and dove inside a thick clump of bushes. Just then, the enemy attacked. The war cries and crack of enemy "fire sticks" echoed in her head.

Suddenly, a hand reached into the bushes and tore Naya Nuki from her hiding place. She kicked and screamed, but it was no use. Her captor was a grown man—a warrior—and she was a small girl. He yanked her up onto his horse and galloped off. Through her tears of frustration and fear, Naya Nuki saw another horse and rider following them with another prisoner. She wasn't sure whether to be happy or sad when she recognized Sacagawea. As the horses rode swiftly east, and their home and people became more and more distant, Naya Nuki vowed that she would escape. Nothing would stop her from returning to her beloved home.

The attack was over in minutes, but those minutes changed the lives of Sacagawea and Naya Nuki forever. It would even change the history of the United States. One of those girls would become world-famous for her heroic deeds but would suffer estrangement from her people. The other would never be famous, but her strength and courage would bring her lasting happiness with her family and friends. As the two eleven-year-olds were carried off to uncertain futures, neither knew what different roads their lives would take.

Like her more famous friend, Naya Nuki was born sometime around 1788 to the Shoshoni (*shuh-SHO-nee*) people of what is now Idaho. The Shoshoni were a peaceful tribe who struggled to survive the harsh winters of their mountain home. In the fall each year, they had to move from the protective peaks into the vast, open prairies of western Montana to hunt bison. They needed the meat, skin, and bones of the bison for food, shelter, clothing, and tools. Without bison, the Shoshoni could not survive.

But these journeys were extremely dangerous. When white people first arrived in North America decades before, they brought horses and guns to the tribes. The Shoshoni got horses but no guns, so they were vulnerable to attack from their enemies. Many of the more warlike tribes of the prairie—the Crow, Blackfoot, and Hidatsa (*hih-DAHT-sah*)—knew the Shoshoni would come for bison each year. They sent raiding parties to steal their horses, kill warriors, and kidnap women and children.

When Naya Nuki and Sacagawea were eleven, the Hidatsa attacked their tribe near Three Forks, Montana. When the raid was over and the dust settled, the Shoshoni mourned their losses: many people were killed, and fifteen women and children were kidnapped. Naya Nuki, Sacagawea, and the other captives were marched from western Montana to present-day Mandan, North Dakota (home to the Hidatsa)—over one thousand miles on foot!

There is no written record of their march, but from the journals of Lewis and Clark, who traveled the same route a few years later, we can imagine what it must have been like for the prisoners. They hiked in deerskin moccasins across a land covered in prickly pear cactus. Escape would have been impossible with the Hidatsa watching their every move, the open plains offering few hiding places. Prisoners who tried to escape would've been killed on the spot.

Naya Nuki surely knew this, and instead of trying an immediate escape that was sure to fail, she spent her energy memorizing their route. As they followed the Missouri River, she must have noted each turn of the river and the major landmarks, scoping out good hiding places for a later escape. The journey would've taken the group more than a month to make. Imagine being forced to march over thirty miles a day, your feet burning and your heart crying in silent frustration. When they arrived at the Hidatsa village, the warriors distributed the prisoners to various families as slaves.

> Indian slaves did everything from gathering wood, lighting fires, carrying water, collecting and preparing food, and curing hides to cleaning and repairing the Hidatsa longhouses.
>
> ᴪᴪ

Indian slaves, like African slaves on white plantations in the South, lived their lives at their master's whim. They were beaten regularly and had to work from dawn until dusk. Friends and relatives were split up forever when slaves were traded to other tribes or even to the white people.

Not long after bringing the Shoshoni prisoners to their village, a few Hidatsa warriors lost a card game with Pierre Charbonneau, a French fur trapper. In order to pay their debt, they offered him eleven-year-old Sacagawea to take as his "wife." Although Charbonneau already had several other young Indian wives, he accepted their payment. Sacagawea had no choice but to leave for even more distant lands with this white stranger, her new master.

The loss of her best friend undoubtedly panicked Naya Nuki, who realized she, too, could be traded away at any time, making her chances of returning home almost impossible. How she escaped we can only guess, but we do know she was kidnapped in August, so she likely fled that fall. If Naya Nuki merely bolted, with no plan or supplies, she would never have made it back to Idaho. To survive the long, difficult journey, she needed the courage to not only escape her captors but also to steal what she would need to make it home: warm clothing, something to hunt with, and a supply of food to last until she was far away from the Hidatsa village.

Naya Nuki must have been terrified when she sneaked away—she would have been killed if she was caught. And yet the dangers were only beginning. When Lewis and Clark covered the same ground a few years later with more than a dozen armed men, they barely survived. Naya Nuki had to be on constant alert for other Indians who might enslave her again and for wolves, grizzly bears, stampeding bison, snowstorms, and even mosquitos, which carried deadly malaria. For a lone girl to survive, she had to be not only brave but very smart.

It is hard to imagine an eleven-year-old girl walking from North Dakota to Idaho by herself! And Naya Nuki did it with no roads, no signs, no maps, no McDonald's, no tent, no boots, no raincoat—nothing. She followed the Missouri River, probably remembering the landmarks she'd seen before. For at least a month, she had to find or kill anything she ate. Even cooking would've been a long, difficult ordeal to people today—no matches, no pans!

> On her journey, Naya Nuki would have seen bison herds that stretched from one side of the horizon to the other. At that time, there were millions in North America. A hundred years later, whites had hunted the bison almost to extinction to starve out their Indian enemies.

But Naya Nuki did it—she made it across North Dakota and Montana all by herself. Sometime that winter, she crossed the snow-covered mountains between Montana and Idaho (the same mountains that nearly killed several men in the Lewis and Clark group). Less than a year after her capture, the determined girl made it back to her village. She was home. The Shoshoni were so surprised and delighted by her courage and miraculous return that they gave her a new name: *Pop-pank*, or Jumping Fish, because of the way she raced through the stream during the Hidatsa raid. She was a hero, and her story was told for years to come.

In 1805, four years later, the Lewis and Clark expedition arrived in Shoshoni country. The Indians were shocked to see the white men's pale skin. But Naya Nuki was even more shocked when a young Indian woman stepped out from the crowd of men. It was her friend Sacagawea! Captain Lewis described their reunion:

> *The meeting of those people was really affecting, particularly between Sah cah-gar-we-ah [Sacagawea] and an Indian woman who had been taken prisoner at the same time with her, and who had afterwards escaped from the Minnetarees [another name for the Hidatsa] and rejoined her nation.*[1]

Fourteen-year-old Sacagawea traveled the same exhausting trail as Naya Nuki, with an infant strapped to her back. She had given birth to a son just before leaving on the long, dangerous journey.

The two girls hadn't seen each other in years and hadn't expected to ever see each other again. They had a lot of catching up to do.

After a great deal of laughing and crying, they shared their stories. Naya Nuki finally heard the strange path her friend's life had taken: After living with Charbonneau for years, Sacagawea had met Lewis and Clark. The explorers were looking for someone to guide them to the Shoshoni—the only friendly Indians who would sell them horses so they could make it to the Columbia

River and the end of their journey. They realized that Sacagawea would be an invaluable guide and translator since she was practically the only person who had been west, and she also spoke the Shoshoni language. Against their better judgment, they also brought along Charbonneau, who lacked any needed skills.

Each girl survived her share of amazing adventures during those four years apart. But after their brief reconnection, their lives would again take different paths. Lewis and Clark's party stayed with the Shoshoni for a few weeks, and after buying the horses, they left to continue their journey to the Pacific. Sacagawea left with them and never returned to her people. Naya Nuki, on the other hand, never left her people again, a survivor and hero who risked her life to return to her nation.

HOW WILL YOU ROCK THE WORLD?

I will rock the world by being an open-heart surgeon. I'll travel around the world and give people in remote places the help and surgery that they need. It might save lives that might not have been saved without heart surgery. I will do whatever I can to help people who need it.

IZZYIE SANDOZ · 🔆 · AGE 12

MARY WollstoneCRaft Shelley

1797–1851 ✦ WRITER ✦ ENGLAND

Beware; for I am fearless, and therefore powerful.

—FROM MARY SHELLEY'S *FRANKENSTEIN*

Mary closed her eyes and tried to sleep, but sleep wouldn't come. She was worried. All her friends had shared their ghost stories already; she was the only one left who hadn't met the challenge. She didn't want them to think she couldn't do it; she didn't want to seem like a less-talented writer.

As she drifted off, images swirled through her mind. These visions seemed different than her regular dreams. More real. Eventually, one image stayed.

A pale young man kneeled beside a bed. In the bed lay another figure.

Mary trembled in her sleep, for the figure was hideous and unnatural.

It was a giant man with black hair, yellow skin stretched tight over nearly visible muscles and arteries, and dull, milky eyes that stared lifelessly.

In her dream state, Mary knew that the first man was a student who had created the second man.

As the student worked a powerful engine, the monster stirred to life. The student, terrified by his success, fled the machine and went to bed. He slept but was awakened by a noise. When he opened his eyes, his monster was standing beside the bed, staring at him with those same dull eyes. It was alive!

Mary jerked awake, shaking from the terror of her nightmare. She tried to go back to sleep, but the horrifying images wouldn't leave. The young writer thought to herself, *If only I could come up with a story to frighten readers as I've just been frightened!*

And then it hit her: the nightmare was her story!

Eighteen-year-old Mary Shelley had just dreamed up *Frankenstein*. It would become one of the most famous stories of all time.

—◦◦◦—

Mary Shelley was born in London, England, to two famous thinkers and writers of the time. Her father, William Godwin, was a philosopher who argued that the wealthy aristocracy should not control politics— that everyone should have that power. Her mother, Mary Wollstonecraft, was a feminist who argued for equality of the sexes in a time when women couldn't vote or own property and had few education and work opportunities. Both parents were controversial figures with radical ideas and their daughter grew up to be just as notorious.

> Mary's father taught her to read in the cemetery, using her mother's gravestone. She learned her letters by tracing her mother's epitaph with her fingers.[1]
>
> —◦◦◦—

Mary's mother died just after giving birth to her. Her father raised her, providing Mary with an informal but rich and varied education. When Mary was eight, her father started a publishing company that produced mostly children's books. Their home was filled with writers and artists and thinkers, so it isn't much of a surprise that Mary began writing at a young age. "As a child, I scribbled; and my favorite pastime during the hours given to me for recreation was to 'write stories,'" she explained.[2]

Mary's father was usually broke and didn't feel he could raise his children alone, so he remarried a wealthy widow. But Mary and her new stepmother didn't get along; the two competed for her father's affections. Mary's teen years were especially tense—so much so that Godwin sent her to Scotland to live with a family he'd never met but knew only through letters. The travel and freedom from family gave Mary more independence and courage than her father ever imagined.

Free love? No one knows exactly what the relationship was between Shelley and Claire, but we know Claire was also attracted to Shelley and that Mary was jealous. We also know the trio liked to read aloud from *The Empire of the Nairs* about a community where women had equal rights, sex was free and uninhibited, and no one wore any clothes! What is known is that the trio traveled and lived together for years.[3]

Because of his debts, Godwin was constantly looking for investors. One of these potential investors was Percy Bysshe Shelley, a poet and the son of a wealthy British family. Shelley was also a radical who wanted to donate large amounts of his family's fortune to help those less fortunate. He had been expelled from Oxford for writing an essay called "The Necessity of Atheism," and his poetry was political as well, attacking the monarchy, war, and religion.

In 1814, after returning from Scotland, Mary met Shelley at the Godwin home. Shelley was everything Mary wanted in a man: an artist, a revolutionary, and someone who could free her from her family. For weeks, they met secretly at Mary's mother's grave, where they read her political writings to each other and fell in love.

When they announced to Mary's father that they were in love and intended to travel together to Europe, he was furious. Mary was sixteen and Shelley was twenty-one. Even worse, Shelley was already married and his wife was pregnant! When her father tried to keep the lovers apart,

Mary and her stepsister, Claire, dressed in black dresses and bonnets and snuck out of the house in the middle of the night. They joined Shelley and sailed a small boat to Calais, France.

In France, Mary and Shelley kept a joint journal, read aloud to each other, and critiqued each other's writing—a working relationship that would continue for years. Their antiwar beliefs were also strengthened as they traveled through war-torn France. Mary wrote in her journal, "The distress of the inhabitants, whose houses had been burned, their cattle killed, and all their wealth destroyed, has given a sting to my detestation of war . . . which, in his pride, man inflicts upon his fellow."[4]

During their six-week trip, they had no money. Mary's family was poor and wouldn't have helped her anyway, so Shelley had to borrow against his future inheritance. They scraped together enough to buy a mule to carry their luggage, which they later traded for a cheap open carriage. They ran out of money entirely in Switzerland but managed to convince a ship captain to take them home without paying for their tickets. Shelley's wife, Harriet, had to pay the bill—for Mary and Claire as well—when they arrived back in London![5]

And they arrived back to an epic scandal. Unwed, teenage Mary was pregnant with Shelley's child. London society and their families shunned them. Mary's beloved father refused to let her into their house and ignored her on the street! She was devastated.

> Percy and Mary were part of what was later called the Romantic Movement. The art of the time, including their poetry and prose, is characterized by valuing intense emotion (including horror and terror), nature, and the individual. It was the liberal, radical viewpoint of the time.

Life for the couple worsened. Unable to borrow from his family, Shelley was constantly on the move to avoid creditors. Mary had to live with Claire, whom Mary knew had feelings for Shelley. And while Shelley's wife, Harriet, gave birth to his son, Mary miscarried their daughter.

The next year was a bit better. Mary and Shelley were able to move in together, and Mary got pregnant again and gave birth to their son William. Claire began an affair with an even more famous poet, Lord Byron (see the Ada Lovelace chapter) and invited herself to visit him in Europe. When Byron said yes, the trio set off again, hoping to recapture the magic of their earlier adventure.

In May 1816, Mary, Shelley, their son William, and stepsister Claire traveled to Geneva, Switzerland, where they joined Lord Byron in a large villa on the shore of Lake Geneva. It was a rainy summer, which trapped them indoors much of the time.

One dark and rainy June night, Byron proposed a contest: they should each compose a ghost story and share it with the group. Each night, someone shared a tale—everyone but Mary. She couldn't think of anything! It was stressing her out. Then one night, as she drifted to sleep, she had a nightmare: "I saw the pale student of unhallowed arts kneeling beside the thing he had put together. I saw the hideous phantasm of a man stretched out . . ."[6] She awoke terrified and knew she had the start of her story.

> Although Mary claimed she invented the name Frankenstein, she had visited Castle Frankenstein in Germany during her 1814 trip. The castle had been home to Doctor Johann Conrad Dippel, who was infamous for his attempts to reanimate corpses![7]

Eighteen-year-old Mary worked on her short story for the rest of the summer, expanding it into a novel. She set the tale amid the great, desolate Swiss mountains surrounding them and incorporated the scientific discoveries she had discussed with her friends—the spark of life and the possibility of using electricity to reanimate the dead. She also worked in themes of slavery, social justice, class, and even the abandonment she felt as a young girl.

At the end of that magical summer, they returned to Bath, England, hoping to keep Claire and Byron's pregnancy a secret from London society. There, Mary's life turned into a roller coaster again. Her half sister,

Fanny, committed suicide. Then Shelley's wife drowned herself. The end of Shelley's first marriage, however, meant that he and Mary could finally marry. Mary got pregnant again and gave birth to their daughter, Clara. Now a respectable couple in the eyes of society, Mary and Shelley's families resumed talking to them. The shunning was over.

In 1817, Mary finished her manuscript and submitted it to publishers. She didn't put her name on it because she was worried about the public reaction to its controversial themes and ideas. The first three publishers rejected it, but eventually, a publisher specializing in books about ghosts and the occult said yes. *Frankenstein: or, The Modern Prometheus* was published in 1818 to mostly bad reviews. *The Quarterly Review* described it as "a tissue of horrible and disgusting absurdity."[8] In spite of the bad reviews, the book was quite popular and sold well. Most important to Mary, her father loved it.

After *Frankenstein*, Mary's personal life got even rockier. Within a single year, her two children died in her arms at ages one and three (she and Shelley had one more son who survived into adulthood). Then Shelley died when his boat sank off the coast of Italy. Mary was heartbroken and depressed. She never remarried and had no more children. She was sickly for the rest of her life and died of a brain tumor at age fifty-three.

But what saved Mary from utter despair was her work. Through each catastrophe, Mary did what made her happy: she wrote. She wrote five more novels, several travel books, and dozens of biographies, short stories, and articles.

As you know, the creature from *Frankenstein* became one of the most well-known monsters ever. Mary's book has never been out of print, is translated into dozens of languages, has sold millions of copies, and is one of the most famous stories of all time![9] It is much more famous than anything ever written by her husband or her other, more famous friends. *Frankenstein* has been adapted into countless plays, movies, TV shows, and even cartoons. It is considered by many to be the first science-fiction novel ever, as well as the origin of the "mad scientist" character. In fact, *Frankenstein* basically invented the entire horror genre.[10] And all from the imagination of a freethinking eighteen-year-old!

At a time when most women couldn't follow their passions, Mary Shelley followed hers, no matter the consequence. She wrote until the day she died and made a living at it. And she lived the life she wanted— relatively free from the social rules of her time, from the constrictions forced on women. It was a life her mother would have been proud of.

HOW WILL YOU ROCK THE WORLD?

I will rock the world by becoming a nurse, helping those around me by saving lives and bringing new lives into the world.

TIERRIKA HUTTON ☼ AGE 18

Ada Byron Lovelace

1815–1852 ✦ MATHEMATICIAN AND COMPUTER PROGRAMMER
ENGLAND

*The more I study, the more insatiable
do I feel my genius for it to be.*

—ADA BYRON LOVELACE

Ada wandered around the party feeling bored. Many of the greatest minds in England were there at Charles Babbage's invitation, but they were all so old! Whom could she possibly talk to?

Suddenly, a gleam of metal caught her eye. There it was: the Difference Engine! Ada practically sprinted to it (very unladylike).

Babbage's famous mechanical calculator was as beautiful as Ada had imagined. All gleaming brass, gears, and wheels . . . and the whole thing *covered* in numbers! Ada's head practically exploded imagining all the calculations this machine could do! If Babbage ever finished building it.

"You understand it?" Babbage himself was standing beside her.

"Of course," answered Ada. The seventeen-year-old math whiz proceeded to explain in detail to the forty-two-year-old inventor the various calculations she could accomplish with his machine. Charles was amazed. No one understood his Difference Engine. *No one.* Ignoring the rest of the partygoers, Charles and Ada discussed the machine's possibilities well into the evening. It was the beginning of an unlikely friendship and the spark of Ada's greatest contribution to science.

Ada was looking at a prototype for the world's first computer, and soon, she would become the world's first computer programmer.

―――∿∿―――

It's not surprising that Ada was a trailblazer, a young woman who thought "outside the box." Her father was Lord Byron, the most famous poet, philosopher, and adventurer of his time—a superstar of the Victorian age. And her mother, Anne Isabella Milbanke, was an abolitionist (someone who fights to end slavery) and an amateur mathematician at a time when math wasn't really an option for women. Byron called her "the Princess of Parallelograms."[1]

Ada's parents' marriage was short and stormy. Like some superstars today, Lord Byron was kind of a jerk, and his brainy wife quickly got fed up with his shenanigans. One month after Ada was born, Lady Byron left her husband and returned to her parents' home in London. Ada never saw her father again.

After leaving Lord Byron, Ada's mother was terrified her daughter would inherit his "poetic nature," thus leading her down the same road to ruin.[2] Her cure? Math. Ada was introduced to math at a very early age and took to it like a duck to water. Lady Byron traveled a lot, so Ada spent much of her childhood alone. Plenty of time for math.

> Ada's education was odd, to say the least. Her mother insisted her teachers speak only the truth to her—no nonsense stories for young Ada! When she was just five or six, she did her lessons while strapped to a "reclining board" to improve her posture. And if she fidgeted, they tied her hands inside bags and put her in a closet.[3]
>
> ―――∿∿―――

Ada loved numbers and kept herself occupied with math and inventing. She filled sketchbook after sketchbook with calculations, puzzles, and designs for all kinds of inventions.

When she was twelve, Ada designed a flying machine. She built a set of wings and calculated the amount of power it would take to make her creation fly. To test her math, she took a model sailboat out into a storm. The boat's sails were like wings, so she tested the speed of the ship over and over again, each time making small changes to the sail and adjusting her calculations.

Before she could build her flying machine, however, she got sick with the measles. Very sick. Nowadays, we have a vaccine for the measles, but back then, more children got it. And the results were dangerous and sometimes even deadly. Ada had a high fever for many days, and when the fever left, she was blind and paralyzed. Her sight returned after a few weeks, but she couldn't walk for three years. During this time, Ada spent even more of her time doing math. Her mother quizzed her with harder and harder problems. Ada could do them all.

Ada's mother recognized her daughter's passion and gift for math, so she hired tutors to challenge her further. One of her tutors was Mary Fairfax Somerville, herself a well-known scientist and mathematician who wrote books on both subjects. It was Mrs. Somerville who invited Ada to one of Charles Babbage's famous gatherings.

Charles Babbage was a well-known scientist and inventor of the time. He had spent years working on his Difference Engine, a revolutionary mechanical calculator. Babbage was also known for his extravagant parties, which he called "gatherings of the mind" and hosted for the upper class, the well-known,

> The Difference Engine was finally built to completion in 2000. You can see it, in all its glory, at the Science Museum of London.

and the very intelligent.[4] Many of the most famous people from Victorian England would be there—from Charles Darwin to Florence Nightingale to Charles Dickens. It was at one of these parties in 1833 that Ada glimpsed

Babbage's half-built Difference Engine. The teenager's mathematical mind buzzed with possibilities, and Babbage recognized her genius immediately. They became fast friends.

Babbage sent Ada home with thirty of his lab books filled with notes on his next invention: the Analytic Engine. It would be much faster and more accurate than the Difference Engine, and Ada was thrilled to learn of this more advanced calculating machine. She understood that it could solve even harder, more complex problems and could even make decisions by itself. It was a true "thinking machine."[5] It had memory, a processor, and hardware and software just like computers today—but it was made from cogs and levers, and powered by steam.

> The US Department of Defense uses a computer language named Ada in her honor.
>
> ᴧᴧᴧ

For months, Ada worked furiously creating algorithms (math instructions) for Babbage's not-yet-built machine. She wrote countless lines of computations that would instruct the machine in how to solve complex math problems. These algorithms were the world's first computer program.

In 1840, Babbage gave a lecture in Italy about the Analytic Engine, which was written up in French. Ada translated the lecture, adding a set of her own notes to explain how the machine worked and including her own computations for it. These notes took Ada nine months to write and were three times longer than the article itself!

> Ada had some awesome nicknames. She called herself "the Bride of Science" because of her desire to devote her life to science; Babbage called her "the Enchantress of Numbers" because of her seemingly magical math brain!
>
> ᴧᴧᴧ

At age twenty, Ada married William King-Noel and had three children. Her husband was named Earl of Lovelace, which made Ada the Countess of Lovelace (hence her name). Sadly, at the young age of thirty-six, Ada died of cancer, but her influence on the world didn't die with her. There have been movies and plays made about Ada, steampunk stories and graphic novels written about her. Did you know that October 11 is Ada Lovelace Day? It's a day that celebrates Ada by showcasing women in science, technology, engineering, and math and by creating role models for girls in these fields.

Young Ada Lovelace imagined the future of computing long before the first computer was ever built. She could see where the Analytic Engine would lead to: computers that could help with schoolwork, play games, and even design the flying machines she imagined as a girl! And although Babbage never finished building his Difference Engine, Ada inspired future computer scientists around the world.

When Ada's notes were first published in a scientific journal, she signed it with her initials, "A. A. L.," so the public wouldn't know her gender. Scientists of the day might not have given stock to Ada's ideas if they'd known a girl wrote them!

ROCK ON!

KARLIE KLOSS

Sure, Karlie Kloss is gorgeous, and a rich and famous runway model. Sure, she's graced the covers of every fashion magazine from *Elle* to *Vogue*. But did you know she's also a kick-ass computer coder? As smart as she is beautiful, Karlie is passionate about getting more girls into computer programming, a field currently dominated by men. In 2015, she partnered with the Flatiron School and Code.org to create a scholarship called Kode With Klossy. Each month, one young woman wins the scholarship—free tuition to learn how to code and prepare for a tech career. To learn more and maybe apply, check out KodewithKlossy.com.

Annie Oakley

1860–1926 ◦ SHARPSHOOTER ◦ UNITED STATES

I ain't afraid to love a man. I ain't afraid to shoot him either.

—ANNIE OAKLEY

Annie was hungry. Her sisters and brother were hungry too. They had been hungry a lot since their father died. The birds and squirrels seven-year-old Annie caught in her traps just weren't enough. She glanced at the rifle hanging over the mantel. Annie's mother didn't believe a girl should be shooting a gun, but her mother wasn't home.

Although Annie had never shot a gun before, she had been hunting with her father countless times. She was sure she could figure out how to load and shoot it. Annie pulled a chair over to the fireplace, climbed up, and lifted the rifle off its perch. It felt good in her hands. It felt right. That day, young Annie went out and shot herself a squirrel, which her mother happily cooked up for dinner.[1] It was her first time shooting a gun, but it would certainly not be her last. In fact, little Annie went on to become one of the most famous and best shots in the world. All because she was hungry.

~~~

Annie Oakley was born Phoebe Ann Moses on August 13, 1860, in a rugged cabin a few miles outside the tiny town of Woodland, Ohio. It was close to the woods, where Annie spent most days tagging along with her father as he hunted for food.

When she was five, Annie's father was caught in a blizzard and died soon after of pneumonia. That left Annie's mother supporting six children on her small nurse's salary ($1.25 per week).[2] It wasn't enough. They were poor, and the family often went hungry. Fortunately, Annie's father had taught her how to make animal traps, and the five-year-old was able to catch something small for their dinner nearly every day. Once she got ahold of her father's rifle, Annie brought home bigger game, like turkey and rabbit, to feed her family.

In spite of her mother's protests, Annie was a crack shot by the age of ten. "My mother . . . was perfectly horrified when I began shooting and tried to keep me in school, but I would run away and go quail shooting in the woods."[3]

While Annie's early years might seem hard, her life soon got even harder. Annie's mother felt she couldn't afford to take care of her children anymore, so she sent them away. Nine-year-old Annie was sent to work at the Darke County Infirmary, a "poorhouse," where orphans or homeless people lived and worked when they had nowhere else to go. Annie was such a good worker that it wasn't long before she got what she thought was a lucky break: a couple offered her a job working for them. They said they'd give her time off to hunt and go to school, and they promised her fifty cents a week.

For the next two years, Annie's life was a nightmare. The couple didn't pay her a dime, working her like a slave, beating her, and keeping all the letters

> If there's a gun in your or someone else's house, don't do what Annie did! Guns are very dangerous, and you should never touch one unless you are trained and have a license. And have your parents' permission.
>
> ~~~

she wrote her mother. Soon, Annie had had enough. One day when they left her alone in the house, she snuck away and hopped on a train back home.

Annie soon began bringing home the bacon by entering local shooting contests called "turkey shoots." In turkey shoots, you didn't shoot an actual turkey but a bull's-eye, from fifty-eight feet away.

"It kind of galled me," she said, describing her competition, "to see those hulking chaps so tickled in what was no doubt to them my impertinence in daring to shoot against them—and I reckon I was tickled too when I walked away with the prize."[4]

> Once, the family Annie worked for, or "the wolves" (as she called them), put Annie outside barefoot in the freezing cold to punish her for falling asleep during her chores.

Soon, Annie won so many prizes that she was banned from entering any more contests. Instead, she started selling the game she hunted to local shops in Ohio. The shopkeepers sold her turkeys and pheasants to fancy hotels and restaurants in the bigger cities nearby. Unlike most hunters who killed birds with buckshot that had to be painstakingly removed before you could eat it, Annie was such a good shot that she could kill a bird with one bullet. Much easier to prepare for dinner! Annie's birds were in high demand, and she was soon making more money than she'd ever seen. At age fifteen, Annie proudly presented her mom with $200 . . . enough to pay off the mortgage for their family's house!

Believe it or not, Annie's shooting skill not only bought her a house, but it brought her true love! In 1875, a shooting match was organized in nearby Cincinnati with a cash prize of one hundred dollars (a fortune back then). Annie couldn't resist. What she didn't know was that she'd be up against a professional sharpshooter: Frank Butler.

Frank was surprised by his competition as well: "I almost dropped dead when a little slim girl in short dresses stepped out to the mark with me."[5] The two were neck and neck for most of the match, each hitting all their flying targets . . . until Frank missed and Annie didn't. She won the match with a perfect score. She also won Frank's heart.

Frank and Annie married a year later.

Frank earned a living by performing in a traveling show (part of his act was shooting an apple off the head of his poodle, George!). He invited his new wife to join him, and the sharpshooting teen was an instant hit. She shot the flames off candles, the corks out of bottles, and the end of a cigarette out of her husband's mouth! "Butler and Oakley" toured the Midwest, and before long, Annie was the main attraction.

In 1885, she and Frank joined a new act called Buffalo Bill's Wild West show. It was a combination rodeo, circus, and theater that aimed to show audiences around the world what life in the Wild West was supposedly like. The show had a huge cast of cowboys and Indians, as well as hundreds of horses, elk, and bison.

Annie performed with the Wild West show for the next seventeen years. In her act, Annie skipped into the arena wearing a hand-embroidered Western dress and cowgirl hat, blowing kisses to the crowd. She played up her playful, girlish persona so that what came next was even more surprising to the audience: Annie could shoot with her right hand or her left! She blasted clay targets that Frank tossed in the air—first one at a time, then two, then three, then four. She never missed.

Annie could toss a couple of glass balls in the air, spin around, and shoot both before they hit the ground. She could lie on her back

One of Annie's biggest fans was the great Lakota chief, Sitting Bull. He was so impressed with her that he lavished her with gifts (including the moccasins he'd worn when he battled General Custer), and insisted on adopting her as his daughter. He named her *Watanya Cicilla,* which means "Little Sure Shot." Later, he joined Buffalo Bill's Wild West show just so he could spend more time with her.[6]

Annie loved to sew and took great pride in creating and decorating her own costumes. She embroidered them with flowers and other designs and added intricate beadwork. By the end of her career, she had 35 in all.

Annie rode more than just horses. She once hitched up a moose to a sled and took him for a spin down a snowy New York City street. The moose crashed into an apple cart and gobbled up all the fruit, leaving Annie to pay the bill!

⎯⎯⎯⎯⎯

Just like celebrities today, Annie had to deal with false stories in the media. While in France, newspapers around the world reported that Annie was dead. She had to telegram to her parents in Ohio explaining that she was, in fact, still alive.

⎯⎯⎯⎯⎯

across a chair and hit a target upside down, and she could hit a target while turned away from it, looking in a mirror and shooting over her shoulder. As if that wasn't hard enough, she would up the ante by hitting targets while riding a galloping horse, and then hit targets while *standing* on a galloping horse! Crowds were amazed—they'd never seen anything like Annie Oakley.

Before long, this country girl was traveling the world. The Wild West show went to New York City to perform, and officials threw them a parade right through downtown. Tens of thousands of spectators came to the show, making it the most popular entertainment in New York history.[7] Next, they headed to Europe, loading all the cowboys, Indians, and hundreds of animals onto a ship. Think how that must have smelled belowdecks!

Annie spent years touring Europe. In England, she met and performed for Queen Victoria, who called her a "clever, clever little girl."[8] She won a shooting match against the Grand Duke of Russia. And in Germany, she rescued a prince by pulling him out of the way of a stampeding horse.

Annie's life was filled with adventure. When she returned to America, Annie Oakley was one of the country's biggest stars. Her shows drew record crowds wherever she went, and she continued to add new and more daring tricks to her act. She "scrambled" eggs by shooting a batch of them midair. She shot a playing card, cutting it in half. Annie never rested on her reputation.

Annie spent her later years giving back, donating her time and skills to those in need. She performed in benefits for the Red Cross, for veterans' hospitals, for soldiers wounded in World War I, and for many other causes. She also discovered a passion for teaching and taught more than fifteen thousand women how to shoot (without charging a cent!).[9]

Even at the end of her life, Annie was still a "crack shot," as Frank called her, able to hit every target he threw. She died of pernicious anemia in November 1926 at age sixty-six. Her beloved Frank died eighteen days later.

Annie Oakley loved to shoot and went after her dream with a laser focus. Although her near-slavery childhood was a lot like Cinderella's, Annie made her own magic to escape. Through skill and determination, she traveled the world and became a sharpshooting superstar.

Any woman who does not thoroughly enjoy tramping across the country on a clear, frosty morning with a good gun and a pair of dogs does not know how to enjoy life. God intended woman to be outside as well as men, and they do not know what they are missing when they stay cooped up in the house.

—ANNIE OAKLEY

HOW WILL YOU ROCK THE WORLD?

I plan to rock the world by becoming an outstanding track athlete. I have run track for many years, and my goal is to develop my skills so that I can reach the Olympics. I will inspire girls younger than me to follow their dreams and reach for the stars.

DENEE HUCKABY AGE 14

Nellie Bly

1864–1922 ◈ JOURNALIST ◈ UNITED STATES

Could I pass a week in the insane asylum at Blackwell's Island?
I said I could and I would. And I did.

—NELLIE BLY, *THE EVENING-JOURNAL* 1922

Nellie was furious. She reread the column in the *Pittsburg Dispatch* written by "Mr. Quiet Observations" that he had titled "What Girls Are Good For." According to QO, not much. He argued that the working woman was a "monstrosity" and that her only proper place was in the home, caring for children and doing housekeeping.[1]

"Rubbish!" thought Nellie. What about widows with no men to provide for them? How could those women survive if they didn't earn money? Nellie and her mother had been working outside the home for years, ever since Nellie's father had died. What choice did they have? And exactly *how* were men more qualified to work than women? How dare this writer judge them!

Nellie grabbed a pen and paper. QO was an idiot and she wanted him to know it. She began writing a letter in response.

"Dear QO," she began. "What shall we do with the girls? Those without talent, without beauty, without money."[2] She went on to explain what it was like to be a poor single woman in American society, struggling to put food on the table for hungry children in a world with few options for women who needed work.

Nellie's arguments poured out onto the page. And solutions too:

Here would be a good field for believers in women's rights. Let them forego their lecturing and writing and go to work; more work and less talk. Take some girls that have the ability, procure for them situations, start them on their way, and by so doing accomplish more than by years of talking.[3]

She finished her letter, sealed it, and mailed it off to the newspaper. Eighteen-year-old Nellie Bly had no idea that this was just the beginning of her long and renowned career in journalism.

—〰〰—

Nellie was born Elizabeth Jane Cochran in 1864, in Cochran's Mills, Pennsylvania. Her family was wealthy since her father owned the town mill and most of the land around their farmhouse. Indeed, the town was named for him! But it didn't last long. When Nellie was just six years old, her father died and the family was plunged into poverty. Nellie's mother was not allowed to run the mill and had to sell their house to survive. Later, her mother remarried, but her new husband was abusive and couldn't support their family. After six horrible years, Nellie's mother filed for divorce and fourteen-year-old Nellie had to testify in court.

Those awful years made Nellie realize that she never wanted to depend on a man to take care of her. She wanted to earn her own money, to be independent. The only career open to women back then was teaching, so Nellie enrolled in a teacher's college. But after one semester, her money ran out and she had to quit.

Nellie's childhood nickname was "Pink." While other girls wore drab brown or gray dresses, Nellie's mother always dressed her in bright pink. Although she later dropped the nickname, Nellie learned early the value of standing out from the crowd.

At sixteen, Nellie and her family moved to Pittsburg. Her younger brothers quickly found good, white-collar jobs, but Nellie looked for five years and found nothing suitable. The only nonteaching work for women was hard labor in factories or sweatshops. When she was eighteen, Nellie wrote an anonymous rebuttal to a sexist column in the *Pittsburg Dispatch* in which she vented her frustration with the inequalities she'd faced.

The editor of the paper was impressed with Nellie's passion and printed an ad asking the author to identify herself. When she came to the office, he was even more impressed and offered her a full-time job writing articles for the paper. This was an incredible feat at a time when female reporters were unheard of. Her boss gave her the pen name Nellie Bly, after a popular song.

Nellie began her journalism career with a bang. She wrote a series of articles about the challenges of working girls and women—something she knew a lot about—and about the horrible conditions for female factory workers. Determined to set herself apart from other reporters, she caught a train to Mexico and sent home articles about the lives and traditions of the people there. When she criticized the corrupt Mexican government, she had to flee the country to avoid being arrested.

Though Nellie's articles were popular, her editor decided to move her to the so-called "women's pages," where she had to write about fashion, gardening, society, and the arts. Nellie was not pleased. She wanted to report "real" news. So one day, she just didn't show up for work and left a note saying, "I am off for New York. Look out for me. Bly."[4]

Finding a job in New York City, however, proved challenging, even for Nellie Bly. After six months of looking, Nellie finally talked her way into New York's biggest paper, the *New York World*. Lucky for her, they happened to be looking for a reporter to go on a dangerous assignment:

sneak undercover into the Women's Lunatic Asylum at Blackwell's Island! (Blackwell's Island is now known as Roosevelt Island.) There were rumors of horrible conditions and abuse—conditions which Nellie would have to live in for ten days and then report on. She was scared, but she knew a great opportunity when she saw one. She accepted.

It turned out Nellie was also a good actress. She convinced judges and doctors she was insane. "Positively demented," wrote one doctor. "I consider it a hopeless case."[5] And they locked her up.

Inside the asylum, Nellie experienced its horrors in person. She was fed gruel, rotten meat, and dirty water. Some patients were tied up with ropes, while others were forced to sit all day on hard benches. The asylum was filthy and overrun with rats. Nurses poured freezing water over patients to bathe them, and also yelled at and beat them. "What, excepting torture, would produce insanity quicker than this treatment?" Nellie later wrote.[6]

After her release, Nellie's scoop made the front page of the paper: "Inside the Madhouse." The story caused an uproar that made Nellie Bly a household name. She was the *World*'s star reporter, and she was just twenty-three years old! But more important, Nellie's reporting led to better living conditions in New York's asylums.

Nellie's editors let her come up with her own story ideas after that. She soon had a doozy. There was a popular novel called *Around the World in Eighty Days*, and Nellie wanted to beat that fictional record. This was not an easy task in the late 1800s; you couldn't just hop in an airplane and fly around the world. Nellie would have to take steamships and trains, which were slow and rarely on schedule.

To make traveling faster and easier, Nellie took almost nothing with her. She took one dress, which she wore, a long, sturdy coat, and several pairs of underwear. She carried just one small handbag with her bathroom necessities and a smaller bag around her neck for her money. That was it for over two months of hard travel![7]

The race was on starting at 9:40 AM on November 14, 1889, when Nellie sailed out of Hoboken, New Jersey. Nellie traveled across the Atlantic, through Europe, across the Mediterranean Sea, through the Suez Canal, and into the Middle East. She crossed the Arabian Sea to India and then went on to Southeast Asia, China, and Japan. She sailed across the Pacific Ocean to San Francisco, where she rode trains across the country. On her trip, she battled seasickness, monsoons, snowstorms, and endless, maddening delays. But all the while, Nellie sent stories about her journey and adventures back to the *World*.[8]

> While delayed for a day in Singapore, Nellie had time to buy herself a monkey, which she named McGinty.
> —ᴡᴡ—

On January 25, 1890, Nellie Bly arrived back in New Jersey, where a cheering crowd greeted her at the train station. The journey had taken her seventy-two days, six hours, and eleven minutes.[9] She had done it—*and* she had beaten the record! If Nellie had been famous before, she was a superstar now. Tens of thousands of people had followed her adventures for months, increasing the *World*'s circulation by twenty-four thousand readers. The paper described Nellie as "the best known and most widely talked of young woman on earth today." Her face was everywhere—on toys, games, cigars, and soaps—and her name was recognized around the world![10]

> While Nellie was running her dead husband's business, she invented and patented an improved milk can and a stacking garbage can.[11]
> —ᴡᴡ—

In her thirties, Nellie did finally marry—to a millionaire who was forty years older than her! When he died, she took over his business, becoming president of Iron Clad Manufacturing Co., which made metal containers. She spent some years as an inventor and became one of the top female industrialists in America. But when employee embezzlement led to bankruptcy, Nellie was ready to go back to her true calling. She wrote and reported for the rest of her life. At age fifty, she was the first female journalist to report from the Eastern Front of World War I. She continued to write about the rights of women and the working class, and the plight of orphans.

Nellie Bly died in 1922 at the age of fifty-seven. Her editor at the *New York World* wrote of her, "She was the best reporter in America."[12] Nellie Bly's own motto was an excellent summary of her life: "Energy rightly applied and directed will accomplish anything."[13]

HOW WILL YOU ROCK THE WORLD?

The best way to rock the world is to bring unity to it. Unity can stop war and bring peace. I want to help stop the hate and bring love. I will rock the world by spreading the motto of the United States: *e pluribus unum*—out of many, we are one!

RACHEL TIPPENS ⚛ AGE 16

Eleanor Roosevelt

1884–1962 ☀ ACTIVIST AND UNITED NATIONS DELEGATE ☀ UNITED STATES

You gain strength, courage, and confidence by every experience in which you really stop to look fear in the face....
You must do the thing you think you cannot do.

—ELEANOR ROOSEVELT

The little girl held tightly to Eleanor's hand as they walked through the dark slum. She was coughing and shivering in the cold night air.

"Will she be all right?" asked Franklin, wrapping her in his coat.

"I think so," answered Eleanor, her voice heavy with worry, "but we need to get her home and into bed."

Home, however, was not much better than the street. They took the girl to the dirty, overcrowded tenement room she shared with her large family. The ceiling was a sheet of tin, the floor a few rough planks, and the walls tarpaper; the cold wind whistled through many holes. They could see one stained mattress in the corner and a small table with no chairs. Otherwise, the room was bare. A single candle lit the faces of the girl's parents and siblings. They looked hungry and tired.

Eleanor was used to seeing this kind of suffering; she'd been working with poor immigrant families for months. But Franklin was shocked. All the way home, he said again and again, "I can't believe human beings live that way." Nor could he believe that a girl of his social class was immersed in that world. But Eleanor wasn't like the other girls he knew.

Eleanor was just eighteen when she introduced Franklin Roosevelt—the man who would become her husband and, later, president of the United States—to a world he had never seen. (And she would continue to enlighten her husband and affect change upon the world for the rest of her life.) As a teen, she changed lives one at a time; as an adult, she would help people on a grand scale. Historians have called her "the most influential woman of our times," and many would argue that Eleanor did more to fight poverty, racism, sexism, and other injustices than any other woman in history. She was truly the "First Lady of the World."

The self-assurance Eleanor would be known for in later years was virtually nonexistent during her childhood. Born to a well-known, upper-class family, Eleanor was raised to be no more than a wealthy debutante and wife. For this job, a girl's main asset was beauty, not brains. Eleanor's mother was just such a beauty and worried over her daughter's looks. She often hurt the feelings of her serious, shy child by calling her "Granny." Eleanor's father, on the other hand, always let his "little Nell" know she was his favorite.

In spite of their wealth, the Roosevelts were not a happy family. Eleanor's parents fought bitterly about her father's drinking and affairs. And just when things looked like they couldn't get any worse, Eleanor's mother had her father committed to an asylum to receive treatment for his alcoholism. Even after his release, he didn't come home, and Eleanor missed her father terribly. But tragedy really struck when Eleanor was eight: her mother came down with diphtheria and died. The children saw their father briefly for the funeral but were packed off to live with their grandmother, as their father was still deemed unfit to raise them.

Grandmother Hall was a stern woman. Her house was a big, drafty, depressing place where noisy playing was forbidden; Eleanor retreated even further into herself, and books became her escape. Her only joy was visiting her father, but this was also stressful, as he grew more and more unpredictable. Once, he took Eleanor to his private men's club in New York City and left her sitting out on the sidewalk. Six hours later, the doorman finally figured out who the girl was and told her Mr. Roosevelt had left hours before. She had to take a cab home. Two years after her mother's death, Eleanor's father died after taking a bad fall while drunk. Any happiness Eleanor had known disappeared. This sadness would plague her for the rest of her life, but from her painful childhood sprang her empathy and desire to help others who were suffering.

She finally escaped the dreariness of Grandmother Hall's house when she was sent away to boarding school in England. Allenswood Academy, a girls' school outside London, was run by a free-thinking French woman named Marie Souvestre, who believed women should be more than ornaments—they should think for themselves. She taught her girls not only about literature and art but also about social and political issues.

Sou, as the students called her, took a special interest in her shy American student. She brought Eleanor with her to Europe and encouraged her self-reliance by having the young girl make all their travel arrangements. Eleanor recalled, "I felt that I was starting a new life, free from all my former sins and traditions. . . . This was the first time in my life that my fears left me."[1] Eleanor learned, explored, debated, and began to find herself; she was happy for the first time in her life.

Eleanor's happy freedom did not last long, however. Before she could start her senior year at Allenswood, Grandmother Hall called her back to America. Again, it was not her intellect that mattered to her family. Eleanor was a debutante, after all, and at age eighteen, it was time for her to make her official introduction to society. Although she was horrified, Eleanor had to obey. She returned to New York and began her rounds of parties and dances. Never good at small talk, Eleanor preferred to discuss serious issues, which was not considered ladylike.

But school had begun a transformation in young Eleanor that could not be stopped. Despite the endless social events on her calendar, she always found a way to bring meaning into her life. She volunteered in settlement houses—shelters for the thousands of immigrants flooding into New York at that time. Working with poor families was a revelation for Eleanor. At Allenswood, they had discussed poverty and injustice, but this was the first time she saw the reality of it. Unlike other high-society women, who just donated money, Eleanor gave her time—and lots of it. She had always wanted to be useful, and now there were people who really needed her. She dove in.

Many of the families Eleanor worked with labored in sweatshops—factories that forced people to work long hours in terrible conditions for very small amounts of money. Eleanor began visiting these places and reporting her findings to the National Consumers League. She was terrified at first but found strength in the anger these visits made her feel: "I saw little children of four or five sitting at tables until they dropped with fatigue."[2]

During her social debut, Eleanor did meet one young man who was attracted to her ideas and opinions: handsome Franklin Delano Roosevelt, her fifth cousin, once removed. Franklin loved talking with her and thought she was the most fascinating woman he'd ever met. When he picked her up at the settlement houses, she opened his eyes to the world that existed outside their privileged cocoon. He'd never realized how much his fellow Americans were suffering, right under his nose. Franklin was deeply interested in the realities of life, and Eleanor showed him those realities. When he proposed, she was surprised and asked why he would choose someone so plain. He told her that with her by his side, he might one day amount to something.

But after marriage, Eleanor buried her newfound independence and social passion. Her domineering mother-in-law, her husband's career, and her constant pregnancies discouraged her from pursuing her own dreams. Over the next ten years, Eleanor gave birth to six children, five of whom survived.

As Franklin's political career took off, Eleanor's life improved. They moved away from his overbearing mother, and Eleanor began to emerge from her shell. When the United States joined the fight in World War I, she got involved in her social causes again. She joined the Red Cross and cofounded the Navy Relief Fund, which served meals to hungry soldiers traveling through Washington, DC. While inspecting hospitals for the Red Cross, she discovered the horrible living conditions and treatment of the mentally ill (many of whom had suffered breakdowns while fighting in the war). For the first time, Eleanor utilized her husband's political connections and was able to get increased funding to these institutions.

During this time of rebirth, Eleanor was dealt another blow: she discovered Franklin was having an affair. For a woman whose childhood love had been uncertain, her husband's lie was crushing. "The bottom dropped out of my own particular world,"[3] she recalled. She had lived her life according to Franklin's needs for over a decade; now she would have to stand on her own again. She offered Franklin a divorce, but he refused—partially because it would ruin his career but also because he still cared for her. From then on, however, their marriage was more of a business partnership.

> After discovering Franklin's affair, Eleanor had him build her a country house, which she named "Val-Kill" for a nearby stream. It was her haven and a hangout for her women friends. Franklin was only allowed to visit.
>
> ~~~

Eleanor dove into politics. Women had recently won the right to vote (in 1920), so she joined the League of Women Voters to help them make intelligent voting choices. She kept members up to date on issues like labor reform and children's rights, and she helped edit the *Women's Democratic News*. She even worked for the Women's Trade Union League, a radical feminist group fighting to decrease the workweek, raise minimum wages, and end child labor. When she and some friends took over the Todhunter School for Girls, Eleanor discovered another passion: teaching. As a teacher, she could push and inspire her students as Sou had pushed and inspired her.

In addition to her own interests, Eleanor continued to assist her husband and his career. In 1921, Franklin was diagnosed with polio, a paralyzing disease. He had difficulty walking for the rest of his life, relying on a cane, bulky leg braces, or a wheelchair. He also relied on his wife. When Franklin was elected governor of New York in 1928, she began visiting state institutions he could not access, doing on-site inspections for him, reporting on what needed to be improved.

In 1929, the stock market crashed; banks and businesses failed, farmers lost their land, people lost their homes, and twelve million Americans lost their jobs. It was the start of the Great Depression. Franklin decided to run for president during this difficult time, promising to give the voters a "New Deal": new relief programs, new jobs, new houses. Eleanor, however, was not excited about the idea of becoming First Lady. At that time, the wife of the president was expected to host dinners, make small talk, and look good on her husband's arm—tasks Eleanor had hated since she was a teen. And she dreaded giving up her political and social work. But when Franklin won in 1932, Eleanor made the most of her new role.

Just as young Eleanor was unlike any girl Franklin had ever met, Eleanor was unlike any First Lady the nation had ever seen. As one Maine lobsterman put it, "She ain't stuck up, she ain't dressed up, and she ain't afeared to talk."[4] Franklin held press conferences and so did Eleanor—that was a first. And to encourage newspapers to employ more women, she only allowed female reporters into her popular press conferences. She also felt that struggling Americans needed some encouraging contact from the White House, so Eleanor gave radio talks, wrote monthly magazine articles, and wrote a popular daily newspaper column called "My Day." She wrote the column for nearly thirty years; at its height, it appeared in ninety papers across the country and was read by more than four million Americans.[5]

She did not give up her political work either; she now played a more powerful role from behind the scenes. As always, she had a considerable influence on her husband, convincing him to put women into top

Eleanor was the first
president's wife to
earn her own money
through her writing,
lecturing, and radio and
TV broadcasts. Her
salary was usually higher
than her husband's,
but she donated most
of it to charity.

government posts. She traveled the country, reporting back to him on how Americans were surviving the Depression and whether government programs were helping. And Eleanor brought comfort and reassurance to the communities she visited, becoming a champion of the poor.

Eleanor also fought racism. She invited black political leaders and poor farmers to the White House to discuss issues, and she supported the National Association for the Advancement of Colored People (NAACP) in their fight for equal rights, as well as a controversial federal law against lynching (the hanging to death of blacks without trial and often without any reason besides racial hatred). She was harshly criticized for her beliefs, and not even Franklin had the courage to pass the anti-lynching law (he needed the support of racist politicians for the New Deal programs). Politician Adlai Stevenson II applauded her courage: "Long before the civil rights issue moved to the forefront of the nation's consciousness, she was there, earning public abuse for her quiet reminders of the inequalities practiced in our land."[6]

In 1939, the strength of her convictions was put to the test. Eleanor belonged to a prestigious group called Daughters of the American Revolution (DAR); members were women from old, important families like the Roosevelts. When the DAR refused to let Marian Anderson, a world-famous singer and friend of Eleanor's, perform at the DAR's Constitution Hall because she was black, Eleanor was outraged and took a very public stand.

She announced her resignation from the DAR and condemned their racism. Her action drew worldwide attention to the cause and got all of America talking about equal rights. She then helped arrange for Marian to sing a free concert at the Lincoln Memorial. In front of an enormous statue of the president who freed the slaves, Marian gave an electrifying performance to a crowd of seventy-five thousand people. As she sang the spiritual "Nobody Knows the Trouble I've Seen," the audience was moved to tears.

But the trouble brewing in America was eclipsed by the war exploding in Europe. By 1939, World War II was underway, and a year later, Franklin was elected to an unprecedented third term as president (presidents now can only serve two terms). Although Eleanor was generally a pacifist, she believed that America had to stop Hitler's quest for world domination and his extermination of the Jews. She took on her first official government position when she became the director of the Office of Civil Defense.

At fifty-nine, Eleanor traveled to the war front in the South Pacific to check on the troops and boost morale. At first, Admiral William "Bull" Halsey was against her visit, thinking a woman on the battlefield would be a nuisance. But Eleanor proved him wrong by conducting a thorough inspection of the hospitals and visiting each wounded soldier, asking his name, if he needed anything, and if she could take a message home for him. Admiral Halsey changed his tune, saying, "She alone had accomplished more good than any other person, or any group of civilians, who had passed through my area."[7] Eleanor worked so hard—traveling twenty-three thousand miles to visit seventeen islands and four hundred thousand men—that she lost thirty pounds!

Franklin's health held out just long enough to make sure America and its allies won the war. After he died in 1945, most people expected Eleanor to pack her bags and retire from public life. Instead, she began working for world peace. Since the end of World War I, she'd been advocating for an international peace-keeping organization, and in 1945, her dream came true when the United Nations (UN) was formed and President

During her trip to the South Pacific, Eleanor visited the indigenous people of New Zealand, the Maori. They were so taken with the friendly First Lady, they named her *Kotuku*, or "White Heron of One Flight," after a magical creature from their legends that is seen just once in a lifetime.

Truman asked her to be a delegate. During her seven years with the UN, Eleanor was the only woman to represent the United States. Though other members had doubted her abilities when she started, she quickly changed minds, working to create and fight for a Universal Declaration of Human Rights. And when it was finally passed, the delegates gave Eleanor a standing ovation.

When Eleanor's Universal Declaration of Human Rights was finally adopted by the UN after years of hard work, she was so elated that she—a 64-year-old—took a running slide down the UN's marble hallway!

As she entered her seventies, Eleanor never slowed down. After the war and her work in the UN, she passionately believed that America needed to stay involved in the world, not retreat. Realizing her diplomatic expertise, Truman sent her to India, Pakistan, and the Middle East to build relationships for the United States. And in 1961, Eleanor was again appointed as a UN delegate by newly elected president John F. Kennedy. When she returned to her old job, she was greeted by her *second* standing ovation!

After her husband, Franklin, died, it was suggested that Eleanor run for president herself. She laughed it off—she didn't think America was ready for a woman president. But she believed that in a few years, a younger woman could run and win.

At a time in life when most women in her generation would be sewing quilts or relaxing in a rocking chair, Eleanor stayed active, both physically and mentally. "I could not, at any age, be content to take my place in a corner by the fireside and simply look on," she said. "Life was meant to be lived."[8] And she continued to live her life—working as a professor at Brandeis University, lobbying for the Equal Rights Amendment, campaigning for her favorite candidates—until her very last day. In 1962, just after her seventy-eighth birthday, she died of tuberculosis, and the world lost one of its greatest heroines.

Eleanor devoted her life to improving the world—first, as a young woman, volunteering for those who needed her help; then as First Lady, advising her husband and responding to the needs of America; and finally on her own, as a delegate to the United Nations. She entered politics because of her husband but remained because of her own beliefs and passions. Even when her outspoken opinions on controversial issues— women's suffrage, civil rights—got her in trouble, Eleanor refused to back down. She stood up for what she believed in and what she thought was right. This courage and strength of character made her one of the most admired, respected, and powerful women in the world.

> If anyone were to ask me what I want out of life, I would say the opportunity for doing something useful, for in no other way, I am convinced, can true happiness be attained.
>
> —ELEANOR ROOSEVELT

ROCK ON!

NADYA OKAMOTO

When Nadya Okamoto was a high school sophomore, her mother lost her job, the family lost their apartment, and they had to live on friends' couches. Nadya worried about how she would get to school, how her family would afford food, and how they would cover other basic needs. Months later, they got their apartment back, but the experience changed her. Nadya began volunteering with homeless groups and realized that one tough challenge homeless women and girls face is getting feminine hygiene products. They told her about using towels, pillowcases—whatever they could find. So Nadya started Camions of Care, which provides "natural needs" care packages to homeless women and girls. Nadya runs the group, with the help of mostly teen volunteers, and is expanding it nationally and internationally. Learn how you can help at CamionsofCare.org.

Dora Thewlis

1890–1976 ❀ SUFFRAGETTE ❀ ENGLAND

Let me go, Mother. I am quite capable. I understand what I am fighting for and am prepared to go to prison for the cause. I feel that women ought to have their rights, and it will be an honor to go to prison.

—DORA THEWLIS, ASKING HER MOTHER TO LET HER JOIN A PROTEST MARCH

Dora heard it clearly. The great clock, Big Ben, struck four. It was time. She linked arms with the women beside her, forming a human chain. "Ready . . . march!" she heard called from up ahead. It was too crowded to see.

She and the others began to march up the street toward the Palace of Westminster, which housed British Parliament. It was a magnificent procession. The girls and women, all dressed in clogs and shawls—the suffragette uniform—were a thousand strong! How could the police stop them?

Dora chanted along with the other protestors: "Rise up! Votes for women!"

The women of England had waited far too long for their right to vote. Dora was tired of working long hours in a factory with no other opportunities—no school, no other job prospects. She wanted to have a say in her future! Getting to vote was the only way.

"Rise up! Votes for women!" she yelled again.

Suddenly, the police descended on the suffragettes, blowing whistles and shouting, "Break it up, ladies! Move along now." There were hundreds of them! Many protestors broke ranks and ran as police grabbed women out of the crowd and began hauling them away.

Dora tightened her grip and kept marching. She wouldn't let them stop her—not yet. She had to make it to the House of Commons, where the backstabbing politicians could hear her voice. That was the goal. *Then* they could arrest her, not before.

"Rise up! Votes for women!"

Whenever a policeman got near, Dora and her line dodged and ran. Miraculously, they made it all the way to the Old Palace Yard without being captured. Dora could see the House of Commons dead ahead. Perhaps the men inside could see her as well. She hoped so.

"Rise up! Votes for women!" she called up to the windows.

Suddenly, Dora felt a hand grip her arm firmly. A policeman. She tried to shake him off. "Let go!" she cried.

"Why, you're just a child," he said in surprise. "Time to go home to your mum."

Dora struggled, so a second policeman gripped her other arm. They were big and burly—twice her size—but Dora fought anyway.

She twisted and pulled and shouted, "Rise up, women!" at the top of her lungs as they hauled her off to jail. The next day, sixteen-year-old Dora made the front page of the *Daily Mirror* newspaper. In the picture, her hair is a mess, her skirt and shawl askew, her face angry. The headline read: "Suffragettes Storm the House—Desperate Encounter with the Police—Wholesale Arrests."[1]

The "Baby Suffragette" was born.

In 1890, Dora Thewlis was born in an industrial town in northern England. Her parents were poor, which meant the women and children had to work to help pay the bills and buy food. Dora's father was a weaver, and her mother and older sister worked in a mill where they made cloth. When Dora turned ten, she joined them, working part-time—an occupation of little interest to her. Dora was really smart. Her mother said, "Ever since she was seven, she has been a diligent reader of newspapers and can hold her own in politics."[2] Yet by age twelve, Dora had to quit school and work full-time to help to support her family.

Some suffragette groups like the WSPU were radical and militant, using force to make their point. Suffragettes led protests and hunger strikes, chained themselves to railings, smashed windows, lit fires, and even set off a few small bombs. It took decades of fighting, but eventually, British women over the age of 30 won the right to vote in 1918 (it was age 21 for men). By 1928, all British women could vote.[3] (American women got the vote slightly sooner, in 1920.)[4]

Dora wanted more for herself. Working conditions were dangerous, and the pay was low. But girls and women had few other options. If they wanted or needed to earn money, they could either teach (if they could afford an education) or they could work in the factories.

Dora's parents may have been poor, but they were passionate about politics. The cause they were most passionate about was women's suffrage (women's right to vote). At that time, British women couldn't vote. Even though they worked, paid taxes, and took care of their households, they had no say in the laws that very much affected their lives. Dora and her family thought that needed to change. Women had been pushing for the right to vote for decades, with no progress from the politicians. Some women were fed up and wanted to take a more active, even militant approach.

In Manchester, another northern industrial city, Lady Emmeline Pankhurst formed the Women's Social and Political Union (WSPU) in 1903, to fight for suffrage.

(The media dubbed them the "suffragettes.") Their motto was "deeds, not words,"[5] and Pankhurst recruited women who were willing to take action—to protest and get arrested, two things women were not supposed to do. The suffragettes were unpopular with many who felt that women voting was a ridiculous notion. The police spied on them, and at protests and gatherings they were often booed, heckled, and spit at. Some critics even threw eggs and rotten vegetables at them.

In 1906, when she was sixteen, Dora saw Lady Pankhurst speak and was inspired. She, too, believed it was time to fight, so she and her mother helped to form a local chapter of the WSPU. Dora passed out leaflets and spread the message. The next year, Pankhurst called on chapters to recruit one thousand marchers for an extraordinary protest. Their mission: to storm the Houses of Parliament, the seat of British government, and take it over until the male politicians agreed to give women the vote. The suffragettes knew that many women would be arrested, but that was the point. They wanted media coverage—wanted to shock England. It was a bold plan, and Dora was dying to be a part of it.

Past protestors had been thrown in jail for months, so Dora's mother couldn't risk going. If she lost her job, who would take care of the children? Dora begged her parents to let her go in her mother's place. They agreed, and in February of 1907, she joined the crowd boarding the train to London. The station was packed with well-wishers. "Mothers said farewell to daughters, aunts wished nieces well," said Jill Liddington, a women's suffrage scholar.[6]

As planned, the march was a media feeding frenzy. Five hundred burly policemen awaited the girls and women who marched on Parliament.[7] Dora was arrested, along with many others, and sent to Holloway Prison. The next day, her face and the story of "the little mill hand" grabbed the nation's attention.[8] Overnight, Dora became a teenage celebrity, but she hated the media's nickname for her. She snapped at one reporter, "Don't call me the 'Baby Suffragette.' I am not a baby. In May next year, I shall be eighteen. Surely for a girl, that is a good age?"[9]

Dora didn't want to be treated any differently just because of her age. When a judge tried to give her a lighter sentence than the older

If you want to learn more about the women's suffrage movement and the girls and women who fought for their rights, check out the excellent 2015 movie *Suffragette*, starring Carey Mulligan and Meryl Streep.

suffragettes, Dora demanded the same punishment. And when a judge actually *ordered* her to go home, she again refused: "I don't wish to go back, sir. I shall remain here as long as the WSPU women want me."[10]

In the end, Dora did go home and back to the mill. Perhaps the media attention was too much for her. Or perhaps she didn't want to work at the mills for the rest of her life. Whatever the reason, Dora left in 1914 for Australia, where she married and had two children. She never returned to England, even after British women finally won the right to vote in 1918. But feisty young Dora's contributions to the suffragette struggle certainly helped to get them there.

HOW WILL YOU ROCK THE WORLD?

I will rock the world by making sure that everyone has the nutrition and resources to survive. I will also make sure everyone has healthcare, even if they cannot pay. I will be an educator and mentor to unprivileged kids.

LEXI SMITH ☼ AGE 11

Josephine Baker

1906–1975 ⚬ DANCER AND SPY ⚬ UNITED STATES AND FRANCE

I shall dance all my life.... I would like to die, breathless, spent, at the end of a dance.

—JOSEPHINE BAKER

Josephine hung by a rope from the stage rigging. Below her, she could see the actors playing Romeo and Juliet. She felt a little ridiculous dangling above them in her pink tights, pink leotard, and pink wings, a harness underneath it all.

She was only thirteen, and she was playing cupid in her very first stage role. She couldn't believe her luck in getting the part. It was a dream come true.

Josephine heard her cue and swung out over the stage. This was it! Her chance to show everyone what she could do. But suddenly her soaring stopped short.

Oh no! Her wings were caught on the scenery!

What could she do? The actors were staring up at her with looks of horror. She was supposed to shoot them with her "arrows of love," but she couldn't get close enough.

In a panic, Josephine jerked her legs around, trying to get free.

I'm going to ruin the show!

She flailed her arms in circles, hoping to dislodge the wings.

I'm going to get fired!

She rocked her body back and forth, grunting with effort.

I'll never work in vaudeville again!

Then she heard it: laughter. *Lots* of laughter. The audience was cracking up!

Josephine looked out at the audience members, who were staring up at her. At her! A feeling like electricity jolted her body. She'd never felt anything like it.

Slowly, a smile spread across Josephine's face. She pretended to run in place. She flapped her arms like a bird. She bugged her eyes and stuck out her tongue. The audience loved her!

And Josephine loved being the star of the show.

From then on, she was hooked on the stage. And during her lifetime, Josephine Baker danced her way into the history books.

〜〜〜

As a girl, Josephine's favorite story was "Cinderella"—probably because it was so much like her own life. She was born in 1906 in St. Louis, Missouri. Her father left when Josephine was born, and her mother struggled to support the family by cleaning houses and washing laundry. Josephine was often hungry, and the family was so poor that they lived in a rat-infested shack with six people sharing one bed!

At just seven years old, Josephine's mother hired her out as a maid. The young girl was responsible for taking care of all the household chores, working from 5:00 AM until she fell into bed exhausted at 10:00 PM.[1] Like Cinderella, Josephine dreamed of escaping her life of near-slavery, but she didn't know how. She *did* know that she loved to dance. "I didn't have stockings," she explained, "[so] I danced to keep warm."[2]

Whenever Josephine had a few extra coins for herself, she went to the all-black vaudeville shows. There, she watched performers play music, sing, and dance. Josephine was spellbound, and she memorized every line and every dance step. At age thirteen, she convinced a vaudeville group called the Dixie Steppers to hire her as a dancer in the chorus line.

The director was so impressed with her dancing that he gave her a solo part in the show: cupid in *Romeo and Juliet*. On her first night, when her costume got stuck and the audience laughed at her midair antics, Josephine was sure she would be fired. But the director could see that the audience loved her and asked her to do it again in *every* show.

When the Dixie Steppers packed up for a tour of the South, Josephine decided it was time to make her escape. Without telling her mother, she snuck out of town with the show and worked as the dresser. When they tried to leave her behind because she was too young and inexperienced, she stowed away in a costume trunk. Josephine wanted to be a dancer and she wanted to see the world—she would not quit!

> Josephine had many nicknames. When she was a child, her mother called her "Tumpy," after Humpty Dumpty, because of her round, chubby face. Later, fans dubbed her the Black Pearl, Bronze Venus, Jazz Cleopatra, and Creole Goddess.

One night, when a chorus line dancer fell and hurt herself, Josephine seized the opportunity. She begged the director to let her take the dancer's place—she knew every step. He agreed, and Josephine got her chance. But the other girl's costume was too big. When Josephine got onstage, the audience laughed at her baggy tights and oversized skirt. Instead of being embarrassed, Josephine hammed it up. She acted clumsy, grinned, and crossed her eyes. The audience loved it, and Josephine quickly became the star of the show yet again.

When Josephine heard about auditions in New York City for an all-black Broadway musical called *Shuffle Along*, she knew she had to go there next. She arrived in the Big Apple with no friends, nowhere to live, and no money, spending her first two nights sleeping on a park bench.

And her audition didn't go well. The producers thought she was too small and too light-skinned, so once again, she got a job as the costumer.

And once again, she learned every song and every dance step from the wings. And once again, when a dancer got sick, Josephine was ready. The director let her replace the sick dancer, and Josephine got to dance in her first Broadway show. "When I saw those watching faces, a giddiness swept over me . . . I let the music carry me away."[3] As usual, Josephine stole the show with her dancing and her comedy.

> Josephine grew up in Boxcar Town, one of the worst slums in America. It got its name because the houses were actually abandoned train cars in which poor black families lived.[4]

Josephine performed all over New York in all-white clubs, where she couldn't even sit at a table or walk in through the front door. She had seen worse segregation during her tour of the south with the Dixie Steppers: whites and blacks used separate train cars, restaurants, bathrooms, and clubs. But at least in New York, she made good money. She began sending money home to her family to help pay for clothes and an education for her siblings—something she did for the rest of her life. But she didn't see her family again for fourteen years.

> A famous French artist designed the poster for La Revue Nègre with Josephine's dancing image on it. The poster was plastered all over Paris. "For the first time in my life, I felt beautiful," she said.[5]

In 1925, nineteen-year-old Josephine was invited to perform in Paris with La Revue Nègre. She was nervous about traveling so far from home, but she had dreams to follow. So she swallowed her fears and set sail for France. From the moment she stepped off the boat, the country amazed her. There was no segregation. Blacks and whites ate together, rode trains together, and sat together in the same clubs. Josephine couldn't believe it.

For Parisians, Josephine's dancing was unlike anything they'd ever seen—it was wild and free. And *funny*. French audiences went wild for her. Practically overnight, Josephine was a superstar. Everywhere she went, people knew her and loved her. Parisians bought Josephine dolls, Josephine lipstick, Josephine perfume, Josephine shoes, and Josephine clothing. French women even tanned their skin to look more like her.[6] And like the superstars of today, Josephine branched out: she made a record, starred in movies, and danced all over Europe.

Josephine returned to America in 1926 and starred in the most popular show on Broadway, *Ziegfeld Follies*. She was the first and only black person in the show. But America hadn't changed much; the country was still racist and treated her like a second-class citizen. She knew she didn't belong there anymore—Paris was her home. She moved back to France for good.

In 1939, Europe got pulled into World War II. Josephine loved France and wanted to help her new homeland. "France has made me what I am," she said. "I am prepared to give my life for France."[7] First, she joined the Red Cross. She had flown as a stunt pilot, so she began flying first aid into Belgium. But France had even bigger plans for their favorite star.

A year later, the Nazis invaded and captured France. The French people were prisoners in their own country—if they were lucky. Jews, resisters, and other "undesirables" were shipped off to the concentration camps, where most were killed. Josephine was recruited by French military intelligence to help her country in a new way: they asked if she would spy on the Germans. Of course, she agreed.

Because Josephine was a famous performer, she had a good excuse to travel around Europe with no trouble. She went to government events, flirted, and eavesdropped on Nazi officials. She wrote secret messages to the French Resistance (those in France who were actively fighting the Nazi invaders) on her sheet music using invisible ink and pinned notes

> Josephine loved animals. In Paris, she had a parakeet, a parrot, two rabbits, a pig, and a snake named Kiki. She even had a pet leopard named Chiquita. She loved to walk Chiquita on a leash down the streets of Paris, with both them wearing matching diamond chokers![8]

When Josephine performed in Europe just before WWII, she saw plenty of racism. In Vienna, posters and flyers called her the "black devil," church bells rang out to warn people to avoid her, and the streets were lined with Austrians protesting her performance.

into her underwear, and then smuggled those messages back home to France. The Nazis didn't dare search a superstar.

The Germans lost the war in 1945—thanks, in part, to Josephine's daring spy work. In fact, it was such a great help to France that the government gave her the *Legion d'Honneur*, the highest honor the country can give.

Josephine tried to have children, but complications from several miscarriages made it impossible. After the war, she began adopting children from around the world. She wanted to show people that different races could live together happily as brothers and sisters. She adopted twelve children in all and called them her Rainbow Tribe.

Josephine loved to dance and kept performing her entire life. At age sixty-seven, she danced at Carnegie Hall in New York City, the most famous theater in America, and embarked on a seventeen-city tour. The show was a huge success. Finally, America loved her. She went back to Paris to launch her new show there and got the best reviews of her life. "This is not just a comeback. This is an eternal return," said a Paris newspaper.[9] In one theater, the fans gave her a standing ovation for thirty minutes!

Josephine married four times but was also bisexual and had relationships with both men and women, black and white. She even had an affair with the famous Mexican painter Frida Kahlo.[10]

After one such evening, Josephine fell asleep and never woke up. Paris, her adopted city, gave her an elaborate funeral. Her hearse was completely covered in flowers and hundreds of fans lined the street.

Josephine Baker fought her entire life for racial equality. Sometimes that fighting was through her art—dance and comedy—and sometimes it was through her words and actions. She always insisted that blacks and whites sit together in her audience, even if a show cancelled her. She convinced banks, TV stations, and stores to hire black workers. She wrote articles about the unfairness of segregation in American magazines and newspapers. She spoke at college campuses and at civil rights gatherings. In 1963, she joined Marin Luther King Jr. at the Washington Monument for his famous March on Washington. She was the only female speaker at this historic event. Here's what she said:

> I have walked into the palaces of kings and queens and in the houses of presidents. But I could not walk into a hotel in America and get a cup of coffee, and that made me mad. And when I get mad, you know that I open my big mouth. And then look out, 'cause when Josephine opens her mouth, they hear it all over the world.[11]

From the boxcar slums of St. Louis to the palaces of Europe, Josephine Baker lived a true Cinderella story. She was a Cinderella who fought her oppressors . . . and won!

HOW WILL YOU ROCK THE WORLD?

I'm going to rock the world by being a salon owner and beautician who is known for her creativity. I work hard every day to enhance my skills by designing, drawing, and using my imagination to make my hands do things with hair that people have never seen. I will be a boss who makes people feel good about themselves through beauty. My clients will rock the hairstyles that I create with great confidence!

ZAMYA TIDWELL · AGE 10

GRace MuRRay HoppeR

1906–1992 ✦ COMPUTER SCIENTIST AND NAVY ADMIRAL ✦
UNITED STATES

A ship in port is safe, but that is not what ships are for.
Sail out to sea and do new things.

—GRACE HOPPER

"How does it work?" wondered seven-year-old Grace. "How does it ring?" She held her alarm clock in one hand and a screwdriver in the other. Carefully, she unscrewed the back, but as she pulled it off, levers, springs, wheels, and gears exploded all over the floor. She hadn't had enough time to see how they fit together.

"What now?" she wondered. She decided that the only solution was to try again.

Grace went to her mother's room and found another alarm clock, which she took apart. Then she got her brother's clock and took that one apart as well. In the end, Grace went through every room in the house and collected four more alarm clocks—seven in all. And she proceeded to take each one apart.

When her mother walked into the living room, there were pieces of metal strewn about everywhere.

"What are you doing?!" her mother cried.

"Figuring out how it works," explained Grace.

Her mother laughed. "Get this mess cleaned up, please."

Grace's face fell. She still hadn't figured out how the alarm clock rang.

"And you may keep *one* clock to put back together."

Grace smiled. One clock would be enough. She would figure it out.

⁓⁓

Grace spent the rest of her life figuring things out.

She was born in New York City in 1906. During her childhood, women couldn't vote and were expected to stay home and have children, not a career. But Grace's parents encouraged all their children (even their daughters) to be curious, to read, and to explore their interests. Her parents also believed their daughters should go to college—very unusual at that time.

Grace was smart in school. At age seventeen, she was accepted to Vassar, a women's college. Vassar offered classes they thought were appropriate for young ladies, like "Husband and Wife" and "Motherhood."[1] Grace skipped those classes and studied math and physics instead.

She graduated from Vassar at the top of her class with a degree in math. Then she went on to Yale for her master's and PhD. She was the first woman in Yale's history to earn a doctorate in math. After graduating, she got a job teaching at Vassar. She was an excellent teacher, always challenging her

Grace's great-grandfather, an admiral in the US Navy during the Civil War, was a role model for her. As a girl, she sailed a small boat in a lake while her mother watched from shore. When a strong wind knocked the boat over, Grace's mother yelled through her megaphone, "Remember your great-grandfather, the admiral."[2] Grace couldn't abandon ship, so she swam it back to shore.

⁓⁓

students to look at things differently. She warned them that the most dangerous thing they could say was "We've always done it this way."[3] Instead, she urged them to innovate.

Grace's life took a turn when the Japanese bombed Pearl Harbor and the United States entered World War II. Grace thought again of her great-grandfather, the Civil War admiral, and decided to enlist. She planned to sign up for the Women Accepted for Volunteer Emergency Services (WAVES), but she was too old and sixteen pounds under the weight requirement.[4] She applied anyway. The navy gave her a waiver for her weight, and she was in.

As with school, Grace excelled in the military. She was the top graduate from training and quickly advanced to lieutenant. Because of her math knowledge, the navy sent her to Harvard University to work on America's first-ever computer, the Mark I. It was enormous: fifty-one feet long, eight feet tall, and five tons in weight![5] For a math whiz who loved to tinker, the Mark I was a dream come true.

> Computers in the 1940s were much bigger and less powerful than computers today. A typical computer might fill an entire room!

On her first day, Grace's boss gave her a codebook and told her she had one week to figure out how to "program the beast" and get it running.[6] She met the challenge and became the Mark I's lead programmer. She spent the next five years programming it to work on math problems related to radar, mines, and atomic bombs. She also wrote a 561-page manual for the Mark I that historians consider groundbreaking. It is one of the earliest examples of digital computer programs.

Back in the 1940s, computers were brand-new, and people couldn't envision all that they would be able to do someday. Universities and the military had them, but that's it. Grace, however, believed computers had the potential to do more than just figure out math problems—way more. When the war was over, her colleagues moved back to regular jobs. Grace was the only one to stay behind to continue.

In 1949, Grace accepted a job as the senior mathematician for Eckert-Mauchly Computer Corporation developing a new computer called the

UNIVAC. The UNIVAC had new technology that made it much faster than other computers, and the company hoped to make computers that could be used by businesses everywhere. Grace knew that for this to happen, computers would have to be easier to use.

At that time, the only way to talk to computers was in binary language. Programmers had to type in long strings of 0s and 1s to tell the computer what to do. Computers didn't understand human language made of letters, so Grace invented a program called a "compiler," which could take simple human commands and translate them into binary code.

Grace's compiler enabled computers to understand letters and words, making it much easier for humans to communicate with them. Her team invented the FLOW-MATIC program for UNIVAC, which could do things like calculate bills and payments for companies. That led to the creation of a whole new programming language called COBOL (common business-oriented language) in 1959—a language still used by businesses and government organizations today.

Grace retired from the navy in 1966, but it didn't last long. A year later, the navy asked her to come back; over the next twenty years, Grace rose to the rank of admiral. During these "post-retirement" years, she helped set up common standards for the navy's programming languages—standards that were adopted by the Department of Defense and eventually made it into all future computers.

When Grace finally retired for real in 1986, she was eighty years old, the oldest active-duty officer in America.[7] The US Congress had granted her special permission to stay in the navy beyond normal retirement age. Even after retiring, Grace continued to work as a consultant for a computer company and lectured at colleges and universities.

> Grace loved collecting: books, stamps, china, dolls, and computer souvenirs. She was also a clotheshorse with seven walk-in closets full of outfits, jewelry, shoes, and gloves. She wouldn't wear the same dress twice in a year. And Grace owned three apartments: one she lived in and two others to hold all her stuff![8]

Nicknamed the "Grand Lady of Software,"[9] Grace earned many honors in her lifetime. She was the first woman chosen as a Distinguished Fellow of the British Computer Society and was awarded America's National Medal of Technology by President George Bush.[10] In Arlington, Virginia, you can stroll through Grace Murray Hopper Park or take a ride on the *USS Hopper*, a ship the sailors call *Amazing Grace*.[11] When Grace died in 1992, she was buried in Arlington National Cemetery with full military honors.

One day Grace was repairing a computer that had shorted out because of a dead moth inside it. Grace removed the moth and joked that she had "debugged" it. A new computer term was born![12]

At a time when there were almost no women working in computer science, Grace made a huge impact on early computing and the development of computers. And her influence is still seen everywhere today, in every computer in every home and business. Including yours!

ROCK ON!

Alyssa Carson

Alyssa Carson wants to be one of the first humans on Mars. She was just three when she first announced her space dreams, and since then, she's gone to NASA's Space Camp seven times in the United States, Canada, and Turkey, making her the first person to complete *all* of the NASA Space Camps. At age twelve, she became the first person to complete NASA's Passport Program by visiting all fourteen NASA US visitor centers. Alyssa is already an ambassador for the Mars One private spaceflight project. NASA plans to launch the first human mission to Mars around 2030. By then, Alyssa will be twenty-nine years old and ready for liftoff!

MARy Lou Williams

1910–1981 ✦ PIANIST AND COMPOSER ✦ UNITED STATES

It's not what you play, it's how you play it.

—MARY LOU WILLIAMS

M ary was out on the sidewalk, skipping rope with her friends, when a man walked up with a boy from the neighborhood. "Where's this piano player you've been telling me about?" he asked the boy.

"Right there, mister," said the boy, pointing to Mary.

"What is this, a joke?" the man said, slapping his forehead. "I asked you to bring me to the best piano player in town! Ours got drunk and took off, and the show's in a couple of hours. It's a real gig, not some school talent show!" He rubbed his hands over his face. "Are you telling me you brought me all the way across Pittsburgh for some *girl*?"

This made Mary angry. What did *he* know about her piano playing?

"She's not just some girl," said the boy, jumping to her defense. "She's the Little Piano Girl. Ain't you heard of her?"

"Nope," said the bandleader, turning to walk away.

One of the jump-rope girls chimed in. "Wait a minute, mister. You came all this way—might as well hear her play."

So Mr. Harris, of the band Buzzin' Harris and His Hits and Bits, asked fourteen-year-old Mary Lou Williams to play for him. Harris's frown quickly turned into a grin. He couldn't believe what he was hearing. This girl could play!

"Can you play this?" he asked, humming the first song of their show.

Mary listened carefully until he finished and then said, "Sure thing."

She proceeded to play the entire song, from start to finish, flawlessly. Harris could barely contain himself. He hummed each song in the show to her and she played each one back to him perfectly, as if she'd been practicing for weeks. As they sat together, Mary memorized the entire set for their show.

Two hours later, Mary joined the Hits and Bits onstage at a Pittsburgh theater. She tore it up with the band, and the audience loved her. The teenage musical sensation brought down the house!

After the show, Mr. Harris begged Mary to join the band. At the end of the summer, they'd be leaving Pittsburgh to tour the country. "Won't you come with us?" he asked.

Mary couldn't wait to get away from home. "Sure thing," she answered.[1]

—————

Mary's musical adventures began in Atlanta, Georgia, where she was born in 1910. As one of eight children, she didn't get much attention from her mother, and she never knew her father at all. When she was young, the family moved north to Pittsburgh, Pennsylvania, and Mary experienced racism for the first time in her life. Because of her dark skin, white and light-skinned-black parents wouldn't let their children play with her. Neighbors threw bricks through the windows of her house.

Mary escaped into music. When she was around three years old, she was sitting on her mother's lap as she played a song on the harmonium (a type of organ). Suddenly, toddler Mary reached up and played the same song, note for note. Her mother was so shocked that she leaped up from the piano bench, spilling Mary to the floor, and ran to get the neighbors to listen to the toddler play. "I never left the piano after that," Mary remembered. "Always played. Nothing else interested me."[2]

Mary's family was dirt poor and her mother an alcoholic. "The kids had to fend for themselves," said Mary's niece.[3] Mary didn't even have shoes until she was four years old. But she learned early on that she could make money playing the piano. Neighbors requested her as entertainment for their parties or just to hear a song (radios and TV were rare then), and they were all willing to pay. Sometimes as much as fifty cents a song![4] At a time when adult jobs paid just a few dollars a day, that was big money. By age six, Mary was playing piano professionally, everywhere from birthday parties to gambling houses to vaudeville stages. But she kept it a secret from her family—she knew her mother would take the money if she found out.

She might have gotten away with it, but then she broke her arm. As she recuperated, neighbors stopped by wondering why she wasn't playing for them anymore. The jig was up. Mary's mother began hiring her out to play at dances, funerals, silent movies, churches, even brothels! Her rates went up to one dollar an hour, and her mother took most of her pay. Soon Mary was supporting their entire family.

Mary was born with the caul, or amniotic membrane (the sack surrounding the fetus), over her face. Some, including her mother, believed it a sign of "second sight"—the ability to see ghosts, visions, and even the future. Mary did have visions: "Everybody was afraid to be around me because I was seeing so many weird things."[5] She believed her strange ability also helped her with music. She could predict the notes coming before musicians played them, so she was a step ahead during rapid jazz improvisations.

Mary's only father figure during her childhood was her stepfather, Fletcher Burley. He gave her the attention she craved and nurtured her musical talent. He was a gambler, and sometimes when he went out, he took young Mary with him: "He bought himself an extra-large coat and would put me underneath and sneak me into one of his gambling joints, most of which had an upright piano against one wall." Mary would play for tips, often earning twenty or thirty dollars a night![6]

> When Mary couldn't get work playing piano, she did other jobs. She did laundry, worked as a maid, and helped make wigs. She even moved bodies for an undertaker!

Before long, young Mary was known across Pittsburgh as "the Little Piano Girl." Her musical gift could not be ignored. Whenever Mary practiced, people on the street couldn't help but take notice: "Everyone would stop on their porch, and truck drivers would stop,"[7] whenever Mary played.

When she was twelve years old, Mary moved out of her house and never went back. First she lived with her big sister; then she got her break with Buzzin' Harris and His Hits and Bits, and hit the road. The band's saxophonist (and Mary's future husband) remembers hearing her for the first time: "I'd never heard nothing like that in my life . . . She outplayed any piano player I'd ever played with. . . . At fourteen."[8] When jazz great Louis Armstrong heard fifteen-year-old Mary playing at a club, he was impressed. Still barely a teenager, Mary was becoming famous in the highest music circles.

She married saxophonist John Williams when she was seventeen, and together, they moved to Kansas City, Missouri. There, Mary joined the band Twelve Clouds of Joy and became part of the growing swing scene (the popular American dance music of the 1930s and '40s). Other bands were always trying to steal her away. She was in high demand to write songs and arrangements for big-time bandleaders like Duke Ellington, Tommy Dorsey, Earl Hines, and Benny Goodman.

In 1942, Mary divorced Williams and left Twelve Clouds of Joy. She returned to Pittsburgh, formed a new band, and married again—this time to trumpeter Shorty Baker. When Shorty left to join Duke Ellington's orchestra, Mary joined as well. They traveled together, playing shows, and Mary wrote several successful tunes for Duke.

Within a year, that marriage was over, and Mary moved on to New York City. There, she got a weekly gig playing piano at the Café Society club in Greenwich Village, and she launched her own weekly radio show called *Mary Lou Williams's Piano Workshop*. All kinds of musicians gathered in her Harlem apartment to try out new songs and jam with her. These up-and-comers would later become the biggest names in jazz, like Thelonious Monk, Charlie Parker, Miles Davis, and Dizzy Gillespie. "During this period, Monk and the kids would come to my apartment every morning . . . after I'd finished my last show, and we'd play and swap ideas until noon or later."[9]

In the 1940s, Mary moved away from swing and into bebop, a new style of jazz that was faster and more complicated, and demanded improvisation from musicians. She also wrote longer pieces, including *Zodiac Suite*, a twelve-movement composition, which was performed at Carnegie Hall in 1946.

In 1952, Mary, who had never been to Europe, was invited to perform in England. She accepted and ended up playing around Europe for two years.

> Teenage Mary once played piano at a high-society tea party. When the hostess asked what she charged, Mary said, "Dollar an hour, my standard fee." She played for a few hours, then as the chauffeur drove her home, she looked at the check. It was for $100! That was a couple months' salary for most people. "My mother almost fainted," Mary said.[10]

But when she returned to the United States, she felt like her life was missing something. She converted to Catholicism and quit playing music altogether. Instead, she focused her energies on helping others, including many of her friends in jazz who had become addicted to drugs. She started a foundation that helped addicted musicians get clean and return to performing.

It took two priests plus Dizzy Gillespie to pull her back into the music world. She finally returned in 1957, when she joined Dizzy's band at the Newport Jazz Festival. She began composing religious jazz music, including several masses. World-famous African American choreographer Alvin Ailey choreographed one of these, *Mary Lou's Mass*; four years later, it was the first jazz piece ever performed at New York City's Saint Patrick's Cathedral.

Mary is finally getting the name recognition she deserves. Duke University established the Mary Lou Williams Center for Black Culture; the Kennedy Center in Washington, DC, has a yearly Mary Lou Williams Women in Jazz Festival; there are several children's books about Mary's life; and in 2015, a documentary film called *Mary Lou Williams: The Lady Who Swings the Band* aired on TV.

Mary also continued focusing her energy and talent on helping others, especially musicians. She opened thrift stores in Harlem and gave the proceeds—along with 10 percent of her own money—to struggling musicians. In the 1960s, when there were only two jazz clubs in all of New York City, she found new venues where jazz musicians could play. She started the Pittsburgh Jazz Festival, as well as Mary Records (the first record company to be started by a woman!) and Cecilia Music Publishing Company. In her later years, she established the Mary Lou Williams Foundation, which teaches children and young adults about jazz.

When Mary hit her sixties, a time when many people are thinking about retirement, her career continued to soar. She recorded numerous albums, played at many prestigious jazz festivals, and was the artist in residence at Duke University. She won two Guggenheim Fellowships and was nominated for a Grammy Award for Best Jazz Performance. She even performed at the White House for President Jimmy Carter in 1978!

Mary died at age seventy-one. Her career and body of work put her at the top of the list of notable musicians, female and male. At a time when women, especially black women, weren't allowed into the music world except as singers or dancers, Mary Lou defied expectations. She wrote 350 songs and recorded more than a hundred records. She wrote and arranged for some of the greatest bandleaders of the era and was a mentor to the future jazz greats. Mary's amazing talent meant she was able to be her own woman—she supported herself doing what she loved and left behind her own jazz legacy.

Looking back at the end of her life, Mary was pleased, "I did it, didn't I? Through muck and mud."[11]

HOW WILL YOU ROCK THE WORLD?

I will rock the world by becoming a teacher. I want to encourage kids to open up and be creative before they get shut down. I think this is one of the most important jobs in the world.

AUGDEN HAYES ☼ AGE 13

Beverly Cleary

1916– ⚭ AUTHOR ⚭ UNITED STATES

*Children should learn that reading is pleasure,
not just something that teachers make you do in school.*

—BEVERLY CLEARY

"Class, Abendroth's Grocery is sponsoring a writing contest for the best animal essay. The winner gets a two-dollar prize." Beverly Bunn's fourth-grade teacher smiled encouragingly at the class.

"Two dollars?" marveled Beverly. "That's a lot of money just for writing."

She could hear her fellow Fernwood Elementary students chattering about which animal they would write about. It sounded like everyone planned to enter the contest.

Beverly wanted her essay to stand out and wondered which animal to write about . . . *Cat? No, too common. Giraffe? Too exotic. Beaver? Yes, that's it!* Beavers were everywhere in Oregon and fascinating creatures by any measure.

That evening, Beverly grabbed a stack of green scratch paper—the leftover check-printing paper from the bank where her father worked—and she wrote down everything she knew about beavers: *They are mostly active at night . . . Their rear feet are webbed, making them excellent swimmers . . . They are second only to humans in how much they change their environment to suit their needs . . .*

Beverly worked on her essay for hours.

The next day, she raced to the store.

"You're the first to turn it in," Mr. Abendroth told her. "Good work!"

Now she just had to be patient and wait for the contest to end.

Days passed, and she tried not to think about it. Finally, the end of the contest arrived, and Beverly ran back to Abendroth's.

"Who won? Who won?" she asked.

Mr. Abendroth scratched his chin, "Hmm, let me think . . ."

Beverly held her breath and crossed her fingers.

"*You* won, Beverly!" he said with a laugh. "And here's your two-dollar prize."

"Really?" Beverly couldn't believe it. "*I* wrote the best essay?"

"Well, you were the only student who turned anything in. But your beaver essay was really good."

Beverly practically floated back to school. She was a writer! A real writer!

Beverly went on to write many, many more stories and to win many, many more prizes. But that day in the fourth grade, she learned one of the most valuable lessons of her entire writing career: you've got to try. "Others will talk about writing but may never get around to trying," she wrote, remembering that day.[1] And thank goodness she did keep trying, or we wouldn't have all of her incredible stories and characters: Ramona, Beezus, Henry, Ribsy, Socks, and Ralph S. Mouse.

Beverly wanted to be a writer her entire life. She was born Beverly Bunn, the only child of a schoolteacher mother and farmer father. She spent her first six years living on an eighty-acre family farm in Yamhill, Oregon, where she was very happy. As a girl, she had a lot of freedom in

One of Beverly's favorite farm activities was tripping chickens! She used a long pole with a hook on the end to snare their feet. Her mother scolded her for it, but Beverly went right on tripping chickens.

the country to roam around on her own. She picked cherries and apples, searched for abandoned bird nests, and got good and dirty. "My parents were much too hardworking to be concerned about a little dirt," she said.[2] She also loved listening to the stories her mother read to her. Beverly always loved a good story.

When she was six, Beverly's family moved to Portland—the big city. She loved her new neighborhood, which was full of children to play with.

We made stilts out of two-pound coffee cans and twine and clanked around the block yelling "Pieface!" at children on the next street and bloodying our knees when the twine broke. . . . We hunted for old bricks among the hazelnut bushes and pounded them into dust in a game we called Brick Factory. With scabs on my knees and brick dust in my hair, I was happy.[3]

Beverly was also thrilled to start first grade at Fernwood Elementary. She was especially excited about learning to read, but the reality was a bitter disappointment. She was used to the exciting stories her mother read to her, but her school readers were filled with boring stories about John and Ruth and Rover. "We wanted action. We wanted a story," she said.[4] Beverly hated them. After she missed a week of school due to chicken pox, she returned to find she was in the lowest reading group: the Blackbirds. Beverly was mortified!

Beverly still has her copy of this much-hated first reader, filled with tear-stained pages.

And her overly strict teacher, Miss Falb, soon made her hate the rest of school as well. When Beverly daydreamed, Miss Falb smacked her hands with a bamboo pointer or stuck her on a

stool facing the corner. "Soon, every school day became a day of fear . . .
I began to beg to stay home from school."[5] Beverly nearly failed first grade.

Lucky for us, Beverly never forgot this challenging first year of school,
and many of her real-life dramas made it into her most beloved Ramona
stories: playing Brick Factory, being teased
about her doll Fordson-Lafayette named for
a tractor (Ramona's doll is named Chevrolet
in the books), and having to sing about
the baffling "dawnzer lee light."[6] Her new
neighborhood in Portland became the setting
for many future books—Klickitat Street
and Fernwood Elementary (now called the
Beverly Cleary School).

> Beverly was so afraid of
> Miss Falb that one day
> she wet her pants. She
> was too scared to ask
> to go to the bathroom!

In the second grade, Beverly got a kinder
teacher, and life improved immensely. She learned to read and gained
back her self-esteem. By third grade, she actually loved reading and spent
a lot of time at the library, but she was still disappointed with her book
choices. Most books at that time were about children who acted noble and
learned something. Beverly knew kids weren't really like that. "I wanted
to read about the sort of boys and girls that I knew in my neighborhood
and in my school . . . I think children like to find themselves in books."[7]

Around this time, Beverly began writing. She entered and won the
essay contest for Abendroth's Grocery. And when a local newspaper, the
Oregon Journal, offered a free book to any child who wrote a book review,
Beverly jumped in. She earned a copy of *The Story of Doctor Doolittle*
(which she loved!) and got her picture printed in the paper, along with
her book review. "Suddenly I was a school celebrity," she remembered.[8]
By sixth grade, a teacher told Beverly that her essays were so good that
she should become a professional writer.

That was Beverly's dream, but her mother had other ideas. "'You must
have some other way of earning a living,'" Beverly recalled her mother
saying. "So I became a children's librarian—the next best thing."[9]

During the Depression, her family was poor (like most families), so
there was no money for college. Luckily, a relative in California offered to

let Beverly live with them, which allowed her to qualify for free in-state college tuition. Beverly went to college and then got her graduate degree in library science at the University of Washington. In 1939, she began her first job as a children's librarian in Yakima, Washington.

Beverly loved working as a librarian but still had trouble finding books with characters that kids could identify with. And books for children who didn't like to read—the same problem she'd had with books when she was a kid. There weren't enough funny stories about regular kids. She vowed that she would write the kinds of stories she knew kids wanted.

> At the bookstore, Beverly often dealt with local authors who became upset that their books weren't better displayed or selling better. Beverly buttered them up, asking them to autograph their titles. But she made a promise to herself that if she ever wrote books, "[she] would never behave in bookstores like Berkeley's local authors."[11]

But first romance got in the way. Back in California, she met and fell in love with Clarence Cleary. Again, Beverly's mother wasn't crazy about her plans (to be with Clarence) because he practiced a different religion than their family. So they eloped in 1940. (And they were married for sixty-four happy years, until Clarence died.)

After the wedding, Beverly and Clarence moved to northern California. Beverly worked part-time in a bookstore, where she learned priceless lessons on which books sold best and what helped them sell. And during World War II, Beverly worked as a librarian at an army base and then at an army hospital. When the war was over, Beverly lost her job and became a housewife, a career that didn't suit her well: "Life as a housewife . . . was a letdown after the stimulating work in the hospital."[10] But the boredom had a positive effect: Beverly started to seriously think about writing a book for children.

The first time she attempted to write, however, she had an experience common to many writers: the terror of the blank page. "When I sat down at my typewriter and stared at the paper I had rolled into it, the typewriter seemed hostile, and the paper remained blank. The longer I stared, the blanker it seemed."[12] She delayed for weeks, instead learning how to braid rugs and carve wood. She made rugs for every room and carved trays, a sewing box, even a mask of a Greek god!

Finally, in 1949, she discovered a ream of typing paper left in the linen closet by the house's former owner. She took it as a sign:

"I guess I'll have to write a book," she told her husband.

"Why don't you?" he asked.

"We never have any sharp pencils," she reasoned.

The next day Clarence brought her a pencil sharpener.[13]

Beverly struggled to come up with a story idea. She remembered her own childhood on the farm in Yakima and later in Portland; she remembered the children she grew up with, the games they played, and the dramas they endured. And then she remembered a story told to her by a coworker at the army hospital about her children taking their dog on a stressful streetcar ride. Beverly took that nugget of an idea and wrote her first book about a boy named Henry and his dog, Ribsy.

Henry and Spareribs was rejected the first time Beverly sent it to publishers—it was too short to be a novel—but she made some changes suggested by an editor, and the next publisher she sent it to accepted it. Retitled *Henry Huggins*, this first book was a hit, and the rest is literary history. Beverly went on to write some of the most beloved children's books of all time—classics like *Beezus and Ramona*, *The Mouse and the Motorcycle*, *Ramona the Brave*, and *Socks*.

> Beverly often baked bread while she wrote. She would mix the dough and then let it rise while she wrote a little. Then she'd take a break and go knead the dough for a while. Then back to the writing. And at the end of a good writing day, she had a new chapter or two plus a fresh-baked loaf of bread!

Beverly has sold eighty-five million copies of forty-one books and has won every award possible in children's literature: a National Book

Award, a Newbery Award, a Laura Ingalls Wilder Award for her "lasting contributions to children's literature," a National Medal of Arts from the National Endowment of Arts, and a Living Legend Award from the Library of Congress.[14]

The reluctant reader who dared to dream of being a writer, Beverly never gave up on it. She spent the rest of her life doing what she loved: writing about real kids. She happily and successfully wrote books for fifty years, and in April 2016, she turned one hundred years old!

If you don't see the book you want on the shelves, write it.

—BEVERLY CLEARY

HOW WILL YOU ROCK THE WORLD?

I will rock the world by creating cool graphic novels. I love to write and draw, and I read graphic novels all the time. My favorites are by Raina Telgemeier, Doug TenNapel, Faith Erin Hicks, and Kazu Kibuishi. My graphic novels will be funny, exciting, and have strong female characters to be role models for girls. I plan to go deeper into this by turning my art and words into comics.

FIONA McCANN · Age 12

Ruth Bader Ginsburg

1933– ⊙ SUPREME COURT JUSTICE ⊙ UNITED STATES

Women belong in all places where decisions are being made.
—RUTH BADER GINSBURG

R uth and her parents were heading home to Brooklyn after a long weekend in the Pennsylvania countryside. Young Ruth kept her mind busy by staring out the window; she saw forests and towns, stores and gas stations flash by. But one bed-and-breakfast caught her eye. Out front, it had a sign that read, "No dogs or Jews allowed!"[1]

Ruth was horrified.

Ruth and her family were Jewish, and although she was young, she had enough experience to know there were people in the world who didn't like Jews. Ruth was well aware that in Europe, millions of Jewish people had recently been murdered in concentration camps. Everyone in America knew. And still there were people who would put up a sign like that.

But what really bothered Ruth about the sign was that it was *unfair*. She was an American, born and raised in this country just like the owners of that bed-and-breakfast. But this sign made it seem like she was worth less than other Americans.

Ruth would spend the rest of her life battling discrimination of all kinds. In fact, she would help create some of America's antidiscrimination laws, along with many others.

–––––~~~–––––

Ruth Bader Ginsburg was born in Brooklyn, New York. Her older sister, Marilyn, died when Ruth was just two, so she was raised as an only child.

When her parents married, her mother, Celia, gave up her job as a bookkeeper to stay home. She instilled a strong work ethic in Ruth, insisting she do well in school and taking her to the library nearly every day.

"One of my greatest pleasures as a child was sitting on my mother's lap when she would read to me," remembered Ruth.[2] She wanted to make her mother proud—and she did. She was an excellent student, always number one in her class. In sixth grade, she published her first legal article in the school newspaper, the *Highway Herald*, entitled "Landmarks of Constitutional Freedom."[3] By eighth grade, she was editor of the paper. In high school, she was in the honor society but also twirled the baton for the pep squad, called the Go-Getters.

Sadly, while Ruth was in high school, her mother was diagnosed with cancer. She died the day before Ruth's graduation but lived long enough to see Ruth get accepted to Cornell University, one of the top colleges in the country, and on a prestigious scholarship to boot. It was all Celia had ever wanted for her daughter.

At Cornell, Ruth was once again top of her class. She also took a first step in her fight against discrimination when she helped a professor do

> Nowadays, Ruth is known as "the Notorious R.B.G.," a takeoff on rapper Notorious B.I.G. There are websites, Tumblr accounts, T-shirts, tote bags— all dedicated to the Notorious R.B.G.
>
> –––––~~~–––––

research on blacklists. In the 1950s, a blacklist named people who were suspected of being Communists—anyone from movie stars to college professors. Whether they actually were communists or not, people on the blacklists lost their jobs, and their reputations and lives were ruined. Ruth watched lawyers risk their careers defending people on the blacklists, in court and in front of Congress.

At Cornell, Ruth also met and fell in love with her future husband, Martin Ginsburg. "Of all the boys I dated," she said, "he was the only one who really cared that I had a brain."[4] Marty was incredibly support-ive of her career, which wasn't common at the time. He was the only person who thought Ruth should become a lawyer instead of a teacher (a more common career for smart women back then), and he convinced her to stick with it. Marty even lobbied behind the scenes in Washington for her Supreme Court nomination. He once told a friend, "I think the most important thing I've done is to enable Ruth to do what she has done."[5]

> When Ruth and Marty had kids, Ruth couldn't cook, so Marty became a master chef. Ruth hasn't cooked a meal since 1980!"

The month Ruth graduated, they mar-ried. Both of them wanted to be lawyers, but that would have to wait. Martin got drafted into the army reserves and the new couple moved to Oklahoma, where Ruth got a job at a Social Security office. There, she experienced sex discrimination firsthand when her boss found out she was pregnant and demoted her.

When Martin's army service ended, he returned to Harvard Law School, and Ruth applied and got in as well. At that time, Harvard Law School only had nine women (including Ruth) out of five hundred first-year law students![6] Female students didn't get much respect there—in fact, the dean of the law school once asked the nine women in Ruth's class how they felt taking spots that should've gone to men!

Sexism wasn't Ruth's only struggle at Harvard; Martin got cancer. The doctors said his chances of survival were almost zero. As he underwent surgery and treatment, Ruth cared for him *and* baby Jane, *and* took notes in all his classes, *and* typed his papers. And she still managed to become one of Harvard's top law students. She was even the first female member of the *Harvard Law Review*, a famous legal journal.

When Martin graduated from Harvard and got a job at a law firm in New York City, Ruth was happy to transfer to Columbia Law School, where they were more accepting of female students. She quickly earned a spot on the *Columbia Law Review*. When she graduated a year later, this working mom tied for the highest grades in her class.

As the top law graduate from two Ivy League universities, Ruth fully expected to have jobs and clerkships thrown at her. After all, that's what would've happened to a man. But that's not what happened to Ruth. About looking for her first job, she said:

> *It was such a rude shock. Employers were saying, "Please don't send us any women. We don't want women in this law firm." My case was particularly difficult, despite my high grades. There I was with three strikes against me: Jewish, woman, and mother.*[7]

Lucky for Ruth, one of her Columbia professors stuck his neck out for her. He arranged an interview with US District Judge Edmund Palmieri.

He told the judge, "If you take a chance on her and she doesn't work out, I'll replace her with a man from the same class. But if you don't give her a chance, I will never send you another Columbia applicant."[8] Ruth got the job and did not need to be replaced.

Years after she left, Harvard tried to give Ruth a belated degree. She turned them down!

Ruth has a positive view of her early struggles to find a job in a male-dominated field and of the discrimination she faced:

> *Suppose I had gotten a job as a permanent associate. Probably I would have climbed up the ladder, and today, I would be a retired partner. So often in life, things that you regard as an impediment turn out to be great good fortune.*[9]

Instead, she clerked for Palmieri for two years and then joined Columbia's Project on International Civil Procedure. In 1963, she got a job as a law professor at Rutgers University and a few years later had her second child, James. At Rutgers, Ruth wore baggy clothing to disguise her pregnancy— she didn't want to give anyone a reason to demote her again.

Soon after James's birth, Ruth began working with the American Civil Liberties Union (ACLU), prosecuting cases of discrimination against women. In 1972, she became codirector of the ACLU Women's Rights Project. That same year, she was also offered a job as professor at Columbia Law School, making her the first woman to get a tenured position there (meaning she couldn't be fired). Throughout the '70s, Ruth battled for equal treatment of women, arguing six women's rights cases before the Supreme Court. She won five of them.[10]

Once she got her foot in the door of America's legal institutions, there was no stopping Ruth. In 1980, President Carter nominated her to the US Court of Appeals in Washington, DC. The thirteen federal appeals courts in America are one step below the Supreme Court. During her thirteen years on the Appeals Court, Ruth wrote *more than three hundred opinions* on all kinds of cases.[11]

Ruth finally got her big break in 1993, when President Clinton got his chance to nominate a Supreme Court justice. Once Ruth met and

> When Ruth found out female faculty salaries at Rutgers were less than their male colleagues, she took it up with the dean. And when he told her that she shouldn't worry about it because her husband had a good job, Ruth joined a lawsuit against the college. They won the suit and enormous pay raises for female professors.
>
> ~~~

> For 200 years, there were *no* female justices on the Supreme Court bench. Ruth was the second ever, and by fall of 2010, there were three (out of nine spots): RBG, Justice Elena Kagan, and Justice Sonia Sotomayor.[12]
>
> ~~~

talked with the president, he was so impressed with her that he knew his search was over. Ruth became the second female Supreme Court justice and the first Jewish female justice.

As part of the Supreme Court, Ruth has been a part of deciding our nation's laws for decades now. Though assertive and vocal in her opinions, she is known as a consensus builder. One of her best friends on the court was the late conservative Justice Antonin Scalia, whom she disagreed with much of the time.

After the Supreme Court ruled to make gay marriage legal in all 50 states, Ruth was the first sitting Supreme Court justice to officiate a same-sex marriage ceremony.

Ruth has always been a trailblazer. And through her legal work and decisions on the bench, she has changed the world for women. For most of her life, she has been fighting against the kind of discrimination she saw on that Pennsylvania sign. "I try to teach through my opinions, through my speeches, how wrong it is to judge people on the basis of what they look like, [the] color of their skin, whether they're men or women."[13] This has always been—and remains—her goal.

When I'm sometimes asked, "When will there be enough [women on the supreme court]?" and I say, "When there are nine," people are shocked. But there'd been nine men, and nobody's ever raised a question about that.

—RUTH BADER GINSBURG

ROCK ON!

JACKIE EVANCHO

Something magical happened when eight-year-old Jackie got her tonsils removed: her voice became amazing! At age ten she performed on TV's *America's Got Talent*. She came in second and launched her singing career. Over the next six years she released seven albums, five of which hit number one on *Billboard's* "Classical Albums" chart. She became the youngest solo artist ever to go platinum. In 2017, Jackie's career hit some turbulence when her sister Juliet came out as transgender around the same time Jackie agreed to perform at the Trump-Pence inauguration. Since that administration does not support LGBTQ rights, Jackie was criticized for endorsing them. Juliet supported her sister, saying that it's an honor for Jackie to sing for her country. Jackie claimed a different motivation—she hoped to "bring people together."

Julie Andrews

1935– ❖ ACTRESS, SINGER, AND AUTHOR ❖ ENGLAND

Perseverance is failing nineteen times and succeeding the twentieth.

—JULIE ANDREWS

Julie hung back, listening. She could hear her mother talking in the next room. She sounded quite upset. "But tomorrow is opening night!" she cried.

"I'm sorry, but Julie is just too young for the show," the producer said. "She's not fitting in."

What he said made sense to Julie. She was just a kid, after all—only twelve years old. *Starlight Roof* was a sophisticated show for grown-ups. Plus, her number, "The Skaters' Waltz," was a silly kids' song.

But her mother didn't give up so easily. She was outraged. "You cannot do this to a young child! She'll be heartbroken!"

The producer didn't answer, but Julie could hear him walking toward the door.

"Wait!" her mother said. "We can make her part better."

He paused. "How?"

"What if she sings something more complicated? Perhaps the 'Polonaise' from *Mignon*."

The producer laughed. "She can't sing that! No twelve-year-old can sing the 'Polonaise.'"

"Julie can."

That made Julie smile. The song was one of the most complicated songs out there, a hundred times harder than "The Skaters' Waltz." She *loved* singing it, and she was thrilled when the producer agreed to her mother's plan.

On opening night, Julie stepped onstage at her cue. The audience was surprised to see such a young girl singing in the show. When she opened her mouth, a strong, beautiful, soprano burst out. Julie's voice skipped up and down the scale like she skipped up the stairs at home. It leapt octaves and shifted keys on a dime. At the cadenza, the most challenging part of the song, Julie held the high C note . . . and then she pushed her voice even higher—up to the high F. It was an impossibly high note. But not for Julie.

When she finished the crowd was silent. *Was I not good enough?* she worried. Then they erupted in applause. They rose to their feet, clapping and whistling for the young girl with the amazing voice. Their standing ovation went on and on, literally stopping the show.[1]

The next morning, reviews called Julie Andrews a "prodigy with pigtails."[2] Her rise to stardom was practically a sure thing after that. But it wasn't always so.

~~~

Julie was born in Walton-on-Thames, a village in the south of England, to two very broke parents. Her father, Ted Wells, taught woodworking and metalworking; her mother, Barbara, played piano; and they shared a tiny house with Julie's aunt, who taught dance lessons. Julie grew up surrounded by music but not money.

When Julie was around four years old, her mother began traveling for long periods of time, playing piano for a singer named Ted Andrews. Within a year, her mother abandoned her two children entirely and took off with her new beau. Julie adored her father and was heartbroken that her mother had left them. A few months after the start of World War II, her mother sent for six-year-old Julie to come live with her in London, but she did not send for Julie's younger brother. Julie was very angry with her and didn't want to leave her father and brother behind to live with her mother and the boyfriend she hated.

Julie's early years in London were tough. It was "a very black period in my life," she said, and added that they were "very poor . . . [we] lived in a bad slum area of London."[3] It was also during World War II, and London was a very dangerous place to live. The Germans bombed it constantly, and Julie spent a lot of time taking shelter in the subways, basements, and bomb shelters. Her mother married Ted Andrews and they were often gone, entertaining the troops. Julie spent many years feeling lonely and scared.

> Julie really did have some amazing pipes. At age seven, a throat specialist declared she had an almost adult larynx. By 12, Julie could sing difficult songs that challenged most professional adult singers. She was a soprano with a four-octave range, meaning she could sing the notes for more than half the keys on a piano.

Julie's stepfather began teaching her to sing when she was seven years old. Her parents were quite surprised to discover that their young daughter had an incredible voice. At age nine, they began paying for a professional singing coach. Julie's voice coach said of her star pupil, "The range, accuracy, and tone of Julie's voice amazed me. . . . All her life she had possessed the rare gift of absolute pitch."[4] Julie was just happy to be taking lessons from someone besides her detested stepfather.

By age nine, Julie was joining her mother and stepfather onstage, singing in their shows. She had to stand on a beer crate to reach the microphone. As the war drew to an end, the act began making more money, and the family was able to move to a larger, nicer home called Old Meuse. Many years before, Julie's grandmother had worked at the same large house as a maid!

Julie got her first big break when she was twelve. Her stepfather got her an audition for a London musical revue called *Starlight Roof*, and Julie got the part. Julie remembered the crowd's reaction to her vocal gymnastics: "I was fortunate in that I absolutely stopped the show cold; I mean, the audience went crazy."[5] Julie's showbiz career was underway.

While Julie's singing career was taking off, life at home was getting much worse. Her stepfather began to drink heavily and fight with her mother. In response, her mother drank more as well. The drinking and fighting hurt their act and the jobs dried up. With no work, they couldn't afford the big house they'd purchased. By the time she was fifteen, Julie's work supported her entire family and paid the mortgage on Old Meuse.

Her relationship with her stepfather hit rock bottom, too. Starting when Julie was nine, he tried to take advantage of her sexually by sneaking into her bed when her mother was gone. Each time, Julie managed to get away, but when she hit her teens, he got more persistent. Julie told her aunt, who installed a lock on her bedroom door to keep him out.

> Julie was often moved to tears when she sang. "Mum would turn around and see me simply bawling my eyes out." Her mother would scold her for being foolish, but her singing coach told her, "You must never be embarrassed when you are moved by music. It shows that you are a sensitive human being, capable of much feeling."[6]

In 1954, when she was eighteen, Julie had her American debut in the Broadway musical *The Boy Friend*. Once again, Julie's voice wowed critics and audiences, and her next role was even bigger: Eliza Doolittle in *My Fair Lady*. The play was a huge success and was later made into a popular movie. While starring in the play, she also got the lead role in a Rodgers and Hammerstein TV musical, *Cinderella*. Her performance was broadcast live in 1957 in front of more than one hundred million TV viewers.[7] Suddenly, Julie Andrews was a household name.

In 1964, Julie made the leap from stage to screen, where audiences loved her even more. Her first movie was *Mary Poppins*, in which she played a "practically perfect" nanny. The movie became the biggest box-office success in Disney history, and Julie won a Best Actress Oscar for her performance.

> Julie wasn't chosen to play Eliza in the *My Fair Lady* movie. Instead, producers gave the role to a better-known actress, Audrey Hepburn. But Hepburn couldn't sing, so they had to dub in a different singer's voice!
>
> ～～～

The next year, she starred as another perfect nanny in another beloved movie, *The Sound of Music*. It was the highest-grossing movie that year, and for her portrayal of Maria, the nanny who gets the von Trapp Family singing again, she earned an Academy Award nomination and a Golden Globe win for Best Actress in a Musical. With those two hit musicals, Julie Andrews became a bona fide movie star.

> Julie initially turned down the role of Mary Poppins because she was pregnant. But Disney wanted her so badly, the movie was postponed until she was ready!
>
> ～～～

Over the next fifty years, Julie starred in many TV shows and movies—some hits, some not. You might recognize her from her more recent movies, *The Princess Diaries 1* and *2*, in which she played Queen Clarisse; or you might know her voice from the *Shrek* movies (she's the queen, of course) and *Despicable Me* (she's Gru's mom).

In 1997, Julie got a hoarse throat while starring in a Broadway musical. She had surgery to remove several nodules from her vocal cords (a relatively common hazard for professional singers), but the surgery did permanent damage to her beautiful voice. She was never able to sing at her full range or strength again. Instead, she shifted to her other talents. Back in 1974, Julie had written her first children's book, *The Last of the Really Great Whangdoodles* (published under her married name, Julie Andrews Edwards); after the botched surgery, she went on to publish more than thirty children's books, going from movie star to bestselling author.

Julie has won more awards and honors than you can count. In 2000, Queen Elizabeth made Julie a dame for her "services to the performing arts." In 2002, the BBC put her on the list of "100 Greatest Britons." And during her fifty-plus years in showbiz, Julie has won an Academy Award, a BAFTA (an award from the British Academy of Film and Television Arts), five Golden Globes, three Grammys, two Emmys, a Screen Actors Guild Lifetime Achievement Award, and a Disney Legend Award.

Back when she was 13, Julie did a screen test for MGM Studios. She sang a song and did a short acting scene, so producers could see if she had what it took to be in the movies. What did they think of the future Oscar winner? "She's not photogenic enough for film."[8]

Even in her seventies and eighties, Julie hasn't slowed down much. She still acts in movies and on TV, gives concerts, and writes bestsellers. Since her first standing ovation, this "prodigy with pigtails" has conquered Broadway, Hollywood, and even our bookshelves, showing the world there's always a higher note to strive for.

HOW WILL YOU ROCK THE WORLD?

I will rock the world by becoming a set designer and producer, making magic come to life onstage for thousands of people. I know that I will impact at least one person in my future. Knowing this, I'm excited to change the world!

KELSI GEORGIA ☀ AGE 16

WaNgaRi Maathai

1940–2011 ⬦ ENVIRONMENTAL ACTIVIST ⬦ KENYA

Trees are living symbols of peace and hope.

—WANGARI MAATHAI

Wangari's eyes opened wide and she craned her head back so far, she worried she might fall over. . . or get knocked down by the rushing crowd. She was in New York City! Cars and taxis beeped their horns, street vendors hollered, glass and metal skyscrapers soared up into the sky. To young Wangari, they looked as if they were swaying in the wind and touching the clouds. It made her dizzy. Back in her African village, Ihithe, the only thing that scraped the clouds was Mount Kenya!

The Big Apple is pretty amazing to most first-time visitors, but for young Wangari Maathai, it was life changing. She had never before been out of Africa. Never been to a big city. Never been on an airplane! As the top student in her high school, she had been chosen by her teachers for an amazing opportunity: Senator John F. Kennedy (soon to be president of the United States) had offered scholarships to three hundred Kenyan students to travel to America and go to college.

In Kenya, few girls attended school at all. And here she was going to college. In America! She could hardly believe it.

But that was just the beginning. This girl from a tiny village in Kenya would grow up to be an environmental leader, would start a political movement across Africa, and would one day win the Nobel Peace Prize!

―――

In 1940, Wangari was born in a traditional mud-walled house with no electricity, running water, or indoor bathroom. She was the oldest of five siblings and a part of the Kikuyu tribe. Back then, Kenya was ruled as a colony by the United Kingdom. White, British colonists owned the land and businesses. The Africans, like Wangari's family, merely worked for the white people on their land for very little money, if any. Her father was a driver for a white landowner, and her mother took care of Wangari's house and the family.

Wangari always felt a special connection to the nature around her. "When my mother would send me to fetch water," Wangari writes, "I would get lost in this fascinating world of nature until she would call out, 'What are you doing under the arrowroots? Bring the water!'"[1] She noticed the streams and plants and trees around her; she noticed the frogs and birds and insects that lived there. And she thought about the larger animals—the elephants and monkeys and leopards—that she couldn't see but knew were living deeper in the forests. Young Wangari noticed how the land and plants and animals were all connected—without one, the others could not survive. Her mother always told her, "A tree is worth more than its wood."[2] This was wisdom she never forgot.

When Wangari was a young girl, her mother gave her a small plot of land to grow a garden of her own. Wangari planted sweet potatoes, beans, maize, and millet (a seeded grass used as grain or cereal). This garden is where she first learned how to dig and plant and tend the earth—skills that would serve her well later in life.

―――

Wangari's younger brothers went to school, but it was very unusual at that time for Kenyan girls to get any education. Girls did women's work with their mothers until they were old enough to marry, and then they did it for their husbands. But Wangari got lucky. One day, her younger brother asked, "How come Wangari doesn't go to school like the rest of us?" Her mother answered, "There's no reason why not."[3] And so, eight-year-old Wangari started school.

She was a quick learner. First, she went to her village school, but at eleven, she left her family to move to a Catholic boarding school in a nearby village. In 1959, Wangari graduated from high school at the top of her class and a few months later was one of three hundred Kenyan students chosen for a scholarship to go to an American college.[4] For four years, Wangari studied science at Mount Saint Scholastica College in Kansas. She loved learning about the life cycles and ecosystems she had so carefully observed as a young girl.

The Green Belt Movement made lasting change in Africa, planting more than 30 million trees and giving jobs to almost a million women. The movement also inspired similar movements in Ethiopia, Tanzania, and Zimbabwe.[5]

The experience wasn't perfect, however. Wangari had witnessed racism in Kenya in the way the colonial white people treated their black workers and neighbors, but she didn't expect it in the United States. She was shocked to see signs forbidding black Americans from using the same bathrooms, restaurants, and stores as whites, or signs segregating blacks into their own section of these public spaces. She realized that even though the countries were different in many ways, in this way, they weren't so different. In America, the civil rights movement was under way, with black Americans fighting for equal rights. In Kenya, her people were fighting to gain independence from Britain, which they did in 1963.

Wangari earned a degree in biology and then returned to Kenya and got a job as the assistant to the director of the veterinary anatomy department at the University of Nairobi. In 1969, she married and had three children but also continued her career. Two years later, she became the first East African woman to earn her PhD; a few years after that, she was promoted to assistant professor and then director of the veterinary anatomy department.

During this busy time in her life, Wangari noticed a change in Kenya. When she was younger, the white colonists were the ones cutting down the forests, but now it was her own people cutting trees to sell. They were also making room for profitable crops like tea, coffee, and tobacco to sell to rich countries. The forests of Kenya were disappearing, and as a result, wild animals were losing their habitats. Rivers were muddy because there were no trees left to hold back the dirt when it rained. Women were having trouble feeding their families because plantations for export crops replaced food-growing farms.

> The people of Kenya call Wangari *Mama Miti*, meaning "Mother of Trees."

Wangari knew she had to do something, but what? In 1977, inspiration struck:

> It just came to me: "Why not plant trees?"... The trees would offer shade for humans and animals, protect watersheds and bind the soil, and, if they were fruit trees, provide food. They would also heal the land by bringing back birds and small animals...[6]

Wangari traveled from village to village, explaining the importance of trees and asking people to think of the future, not just the present. She created tree nurseries across Kenya, putting local women in charge of replanting trees in their area. Her effort evolved into the Green Belt Movement.

Wangari and her Green Belt Movement protested the Kenyan government and its environmental policies. She was not popular with the men in charge, who didn't like being challenged by a woman. They threw her in jail. They beat her. They threatened to kill her. But Wangari never gave up. She organized her own party, she ran for office, and she protested. When president/dictator Daniel arap Moi planned to build a sixty-story skyscraper inside Nairobi's Uhuru Park, Wangari organized a huge demonstration, and the government gave up the project. Every time the government tried to mess with the environment, Wangari was there, fighting.

When Moi finally lost power in 2002 (after being "president" for twenty-four years!), Wangari ran for office and won a seat in Parliament. In 2003, the new president appointed her minister of the Environment, Natural Resources, and Wildlife. A year later, she was awarded the world's most prestigious honor, the Nobel Peace Prize, "for her contribution to sustainable development, democracy, and peace."[7] She was the first African woman to receive it.

Although she died in 2011, Wangari's dream lives on in Africa. Today, thanks to her work, there are way more trees in Kenya than when she started. Wangari's Green Belt Movement has succeeded in planting more than fifty-one million trees since she founded it in 1977![8] And thanks to her fighting, protesting, and organizing, Kenya is now a free democracy. Her political organization is still protecting and planting and building a better future for Africa.

ROCK ON!

DURO–AINA ADEBOLA, AKINDELE ABIOLA, FALEKE OLUWATOYIN, AND BELLO ENIOLA

Duro-Aina Adebola, Akindele Abiola, Faleke Oluwatoyin, and Bello Eniola invented a urine-powered generator that could help millions in their home country of Nigeria and around the world. With their invention, one liter of urine is converted into six hours of electricity. Generators are a common power source in the developing world. In Lagos, where the girls are from, there are daily power outages, and people use generators while power is out. One expert predicted that if they collected urine from a single university (about twenty-two thousand students), they could power 100–150 houses for a year! Pee power, anyone?

Aretha Franklin

1942– ◦ SINGER ◦ UNITED STATES

*We all require and want respect, man or woman, black or white.
It's our basic human right.*

—ARETHA FRANKLIN

Aretha stepped up onto the chair. From this height, she could see the whole congregation at New Bethel Baptist Church. They were all staring at her, some fanning themselves as they waited. It seemed like they were holding their breath.

Aretha was a little nervous. She had been singing in church and at home for as long as she could remember, and she was ten now—practically a grown-up. But there were a lot of people sitting out in those pews, and they were all staring at her. Not at her father. Not at the choir. At *her*.

It made her nervous but also excited. This was her first solo, and she wanted it to be good.

She wished her mama were here. But her mama was dead now. Aretha tucked a stray curl of hair back into place, fidgeted with her skirt. Then the piano player struck the first chord. It was "Jesus, Be a Fence Around

Me," one of Aretha's favorite hymns. She closed her eyes and let the music flow in. Then she opened her mouth and sang. Aretha put her heart and soul into it, as she'd seen famous gospel singers do for years. She felt the spirit and emotion in every word she sang.

The audience was astonished. They knew Reverend Franklin's ten-year-old daughter could sing, but they had no idea she sounded like this.

After the services were over, the congregation mobbed Reverend Franklin. "Oh, that child sure can sing!" they marveled.

And she hasn't stopped singing since.

―――

Aretha Louise Franklin was practically born singing. Her mother was a piano player and singer, and her father was a famous minister with a "million-dollar voice."[1] The whole family sang, in fact Aretha remembered, "The radio was going in one room, the record player in another, the piano banging away in the living room."[2] And because of her father's position in the church, their home was often filled with famous gospel singers.

Aretha's father tried to get her to take piano lessons, but she hated them. Too much like school. Whenever the piano teacher came, Aretha hid. Eventually, he gave up, and Aretha taught herself to play "by ear" (listening to songs and playing them back, without sheet music).

―――

Aretha spent most of her childhood in Detroit, Michigan. Her parents split up when she was six and her mother moved away, so she was raised by her grandmother (Big Mama), aunts, and family friends. When she was around eight, she taught herself to play piano and began singing in her father's church choir. Aretha loved to sing: "I had a piano off the back porch, and sometimes I'd sing . . . all day, every day, with my sisters and friends," she said.[3]

When Aretha was ten, her mother died. At about this time she began singing solos at New Bethel. Audiences loved her and, like a diva in the making, Aretha loved the attention. Her father, with his beautiful voice, was such a popular minister that he was invited to preach all over the country and was paid handsomely for it. He put together a gospel caravan to perform with him on his travels. When Aretha was fourteen, he began taking her too. She was such a hit, her father started managing her, thereby launching her singing career.

Aretha's career took off fast. At age fourteen, she got her first record contract to sing gospel music with JVB Records. Her first album, *Songs of Faith*, came out in 1956—that same year—and Aretha was thrilled to hear her songs on gospel radio stations. By the time she was eighteen, she was ready to do more than just gospel. She loved listening to other kinds of music on the radio and wanted to spread her wings. She told her father her plan, and to her surprise, he was completely supportive. He helped her cut a two-song demo and shopped it around to bigger record labels.

On the road, with no mother and a constantly working father, Aretha pretty much raised herself. She was exposed to a lifestyle that wasn't exactly appropriate for a young girl, surrounded by adult performers who drank, partied, and had sex. Aretha herself had two teenage pregnancies, but she kept both her sons, relying on family to take care of them while she was traveling, building her career.[5]

Columbia Records offered her a contract, and her first single, "Today I Sing the Blues," made it into the top ten of the "R&B" (rhythm and blues) *Billboard* Chart in 1960.[4] Eighteen-year-old Aretha had made it into the big leagues!

At Columbia, Aretha recorded songs in all kinds of styles: jazz, blues, doo-wop, rhythm and blues. But after six years with the label, she wasn't making much progress; she felt like Columbia was holding her back. So in 1967, she switched to Atlantic Records.

It was the right move.

Her first album with Atlantic, *I Never Loved a Man the Way I Love You*, came out in 1967. Her first single with Atlantic, the title song of

Detroit in the 1950s and '60s was chock-full of talented black musicians, and Aretha knew them all. Sam Cooke and Smokey Robinson were family friends, and Diana Ross (of The Supremes) was a neighbor!

the album, shot to number one on the R&B chart and number nine on the pop chart.[6] Her second single, "Do Right Woman, Do Right Man," also climbed the charts. The record with these two singles became her first record that sold over one million copies.[7] Aretha's third single, "Respect," hit number one on both the R&B and pop charts. The album went gold that first year and made *Rolling Stone* magazine's list of *The 500 Greatest Albums of All Time* in 2003.[8]

By the end of the '60s, Aretha had earned herself the nickname "The Queen of Soul." Her next album had two of her greatest hits, "Chain of Fools" and "I Say a Little Prayer," and she won her first Grammy Awards, including Best Female R&B Vocal Performance. In 1968, she not only landed on the cover of *Time* magazine but was also given an award by her good friend Martin Luther King Jr. just two months before his death.

"Respect" became Aretha's signature song. Her empowering lyrics grew into a forceful rallying cry for both the women's movement and the civil rights movement.

Aretha and her amazing voice dominated the charts for decades, smashing records and firmly establishing her spot at the top of the music world. She is the most charted female artist in the world (that's for 112 singles on the *Billboard* charts).[9] She's won eighteen Grammy Awards and sold more than seventy-five million records worldwide, making her one of bestselling artists of all time.[10] Aretha was the first female performer inducted into the Rock and Roll Hall of Fame; she is also in the British Music Hall of Fame and the Gospel Music Hall of Fame. *Rolling Stone* magazine listed her number nine in the "100 Greatest Artists of All Time" and number one for the "100 Greatest Singers of All Time."[11]

Aretha went on tour as recently as 2015–16. Could the seventy-three-year-old legend still rock the house? Let's just say that when she performed "(You Make Me Feel Like) A Natural Woman" at the Kennedy Center in Washington, DC, she brought President Obama to tears.

Aretha's voice has a way of doing that.

Being the Queen is not all about singing, and being a diva is not all about singing. It has much to do with your service to people. And your social contributions to your community, and your civic contributions as well.

—ARETHA FRANKLIN

HOW WILL YOU ROCK THE WORLD?

I will rock the world by being the best lawyer. I will do so by keeping the law enforced and making the world safer by putting bad people in jail. I will work hard and do my best to have fun *and* take my job seriously.

DEJANAEH GETTY · AGE 11

Hillary Rodham Clinton

1947– ❀ POLITICIAN AND SECRETARY OF STATE ❀ UNITED STATES

As long as discrimination and inequities remain so commonplace
everywhere in the world; as long as girls and women are
valued less, fed less, fed last, overworked, underpaid,
not schooled, subjected to violence in and outside their homes,
the potential of the human family to create
a peaceful, prosperous world will
not be realized.

—HILLARY CLINTON

Hillary sprinted to the mailbox and rifled through the bills and letters. *It's here!* she marveled, snatching out the letter with the NASA logo on it.

Weeks earlier, she had written to NASA asking what she could do to become an astronaut. The "space race" between the United States and Russia was in full swing, and it seemed Russia was winning. Everyone knew NASA was recruiting the best and the brightest for its astronaut training program. Thirteen-year-old Hillary was an excellent student, was physically fit, and wanted to serve her country. Becoming an astronaut seemed like a great way to do that.

She tore open the envelope. *Maybe they want me to come to a training program . . .*

As she read the short letter, her hopes crashed back down to Earth. "There will not be any women astronauts,"[1] was NASA's response. Hillary was devastated. But she was also angry.

It isn't fair! she thought. *Why do boys get to do everything and girls' choices are so limited?*

That's right—before she wanted to be president of the United States, young Hillary Clinton wanted to be an astronaut. But back in the 1950s, that wasn't possible; in fact, an American woman didn't go into space for thirty more years (Sally Ride in 1983)! This was a turning point for young Hillary. It was her first real experience with discrimination, and she didn't like it. She has spent the rest of her life showing the world what girls and women are capable of.

mm

Hillary grew up in Park Ridge, Illinois, a conservative suburb of Chicago. Her father owned a business that made and sold curtains, and her mother was a homemaker. Her father had grown up poor, worked in coal mines, and lived as a hobo for a time. He attributed his success to his own hard work and believed that anyone who couldn't do the same wasn't trying hard enough. He once drove the family through the slums of Chicago to show his children what happened to people who didn't work hard.

Hillary's mother was abandoned by her parents when she was very young. She had to fend for herself her entire life, which gave her great empathy for poor, struggling families. She told her daughter, "Things happen to people that they have no control over."[2] She was secretly a Democrat—one of the very few in Park Ridge.

As a child, Hillary was a tomboy who played sports and excelled in school. She ran for school office from elementary school on, and she did things like organize a mock Olympics to raise money for United Way. Her

When a neighbor girl bullied four-year-old Hillary, she tried to hide inside the house, but her mother blocked the door. She told Hillary, "There's no room in this house for cowards. You're going to have to stand up to her. The next time she hits you, I want you to hit her back."[7] Hillary did what her mother asked—she hit back and was never bullied again.

father didn't pay allowances, so at thirteen, Hillary got a job cleaning a local park to earn spending money.

Soon after getting the rejection letter from NASA, she joined the University of Life group at her church. Her pastor, Don Jones, taught the group about life outside of Park Ridge and told them they needed to "put their faith into action."[3] Hillary already had firsthand experience with discrimination against women and girls, but she soon learned about other kinds of discrimination. Don took the kids to Chicago's rough South Side, where they met with an all-black youth group and discussed the civil rights movement, which was fighting discrimination of African Americans. "It just kind of opened my mind,"[4] Hillary said of Pastor Don's teachings.

When Hillary was fifteen, Pastor Don took the University of Life group to hear a speech by Dr. Martin Luther King Jr., the leader of the civil rights movement. He urged his audience to "participate in the cause of justice, not to slumber while the world changed . . ." Afterward, Hillary was invited to shake his hand and speak with him briefly. She called the experience one of the greatest privileges of her life.[5]

During her junior year of high school, Hillary was elected class vice president. When she ran for class president her senior year, the boy who beat her said, "You are really stupid if you think a girl can be elected president."[6] In spite of her mother and Pastor Don's Democratic leanings, Hillary followed her father's politics during high school. She was part of an anti-Communist club, she joined a Republican group called the Goldwater Girls, and she campaigned door-to-door for presidential candidate Barry Goldwater.

Hillary graduated in the top 5 percent of her class, was a National Merit finalist, and was voted "Most Likely to Succeed" by her classmates. She should have had her pick of colleges, but the most prestigious schools still only accepted men. Hillary chose Wellesley, a top all-women's college, and majored in political science. Her political views shifted—she became opposed to the Vietnam War and supported the civil rights movement—so she decided to switch to the Democrats.

Then she ran for president of student government and won! Thanks to Hillary, the college made many improvements. She helped change outdated school rules and curriculum requirements that seemed intended to turn the Wellesley students into educated housewives. She also helped convince the administration to get rid of restrictions on black student admissions and to hire more diverse faculty.

At her graduation, she became the first Wellesley student in history to be invited to speak at the ceremony. In her speech, she criticized the school's guest speaker, Republican Senator Edward Brooke, and spoke out against the war. The audience gave her a seven-minute standing ovation! During her college years, Hillary had learned to speak her mind, even when it was controversial and could get her into trouble. Her speech drew national attention, and she was interviewed on national TV and in newspapers, and was even profiled in *Life* magazine!

After two years, Pastor Don was forced out of Park Ridge by the conservative parents who didn't like him exposing their children to his radical ideas. He remained a mentor for Hillary, however. She wrote to him for guidance after he left and throughout her college years, as her political beliefs changed.

In her Wellesley graduation speech, Hillary inspired her audience with her unifying words: "We are, all of us, exploring a world that none of us even understands and attempting to create within that uncertainty. . . . Fear is always with us, but we just don't have time for it. Not now."[8]

Hillary decided that the best way to serve her country (if she couldn't be an astronaut) was to become a lawyer. She went to Yale Law School. While getting her law degree, she volunteered her time working on cases of child abuse at a local hospital and gave free legal services for the poor. She also worked with Marian Wright Edelman, an activist for children's rights, researching problems migrant workers faced with housing, health, and education.

During her second year of law school, she met fellow law student Bill Clinton, and they fell in love. Bill asked her repeatedly to marry him, but Hillary wasn't sure. He wanted to go into politics, and she wasn't sure she wanted to follow his path. Hillary had her own dreams to pursue.

After graduating from law school, she went to work for Edelman's newly founded Children's Defense Fund, fighting for the legal rights of children and families. She was on the impeachment inquiry staff during Nixon's Watergate scandal. Everyone around her felt she had a bright political future: she could be a US senator, or even the president!

"I chose to follow my heart instead of my head," she explained of her decision to follow Bill to his home state of Arkansas instead of staying in Washington to pursue her own political career.[9] She got a job teaching law at the University of Arkansas and was one of two women on the faculty. In 1975, four years after they met, Hillary finally agreed to marry Bill. But she kept her maiden name—Rodham—a move that was controversial at the time. Five years later, she had baby Chelsea.

In Arkansas, Bill's political career took off. First he was elected the state's attorney general and then, in 1978, governor. Hillary became First Lady of Arkansas, a title she would hold for twelve years, but she didn't choose the traditional path of the supportive, nonworking wife of a politician. Even though she knew it was controversial and might get her into trouble, she continued to pursue her law career. She was the first female lawyer at her law firm, and later, their first female partner. From 1978 until they entered the White House in 1992, Hillary earned more money than Bill.[10] In fact, when he lost his 1980 run for governor, she was the only breadwinner in the family.

But Hillary didn't just want to be a good lawyer and provide for her family; she wanted to change the world. In 1977, she cofounded the Arkansas Advocates for Children and Families, and in 1979, Bill appointed her the chair of the Rural Health Advisory Committee, to help bring healthcare to Arkansas's poorest areas—two moves in the right direction.

When her husband was elected president of the United States, Hillary became a different kind of First Lady as well. She was the first First Lady to have her own office in the West Wing (just like the president). She was also the first First Lady to head up a task force on affordable healthcare for all (with a staff of over five hundred), the findings of which she then presented to Congress.[11] She helped create the Office on Violence Against Women at the Department of Justice, and she helped pass the State Children's Health Insurance Program, which provided services to poor families. In addition, she drafted and helped pass the Adoption and Safe Families Act. Hillary continued making her own difference in the world, following her own dreams as Bill pursued his.

> Hillary was an excellent lawyer. Two times, the *National Law Journal* named her one of "The 100 Most Influential Lawyers in America."

With trips to seventy-nine countries, she added the most-traveled First Lady to her list of achievements too. She wasn't just sightseeing either; she was helping with US diplomacy. In China, she spoke about women's rights around the world. "Women's rights are human rights,"[12] she told the crowd. Her remarks were controversial and could have gotten her into trouble, but she made them anyway.

When her husband's two terms were up, Hillary decided not to go back to Arkansas and her law practice. Instead, she ran for US Senate in 2000, representing the state of New York (the first First Lady to do that), and won. Out of one hundred senators, she was one of *only thirteen women*.

She served in the Senate for eight years, earning a reputation for working across party lines to get things done. One journalist wrote, "Clinton has emerged within the Senate as the unlikeliest of figures: she . . . has turned out to be a uniter, not a divider."[13] A childhood spent navigating between her Republican father and Democrat mother served Hillary well in this work.

In 2008, Hillary ran for president, but she lost in the primaries to exciting newcomer Barack Obama. Obama was so impressed with Hillary's experience and talents, however, that he made her his secretary of state, in charge of America's foreign relations. All the relationships she made during her travels as First Lady and her time in the Senate were put to great use.

As always, Hillary worked her butt off. During her time in the office, Hillary visited 112 countries—more than any US secretary of state in history.[14] She also pushed for women's rights and for equality of the sexes around the world—even when it was controversial. In Egypt, where women have fewer rights than men, she urged equality. In Cambodia, where very few girls are allowed to go to school, she argued for more opportunities. She founded the global group No Ceilings, which works to improve the lives of girls and women. Hillary has become an inspiration around the world. Mu Sochua, Cambodian politician and Nobel Prize nominee, said Hillary gave her the courage to become a politician and change things in her country: "Watching her, I had the sense that I could do it, that other women could do it."[15]

In 2016, Hillary tried for the White House one more time. She beat Bernie Sanders in the primary and became the Democratic Party's nomination for president of the United States—the first woman to ever be nominated by a major US political party. Hillary ran a strong campaign against Republican nominee Donald Trump, business tycoon and reality-TV star. She fought hard and stood up for her beliefs in an extremely unusual and polarizing race. On election night, though she won the popular vote by nearly three million votes, she lost the Electoral College 232 to Trump's 306 votes.[16] Donald Trump became America's forty-fifth president.

Hillary Clinton has spent her life making the world a better place, fighting discrimination and injustice. As a girl, she spoke her mind, even when it went against the grain of popular opinion. And she's continued speaking her mind and rocking the world ever since.

Now, I know we have still not shattered that highest and hardest glass ceiling, but some day, someone will, and hopefully sooner than we might think right now. And to all the little girls who are watching this, never doubt that you are valuable and powerful and deserving of every chance and opportunity in the world to pursue and achieve your own dreams.

—HILLARY CLINTON

HOW WILL YOU ROCK THE WORLD?

I will rock the world by becoming the first female president of the United States. I will give the Mexican people a chance to live here. I would help poor people follow their dreams.

ANGELINA HERNANDEZ ⚛ AGE 15

Sheila Sri Prakash

1955– ✿ ARCHITECT ✿ INDIA

I take my role as an architect seriously because my thoughts and actions are bound to have a lasting impact on people, society, and the planet.

—SHEILA SRI PRAKASH

Sheila sat waiting in the principal's office. He was reading her application, glancing up at her every few minutes. *When will the interview begin?* she wondered.

She rubbed her hands nervously up and down her sari. It was her nicest one—she wanted to make a good impression. She was applying to Anna University School of Architecture and Planning in southern India, and she knew they didn't have any girls at the school. Not yet.

Sheila had wanted to be an architect for many years now. She felt drawn to it and saw it as a way to improve people's lives. Her years as a dancer had given her an idea of how a space could influence your performance; she wanted to design spaces that would help people to be their best.

A sound interrupted her thoughts. The principal had dropped her paperwork on the desk and was staring at her. Sheila stilled her trembling hands. She was ready—she could answer anything he threw at her about design, favorite buildings, influential architects. She wasn't prepared, however, for the question he asked.

"Don't you think you would be wasting a seat?"

What? Sheila didn't understand. She had excellent grades and was considered a child prodigy in several performing arts. *What is he talking about?*

Before she could compose an answer, he continued, "If a *boy* got this seat, don't you think he could pursue a career better?"

She couldn't believe it! This man didn't think she could do it. Just because she was a girl. Sheila gathered her thoughts and her nerve, and then she sat up straight and looked right into his eyes.

"No," she answered. "I am a woman, but I'm quite serious."[1]

Months later, Sheila sat in her first design class. She looked around at her classmates—all boys. They and the teachers seemed a bit baffled to see a girl sitting there. She would show them, and the principal too, that she wasn't wasting a seat. She would use architecture to make the world a better place.

Today, Sheila is one of the top architects in the world. A respected, award-winning innovator known for her sustainable, environmentally friendly designs. But Sheila's path wasn't always clear. As a child, her passion wasn't architecture, but dance.

Sheila was born in 1955 in Bhopal, India. Her parents tried to have a baby for fifteen years before she was born, and Sheila was their one and only child, becoming the center of their lives. At that time, Indian women were not expected to have careers outside the home. But Sheila's father told her over and over again that she could do whatever she wanted. "You just have to dream, and that is enough . . . It will get you there," he told her.[2]

Sheila was smart and loved to learn. She explored everything but was especially drawn to the arts. She learned to sing, play instruments, paint, and sculpt, but it was dance that she fell in love with. At age four, she began training in the classical Indian dance Bharatanatyam. It turned out that she had a gift for it; by age six, she was performing to amazed crowds. People began calling her a child prodigy (someone under the age of ten who achieves to the same level as an adult expert in their field), and child prodigies are rare.

After more than a decade as a celebrated dancer, Sheila switched gears. In 1973, at age eighteen, she went to college to study architecture. Sheila explained the connection between her passions:

Even as an eight-year-old I was extremely intrigued and fascinated by architecture and design. As a trained dancer, we create an ambiance and then we perform. We don't have the props and sets behind us, so we say that a river is flowing, there is a tree here . . . And then you set the scene for what is to come.[3]

> *Bharatanatyam* is a solo dance performed by women wearing bright costumes. It began in Hindu temples in India to express spiritual ideas and stories. Performers must keep their upper torso completely still and legs bent. They move only their feet and arms, conveying story and emotion through complicated hand gestures and eye and face movements. This dance has been performed for over a thousand years. Although it was banned during the British colonial period (1612–1947), it has since enjoyed a rebirth.

There were very few female architects in India at that time, and none at her university. But Sheila knew what she wanted. She thought if people lived in a positive environment, they could be empowered more easily, could perform better. Once out of school, she had to fight hard for her beliefs—and for work. She had to prove herself over and over again; she got threatening phone calls. Some clients thought they didn't have to pay her because she was a woman. Contractors and laborers who were supposed to construct her designs didn't believe a woman could know about building things. She had to work harder than her male colleagues to earn respect.

As Sheila's buildings grew, so did her reputation. In 1979, she was the first woman to start and run her own architecture firm, Shilpa Architects, which is still in business today. During her career that spans more than thirty-five years, Sheila has designed more than 1,200 projects—everything from low-cost housing to energy-efficient office buildings; residential communities, art museums, and sports stadiums to schools and luxury hotels.[4]

> Sheila is considered the founder of "spaciology," the science of environment and behavior, which studies the impact of the built environment on the behavior of society and individuals.[5]

Today, Sheila is the most famous, award-winning architect in India and a world leader in environmentally friendly, sustainable design. She believes that the only way forward in her industry is with design and construction that cares for the earth and the environment. Another passion is well-designed housing for low-income groups. She also incorporates Indian art and culture into her projects, drawing inspiration from the classical dance and temples of her childhood.

Fulfilling her childhood dream, Sheila is indeed making the world a better place through architecture. In 2011, she became the first Indian architect chosen by the World Economic Forum for their Council on Design Innovation. The mission of her sixteen-member team? To brainstorm ways to improve the world. In 2015, *Architectural Digest* named her one of the fifty most influential architects in the world.

> In 1993, Sheila designed a home in Chennai, India, using recycled materials and incorporating a system for gathering rainwater. It was an effective, low-cost solution for the lack of freshwater in India.

Sheila has been called a pioneer and a living legend in architecture. Good thing she didn't give up her university seat to a boy!

When I look back as a dancer, what I learned was wherever your hands go, your eyes must go, and wherever your eye goes, your mind must go. This taught me how to focus. When you have a passion to achieve something that you really desire, and when you have the focus and the tenacity to work hard... you will get what you want."

—SHEILA SRI PRAKASH

HOW WILL YOU ROCK THE WORLD?

I'm gonna rock the world by becoming an environmental architect/designer. I am going to design houses and cities that will help prevent global warming by saving water, gas, fuel, etc., using up as little resources as possible. I will also make designs that are accessible to people whether they have money or not. It's not just rich people who should have good design; everyone should.

IVA BORRELLO ⚛ AGE 13

Arlen Siu Bermúdez

1955–1975 ◦ REVOLUTIONARY, POET, AND MUSICIAN ◦ NICARAGUA

Now we are in a new stage when we have concrete achievements.
They are tangible. There is the fruit of my sister's sacrifice.
It was not in vain.

—MARLON SIU, ARLEN'S BROTHER

Arlen sat at her desk, her pen poised above a sheet of paper. She was feeling angry and frustrated. Her country had so many poor people—so many families without food, without hope. She wanted to help them, *all* of them.

But what could she do? She was just a teenager.

With her church, she often helped poor families—brought them food, helped tutor their children. Sometimes she even did these things on her own. But it wasn't enough. There were thousands who needed help. They needed something bigger.

Arlen remembered a recent trip to *el campo* (the countryside) where she had seen a mother walking down the country road, a crying baby in her arms . . . Arlen's pen began scratching at the paper.

Words flowed out of Arlen like water, like a flood.

"Today I want to sing about you, Rural Maria . . ."[1]

This was how she could help. She would tell the world about the suffering of Nicaragua. She would show them with her words.

Arlen's passionate words became a song, "Rural Maria," about the suffering and poverty of rural mothers in Nicaragua—a song that soon gained fame across the country. In fact, Arlen and her song would become the symbols for an entire revolution! And at the young age of twenty, Arlen would become the first martyr to die in that revolution, fighting for her beliefs.

***

Arlen's father was from China, where he was a soldier in the Communist Revolution army. He immigrated to Nicaragua and married a Nicaraguan woman, and Arlen was born in 1955.

Arlen was raised as a Christian in Jinotepe, Nicaragua. She was always concerned about the poor people of her country and wanted to do something to help. "She gave away everything to the poor," remembered her brother, Marlon.[2] At that time, the government of Nicaragua, run by the Somoza family, was corrupt. The rich families, including the Somozas, kept everything for themselves and not much trickled down to the poorest people. Arlen, like many others in Nicaragua, wanted wealth and property to be more equally distributed between the rich and poor.

> Grupo Pancasán is a Nicaraguan folk band. They are considered an iconic group of revolutionary music in their country. "Rural Maria" was officially released on their 1978 self-titled album.
>
> ***

Arlen was also a talented artist who played the accordion, guitar, and flute, as well as painted and wrote poetry. In the end, it was her art that truly made a difference for her people. As a teenager, she wrote the poem "Rural Maria," which was set to music and performed by Grupo Pancasán. It became a hit with the Nicaraguan people who were fed up with the corruption and looking for a change.

Arlen's fame grew as she continued to write and create music—especially with the revolutionaries. Decades before, university students formed the Sandinista National Liberation Front (in Spanish, it's *Frente Sandinista de Liberactión* or FSLN), which was growing in power and popularity. The Sandinistas stood up for the rights of the workers, rural populations, and the poor. They wanted the Somoza government to change. Arlen began joining in their protests and hunger strikes.

In 1972, the political situation in Nicaragua came to a head. There was a huge earthquake in the capital city, Managua. Ten thousand people died, fifty thousand were left homeless, and 80 percent of the city was destroyed.[3] Arlen Siu went to the capital to help victims and witnessed the corruption of the Somoza government firsthand. They were taking millions of dollars in international relief money and keeping it for themselves instead of giving it to the victims of the earthquake. Arlen spent months helping the victims, living in refugee camps, witnessing their suffering. Her revolutionary beliefs intensified, and at age eighteen, she joined the Sandinistas.

Arlen was already a national celebrity, and the Sandinistas knew she would be a powerful voice to have on their side. They asked her to help recruit young people to the cause, and she agreed. In 1974, the revolution began in earnest as the Sandinista guerillas launched attacks on the national guard. President Anastasio Somoza Debayle (the last member of the family to rule) retaliated by capturing Sandinistas wherever he could. Arlen performed at rallies and protests, her songs condemning Somoza's tactics: mass kidnapping, torture, and execution. She also criticized the government's record: high poverty, illiteracy, and infant mortality rates.[4] Arlen's words fanned the flames of the revolution.

The government wanted to silence her.

In August 1975, as Arlen worked at a Sandinista training school in the city of León, the national guard launched a surprise attack. She and others fought off the attackers in a desperate two-hour armed battle. In the end, Arlen and seven other Sandinistas were killed as they covered their comrades who were making an escape. She was just twenty years old.

WHO WERE THE SANDANISTAS?
HERE'S A QUICK HISTORY:[5]

- The United States occupied Nicaragua from 1912 to 1933 to stop anyone else from building a canal through the country.

- In the 1930s, Augusto Cesár Sandino (the Sandinistas' namesake) led a nationalist revolt against the occupiers and eventually forced them out. However, a United States–supported regime led by the Somoza family took over, and the Somozas' government was corrupt and oppressive to the Nicaraguans, especially the poor.

- A rebellion against the Somozas grew during the '50s and '60s, and in the 1970s, the *Frente Sandinista de Liberación* (FSLN, or Sandinista National Liberation Front) began actively fighting the government.

- In 1979, after five years of fighting, the Sandinistas overthrew the Somoza government and took over running the country.

- Through much of the 1980s, the FSLN had further conflicts with the United States, which, through the CIA, financed and trained former Somoza national guards (renamed "the Contras") to take back Nicaragua. After 10 years of covert operations, the United States finally gave up for good and left Nicaragua alone.

~~~

If the Somoza regime thought they had silenced Arlen, however, they were wrong. After her death, she became an even more powerful symbol for the Sandinistas. To them, she was the first martyr of the revolution (someone who dies for their beliefs), and they proudly displayed her picture at protests and rallies across the country. "Maria Rural" became the rallying cry of the guerillas, and Arlen's essays about Marxism and Feminism were an inspiration to the Sandinistas and to the growing Nicaraguan women's movement. Arlen's voice was louder than ever.

The uprising continued for years, and Nicaragua was plunged into what was nearly a civil war. Finally, in 1979, Somoza fled to Miami, and hundreds of thousands of Nicaraguans celebrated the end of the war. The Sandinistas took over the government and implemented social programs to improve literacy, healthcare, education, unions, and land reform. Finally, Arlen's dreams became a reality.

Today, the Sandinistas are still one of Nicaragua's most powerful parties, holding a majority of seats in the National Assembly. And they haven't forgotten one of their youngest heroes. In cities across Nicaragua, you will find neighborhoods, roads, ports, schools, and parks all bearing the name of Arlen Siu.

ROCK ON!

Anya Pogharian

While volunteering at a hospital, eighteen-year-old Anya Pogharian learned about kidney dialysis: patients whose kidneys don't work have to get their blood filtered by a machine to remove extra water and waste products (what kidneys do) three times a week! Anya also discovered that each dialysis machine cost $30,000, so hospitals in developing countries can't afford them. Anya was inspired. She studied the dialysis machine's manual online and designed a smaller, portable model for her science fair project. Anya's machine cost just $600.00 to make (one-fiftieth of the cost of the hospital's machine) and took only twenty-five minutes to filter blood instead of four hours! The Canadian National Science Fair gave her the bronze prize, but more important, Anya revolutionized dialysis. Her machine will make it affordable for people around the world.

BjöRk

1965– ✹ SINGER, SONGWRITER, AND ACTRESS ✹ ICELAND

It takes a long time to fully become who you are.

—BJÖRK

Björk stood in her living room surrounded by instruments: piano, drums, flute, oboe, guitar. She scowled as she read the letter from Fálkinn, her new recording company. They had given her a contract to make a record, but now they were telling her exactly which songs to sing—not so surprising, considering their singer was just eleven years old.

But Björk wasn't having it. She stomped around the room, growling to herself.

"What in the world is the matter?" her mother asked.

"These songs are crap!" Björk answered. "I won't sing them."

Hildur was used to her daughter's moods. She took the list and scanned it.

"You're right. These songs *are* crap."

That got a grin out of the young singer.

"I'm going to call them and tell them I won't do the record."

"Wait a minute, Björk. What if Sævar and his friends help you choose better songs and write some new ones."

Björk smiled again. Her stepfather, Sævar, was a guitarist in a local band. His friends jammed at their house all the time.

"Yes, that's what we will do," said Björk.

Satisfied, she quit stomping around and picked up her flute. Before the letter had arrived, she'd been working on a song about her favorite Icelandic painter, Jóhannes Sveinsson Kjarval. She loved the landscapes he painted, especially those that focused on moss. Björk decided the song would have piano as well. And it would go on the album.[1]

This quirky first album would introduce Iceland to Björk's unique voice and vision. Just a few years later, the world would discover her as well.

Björk Gudmundsdottir was born in 1965 in Reykjavik, the capital of Iceland. Her mother was an activist and her father a union leader and electrician, but they divorced soon after their baby was born. Björk and her mother moved to a commune. Her mother soon remarried a musician, so Björk grew up in a house full of music. She took to it early: "I've always sung, ever since I was a little kid," said Björk.[2]

> Björk means "birch tree" in Icelandic, which is ironic because the country is known for its complete lack of trees.

At age five, Björk enrolled in a music school where she studied classical piano, oboe, and recorder. At a school recital, she sang the disco hit "I Love to Love," and her teachers were so impressed that they sent a recording to Iceland's only radio station. The station loved Björk's voice and played the recording on air for the whole country to hear. Soon, a local record label came knocking, offering Björk a record contract. She was ten years old.

Björk always danced to the beat of her own drum. One day in elementary school, she decided that getting dressed for school was too much bother. So she took the sheet off her bed, cut a hole in the middle, stuck her head through, and wore that to class. "That was normal for me," she recalled.[4]

~~~

Björk took two weeks off from school to make her first record, the self-titled *Björk*. The label gave her a list of songs they wanted her to record, but headstrong Björk hated their picks and refused. The result was a combination of original tunes, Icelandic folk songs, covers, and the one instrumental written by young Björk herself. It was "a surprisingly eclectic and accomplished album for one so young."[3] Björk is still quite proud of it to this day. One song became a hit in Iceland, and the album sold well in the small country. Overnight, Björk was famous.

Björk didn't like all the attention, however, and promptly retired from music—though not for long. A few years later, when she was thirteen, punk rock hit Iceland, and Björk couldn't stay away. With three friends from school, she started an all-girl punk band called Spit and Snot. (You read that right—most punk name ever.) A year later, in 1980, Björk graduated from music school and switched music genres again. This time she formed an experimental jazz-funk band called Exodus.

From there, Björk moved in and out of a number of bands. She played all different kinds of music and experimented with her singing style as well. She howled. She shrieked. She whispered. She wanted to have a unique sound—something all her own. And she found it. In 1986, she joined a new band called The Sugarcubes and married the guitarist, Þór Eldon. They had a baby together, Sindri, and then divorced. Fortunately, they stayed friends and the band stayed together.

The Sugarcubes were an art-punk band with a sound similar to popular New Wave bands of the day—The B-52s and Talking Heads. Their first album, *Life's Too Good*, came out on Björk's twenty-first birthday. With their quirky lyrics and Björk's unique vocals, the album was unlike anything on the radio at the time, launching the Sugarcubes onto the world stage. Their first single, "Birthday," topped the British music charts and was voted Single of the Week by *Melody Maker* (a weekly British pop/rock newspaper). The album got rave reviews, was played on radio stations in America and Europe, and sold more than a million copies worldwide.[5]

The band did a world tour, and when The Sugarcubes first hit America, *Rolling Stone* magazine had this to say: "Singer Björk . . . is casting a powerful spell of her own with an astonishing voice that is unpredictable yet captivating in its wild extremes. In a single line, she swings from romantic cooing to an angry snarl, punctuating her chorus with Indian war whoops and breathtaking supershrieks."[6] A unique sound indeed! The band also played on *Saturday Night Live* and was the show's first Icelandic band.

The Sugarcubes released a couple more albums and opened for U2 during their 1992 world tour. Lead singer Bono praised Björk's talent: "She has a voice like an ice pick . . . Wherever I was in the stadium . . . it could travel through metal, steel, concrete . . . and straight to my heart."[7] When Björk decided to launch a solo career, The Sugarcubes broke up, but they're still considered "the biggest rock band to emerge from Iceland."[8]

In 1993, Björk recorded a solo album called *Debut* (her first since age eleven). One single reached number two on *Billboard* magazine's "Modern Rock" chart. British music magazine *NME* named *Debut* Album of the Year, and it went platinum in America. And at the 1994 Brit Awards, Björk won Best International Female and Best International Newcomer. Solo Björk was a hit!

> Björk and the Sugarcubes started their own music label in Iceland, called Bad Taste. The company is a record label, art gallery, bookstore, publishing house, and radio station whose motto is "world domination or death" according to vinylhub.com

> Many people know Björk from her strange, artsy music videos. She has collaborated with many award-winning directors. Check them out on YouTube.

From there, she went on to record seven more solo albums, in which she mixed nearly every musical genre—dance, electronic, house, techno, punk, pop, rock, jazz, and hip-hop. She also brought in a variety of sounds to accompany her vocals, everything from Inuit choirs and orchestras to household sounds, like shuffling cards and ice being cracked. Even with her avant-garde sound, several of Björk's albums reached the top twenty on the "*Billboard* 200" chart, and thirty singles reached the top forty on pop charts around the world.[9]

At the 2000 Oscar ceremony, Björk caused a media frenzy when she arrived in a white, feathery swan dress that wrapped around her body.

The iconic dress was later auctioned off for nearly $10,000, with all the money donated to the international aid agency Oxfam.[11]

In 2004, Björk performed the opening song at the summer Olympics in Athens. As she sang, her dress unraveled and flowed over all the athletes in the stadium to show a ten-thousand-square-foot map of the world.

As she gets older, Björk seems to be getting even better. Her 2015 work, *Vulnicura*, was nominated for a Grammy Award for Best Alternative Music Album, and one reviewer wrote of a 2011 concert, "The elemental timbre of her voice has grown more powerful with age."[10]

Björk is also a talented actress. She starred in her first film back in 1986—a witchcraft movie called *The Juniper Tree*. In 1999, she agreed to write the soundtrack for another movie called *Dancer in the Dark*. When the director asked if she would play the lead role, she agreed. Good decision! *Dancer in the Dark* went on to win Best Film at the Cannes Film Festival and Björk won Best Actress. One of her songs was nominated for an Oscar, and she performed it on live television during the show.

Björk uses her art to help change the world for the better, both in other countries and in her own. She did concerts to raise money for tsunami relief in Southeast Asia and spoke out for Tibetan freedom during a concert in China. In Iceland, she raises money for the country's music scene and fights to protect wilderness, both in the sea and on land. She founded a group, the Náttúra Foundation, which protects Icelandic nature and promotes sustainable industry. She's also raising money to establish a national park.

Since this headstrong eleven-year-old made her first album, Björk has always been a star like no other. She has beautifully fused music and art for more than forty years. Her albums have sold millions of copies around the world, and she's won awards and praise for her groundbreaking experimentation. Björk also made *Rolling Stone*'s lists of "100 Greatest Singers of All Time" and "100 Greatest Songwriters of All Time." In fact, she's been called "a true sonic innovator . . . the most important and forward-looking musician of her generation."[12] With her musical talents and one-of-a-kind sense of style, Björk paved the way for a whole new generation of artists. (You're welcome, Lady Gaga.)

ROCK ON!

MAYA PENN

As a young girl, Maya Penn loved to sketch clothing designs and sew. When she was eight, she started a company, Maya's Ideas, selling eco-friendly accessories like headbands, scarves, and hats—all made with environmentally safe, recycled materials. Now in her teens, Maya keeps busy as the company's CEO and with a few other interests. She animated a cartoon series called *The Pollinators* and recently wrote a book called *You Got This!* She also learned to code at age ten so she could design her website, Maya's Ideas. And she gives back: she donates 10–20 percent of her business profits to nonprofit groups and founded her own nonprofit, Maya's Ideas 4 the Planet. Maya's showing the world you don't have to be a grown-up to be a business tycoon!

Selena

1971–1995 ◈ SINGER ◈ UNITED STATES

She really broke the mold in Tejano music with everything from the music she sang to the way she dressed...Selena had a huge talent and sang like an angel. But she also worked tirelessly...

—CHRIS PEREZ, SELENA'S GUITARIST AND HUSBAND

Selena spun and danced across the stage, her feet and hips moving to the beat. It was a sound check, and her sister, Suzette, was tapping on the drums while her brother, A. B., tuned his guitar. Selena danced by and caught the eye of their new guitarist, Chris. He gave her a grin that said, "I have a secret." Selena grinned back, her heart pounding so hard she was sure the band could hear it.

Did they know? Could they tell?

Selena and Chris were in love.

Her father would be furious if he knew! He was a Jehovah's Witness and didn't approve of his teenage daughter dating. Selena and Chris had to hide their feelings even though they were together practically 24/7. It was driving her crazy.

As she danced, Selena hummed nonsense words to herself, "Bidi bidi bom bom . . ." It was the sound of her pounding heart.

Chris's guitar chimed in, playing a riff to go with her silly lyrics. She let out a laugh and sang it again.

"Bidi bidi bom bom…"

Next, her sister added a drumbeat. Then her brother called to Chris, "What key are you in?"

"B flat," he answered. The band jammed, and Selena danced and sang more silly words. She couldn't remember the last time she was so happy.

That night, during the concert, between songs, A. B. shouted to Selena, "Hey, let's play that song you were doing in sound check."[1] Selena's face lit up.

As the band did their best to remember the improvised melody, Selena turned to Chris and her words poured out. She sang about a girl so in love that each time she sees her man, her legs tremble and her heart goes crazy, pounding with excitement. "Bidi bidi bom bom" echoed through the stadium.

Selena's ad-libbed lyrics shocked Chris. He knew how she felt about him, but she sure wasn't doing a good job of hiding it! A stadium full of fans—plus her entire family—was listening.

The applause at the end was deafening. They loved it!

Selena could tell she'd written another hit song—maybe her biggest hit yet.

And she was right. Years later, when she finally recorded "Bidi Bidi Bom Bom" it became one of her most beloved and lasting hits. But she wasn't able to hide her pounding heart for that long. Just a few months after first playing the song together, she and Chris eloped.

Selena was practically born singing back in 1971 in Lake Jackson, Texas. Her Mexican American parents recognized and nurtured her talent from her earliest years. Abraham, her father, worked at a chemical company to support his family, but at night, he played guitar while his

Tejano music is bouncy and upbeat, and unique to Texas. It was created over 100 years ago in the Rio Grande region, along the border between Texas and Mexico. The unique sound reflects the people of the region: a mix of traditional Mexican folk music, polka, jazz, and country and western.[4]

tiny daughter sang along. He could tell immediately that Selena had a gift: "Her timing, her pitch were perfect; I could see it from day one."[2]

When Selena was seven, her father started a family band: Selena was the lead singer, her brother, A. B., played guitar, and her sister, Suzette, played drums. He taught them Tejano music, which was popular in their area. Tejano songs are sung in Spanish, but Selena didn't speak it—she had to learn the lyrics phonetically. It wasn't until later, in her twenties, that she finally learned to speak Spanish and could understand what she was singing!

Selena's parents opened a restaurant where the band performed every weekend. Soon, they also began playing at weddings and parties. But when the price of oil dropped and oil workers in the area lost their jobs, the family had to close the restaurant and move to Corpus Christi, Texas. Without the restaurant income, the band was the only thing supporting the family. Selena said, "We were literally doing it to put food on the table."[3]

Selena had other passions besides singing. She was also a natural athlete, but what she really loved was fashion. She loved to draw clothing designs and dreamed that one day she would design clothing professionally.

The band got a new name, Selena y Los Dinos ("Selena and the Guys"), and played any paying gig they could get: dance halls, weddings, skating rinks. Selena's father bought a beat-up bus they called "Big Bertha" to tour in. The name change may have caused them some difficulty, though, as only men perform Tejano music traditionally. Selena and her band were often turned down for gigs because their lead singer was a girl. For years, the family barely scraped by.

When Selena was nine, Selena y Los Dinos recorded their first album, which got played on local Spanish radio stations. Slowly, she and the band landed more gigs, gained fans, and became more successful. At last, in 1986, fifteen-year-old Selena's hard work started paying off. At the Tejano Music Awards, she won Best Female Vocalist and Performer of the Year. Selena had become Tejano's biggest star.

But Selena wanted the rest of the world to hear her music as well, not just Tejano fans. When she was eighteen, she and the band signed a contract with record company EMI. They also signed a new guitar player, Chris Perez. Working closely together onstage and in rehearsals, Chris and Selena fell in love. But Selena's father wouldn't let her date, especially someone in the band—he didn't want his daughter to ruin her squeaky-clean image. The couple hid their feelings for as long as they could, but in 1992, they snuck off to a Corpus Christi courthouse and got married. They didn't tell their families until it was done.

> Although Selena was an excellent student, she and the band were on the road so much that she had to quit school in eighth grade. Later, she did complete high school through a correspondence course.

Just as Selena's love life was taking off, so was her career. Between 1989 and 1995, she recorded six albums, each more successful than the last. Her 1990 album *Ven Conmigo* (*Come With Me*) went gold, making her the first female Tejano artist to have a gold record.[5] In 1992, she did it again with *Entre a Mi Mundo* (*Enter My World*), which also went gold. Her 1993 album, *Live!*, won a Grammy for Best Mexican American Album (the first Tejano album to do so).[6] *Amor Prohibido* (*Forbidden Love*), released in 1994, was the first Tejano album to hit number one on *Billboard's* "Top Latin Albums" chart, a position it held for

> Selena won the Tejano Music Award for Female Vocalist of the Year a stunning nine years in a row! From 1989 until her death in 1995.[7]

ninety-eight weeks (a record that still stands) and became one of the bestselling Latin albums in the United States.[8] While touring for that album, Selena broke attendance records at arenas in Houston and Miami.

The girl from small-town Texas jumped from Tejano icon to all-around music superstar in just a few years. Fans loved the energy and excitement Selena created onstage. They loved her style. The president of EMI said, "Selena is the closest artist I've got to Madonna. I love artists who know where they want to go and how to get there. She's definitely a pop star."[9]

Selena explored other passions as well. She designed her own clothing line and opened two boutiques, called Selena Etc., in Corpus Christi and San Antonio. Selena had an eye for fashion and her business boomed, earning her more than five million dollars. Selena was ranked as one of the twenty wealthiest Hispanic musicians in 1993 and 1994.[10]

We'll never know how high Selena might have climbed. On March 31, 1995, an employee she suspected of embezzling money from her company shot her to death. Fans were stunned. "It's a real tragedy. We've lost a heroine,"[11] said the publisher of *Teleguia* magazine. Sixty thousand mourners came to her funeral, many traveling from out of the country. Two weeks after the singer's death, Texas governor George W. Bush declared her birthday, April 16, Selena Day in the state.

Selena had many causes she cared about. She visited schools and encouraged kids to get an education and to stay away from drugs. Additionally, she helped raise money for people with HIV. "She was a very loving person," said her father. "She was concerned about so many issues in the Hispanic community, education, drugs, AIDS. She was just so busy."[12]

If you want to learn more about Selena and her life, check out the 1997 movie *Selena*, starring another famous Latina singer—Jennifer Lopez!

Although Selena's life was cut short, her contributions live on. She has sold more than sixty million albums worldwide, and her impact on music and fashion has made her one of the most famous and beloved Mexican American performers of all time.

HOW WILL YOU ROCK THE WORLD?

I will rock the world by becoming a singer. I hope to one day write and sing songs that will touch people's hearts, just like the people who have inspired me to follow this dream of mine.

NATALIA BECERRA ☀ AGE 10

Fawzia Koofi

1975– ☼ POLITICIAN ☼ AFGHANISTAN

I have stared death in the face countless times...
but still I'm alive. I can't explain this,
other than knowing that God has a purpose for me.

—FAWZIA KOOFI

A scream came from inside the shack. A woman inside was giving birth, and her pain was great. She was older and this was her seventh child, so her body was tired. Her heart was too. Her husband, whom she adored, was in love with another woman: his new wife.

She prayed to Allah, "Please give me a boy." Maybe if she could return home proudly carrying a son, who would bring honor to her husband, then she could win back his favor.

Inside, the shack was crowded with the midwife and other village women helping with the birth. The heat was unbearable, the smell of cows and sheep suffocating. The mother labored for hours, drifting in and out of consciousness. She was barely awake when she delivered the tiny, blotchy newborn.

Her eyes fluttered open as a helper brought the baby close to her. "It is just a girl," she whispered sadly. "A poor girl." The mother refused to hold her tiny daughter and turned away.

The helper asked the midwife, "What should we do with it?"

The midwife could see that the mother had no will to live. It would be hard to bring her back.

"The baby doesn't matter. We must save the mother."

And so the women wrapped the newborn baby girl in a cloth and put her outside in the pasture. It was a summer day, and the hot, baking sun would soon take care of the unwanted child. The women went back inside to nurse the sick mother.

By evening, the mother's condition took a turn and she began to recover. Since the baby was still alive—still crying, in fact—the women thought they should try again and brought the baby back to its mother. This time, when she saw the screaming baby, its tiny face burned and blistered, the mother gasped in horror. *What have I done?*

She knew this baby was a fighter. She clutched her daughter to her breast and wept. Again, she prayed to Allah: "It is a miracle that she is still alive. Please spare her, and I promise I will love her and never allow any harm to come to her."[1]

This baby would become her mother's most beloved child, and the two would remain incredibly close through the rest of her life. The mother would keep her word and protect her daughter from all manner of dangers. They both knew that Allah had chosen this girl for a special purpose. She was born in a time and place where girls were unwanted, less valuable. And from that fragile beginning, Fawzia Koofi rose to become a leader of her country, a politician who fights for girls, and the first woman elected to Afghanistan's Parliament.

Fawzia Koofi was born in 1975 in the remote northeastern corner of Afghanistan. Her father was a respected member of the country's Parliament for twenty-five years, and her mother was the second of his

Why do some Afghan families prefer sons? In parts of the country (and other areas of the world), if a son is born, the family knows that when he grows up, he will get a job and represent and help feed the family. So any money spent on his education is a "good investment" because it will help the family in the long run. But when a girl grows up, she will marry and join her husband's family. Any money spent on her education will be lost. In places where girls aren't allowed to work, they can't bring any money into the family, so some families consider them a burden.

~~~~

seven wives. Fawzia was his nineteenth child out of twenty-three. When Fawzia's depressed, exhausted mother saw that her baby was a girl, she did not want her to live. But after Fawzia survived a full day out in the sun (her face was so burned that she still had visible scars in high school), her mother felt great regret and believed her survival was a sign.

The government Fawzia's father worked in during the 1970s was in upheaval. In 1978, there was a Communist coup, and Russia supported the new government. When Fawzia was three, Afghan fighters called the *mujahedeen*, who were against the Soviet-backed government, killed her father. A few days later, the killers came looking for Fawzia's family, but they fled from their home and escaped into Russian-controlled territory.

The family moved in with Fawzia's older brother in the city of Faizabad. Fawzia was seven when she first noticed city girls walking to school. Fawzia asked her mother if she could go too. Her mother thought about it for a long, long time and then answered with a big smile, "Yes, Fawzia, you can go to school."[2]

This decision changed Fawzia's life. She loved school and was so happy to be there that she worked very hard. She caught up to her fellow students who had started before her and soon passed them to become one of the top students in her school.

When Fawzia was eleven, the family moved to Kabul, the busy capital. It wasn't yet illegal for Afghan girls to go to school, but it wasn't normal either. Her brothers teased her, and her mother worried about her: "If this English class makes you president, I don't want you to be president—I want you to be alive."[3] In Kabul there was much fighting between the mujahedeen and government troops. Even when rockets roared overhead and shrapnel exploded around her, Fawzia kept walking to school. She wanted to learn, to get a job someday—to be able to support herself.

In the early 1990s, when Fawzia was a teenager, the mujahedeen forced the Soviet army out and took over Afghanistan. Almost immediately, the mujahedeen began to fight among themselves, and Afghanistan was plunged into a civil war that lasted more than ten years.

During this time, the mujahedeen also cracked down on women's rights. Fawzia had to cover herself with a *burqa*—a loose-fitting dress that covered her from head to toe, with only a slit for her eyes. "I was furious. I had never worn a burqa in my life," she remembered, "And here I was in my nicest clothes, with my hair and makeup done . . . and [my mother] was insisting I cover myself in a heavy blue sack."[4] Before then, burqas were something only older, more traditional women chose to wear. Now *all* women and girls were forced to wear them whenever they went outside.

Still, Fawzia took her exams and graduated from high school. The next year, she was accepted into university—she planned to study to be a doctor.

Afghanistan was changing quickly, however. Fighting got worse, and millions of Afghans fled the country—mostly wealthier people. Those who stayed suffered. Fawzia's brother was shot to death in his home. Her mother got sick and died. A new, more radical group was taking over: the Taliban.

The Taliban was an Islamic militia that wanted to turn Afghanistan into a country ruled by strict Islamic law. At first, they brought some

> Fawzia's neighbors hid her and her mother from the mujahedeen in a very unusual spot: a pile of cattle poop! They piled the poop all around them until they couldn't be seen. Fawzia remembered, "It felt like I was being buried alive."[5] But the killers didn't find them.

order and security to war-torn towns, but they soon made a series of laws changing life for everyone. Afghans could no longer listen to music, watch TV, meet friends at a café, or even have wedding celebrations. Men had to wear turbans and long beards.

These laws were hard on all Afghans but especially on girls and women. They made a law that women and girls had to be fully covered and could only go outside with a male relative. Girls couldn't ride bicycles, wear bright clothes, or laugh loudly. If the Taliban heard that a woman had shamed her husband, they would kill her. For Fawzia, the worst was their law banning girls from going to school or getting jobs. Fawzia had to quit the university. She didn't leave her home for months.

Taliban mobs drove around enforcing these "morality rules." Punishment might be a severe beating. Or they might take a rule breaker to the Olympic sports stadium, where a crowd would cheer as they cut off a hand or stoned the perpetrator to death.

During this terrible time, Fawzia met Hamid, who ran a finance company and taught at the university. Fawzia thought he was kind and intelligent. They had a Taliban wedding—no music, no video, no dancing, no party—but Fawzia was happy that at least she'd gotten to choose her own husband.

Ten days after the wedding, however, the Taliban arrested Hamid and threw him in prison. He was released three months later, but it was too late: he'd caught tuberculosis. The couple fled back to their home village in the northeast and lived together long enough to have two daughters. Hamid died of the disease a few years later.

On September 11, 2001, two airplanes flew into the World Trade Center buildings in New York City and a third hit the Pentagon in Virginia, killing nearly three thousand people. The leader of the worst terrorist attack in US history, Osama bin

The first thing the Taliban did when they took over Kabul was destroy their cultural treasures. They wrecked museums filled with priceless artifacts. They blew up ancient stone Buddhas—considered wonders of the world. They burned schools and universities and books.

Laden, was hiding in Afghanistan under protection of the Taliban. The United States attacked and, by the year's end, pushed the Taliban out of Afghanistan.

Out from under the thumb of the Taliban, Fawzia was able to go to school again. She graduated from college with a master's degree in business and management and then went to work for UNICEF, an international children's aid organization. She helped people forced to flee their homes in Afghanistan and served as the child protection officer, protecting children from violence and abuse.

Soon after, she began her political career. She launched a back-to-school campaign across Afghanistan, promoting education for girls. During meetings with other leaders, the men asked her to take off her burqa so they could communicate more easily. "They respected me for what I did," she said.[6]

When Afghanistan prepared to hold parliamentary elections in which women would be allowed to participate, Fawzia decided to run. She believed that the only way to make big improvements in the lives of women and children was to become a leader in her country. She campaigned in 2005 (without her burqa) and won! Fawzia Koofi became the first woman in history to serve in the Afghan Parliament, a position she's held for more than a decade. She has served as Deputy Speaker of Parliament and as chairperson of Afghanistan's Women, Civil Society, and Human Rights Commission.

Before the Soviet and Taliban occupations, Afghanistan was a fairly liberal country. Women made up 50 percent of government workers, 70 percent of teachers, and 40 percent of doctors. Although the Taliban is gone, Islamic fundamentalism still dominates Afghanistan and there is much work to be done. As of 2016, only 12.6 percent of Afghan women can read. Only 40 percent of girls go to elementary school and 6 percent to high school. And while 200,000 Afghans go to college, only 18 percent are girls. Conservative groups who oppose women's education still regularly attack schools, students, and activists.[7]

In Parliament, Fawzia fights for equal rights and better conditions for women and girls and for universal education for both sexes. In 2009, she drafted the Elimination of Violence Against Women legislation, which was blocked by conservative members but was voluntarily adopted in communities across the country.

In 2014, Fawzia tried to run for president of Afghanistan, but the election commission moved the registration date so that she was too young for their minimum age requirement of forty. At the time of publication, she was planning to run for president in the next election.

No matter what her position in the government, Fawzia has been making Afghanistan better and safer for girls and women for decades now. From the nature of her very birth—when she had to scream to be heard and fight just for a chance to live—it is no wonder that Fawzia is now inspiring a new generation of Afghan girls to use their voices to fight for the life they, too, deserve.

> The Taliban and other conservative Islamic groups in Afghanistan do not like Fawzia and the changes she is making for girls and women. They have tried to assassinate her many, many times. In one recent attempt, her car was shot at for 30 minutes (while she was trapped inside), killing two policemen.[8]

AFGHANISTAN TIMELINE

AFGHANISTAN HAS A LONG HISTORY OF CONFLICT.[9]

- 1921: Afghanistan defeats British colonizers, becomes independent nation.
- 1921–1973: Afghanistan is a monarchy that allows women to go to school and hold jobs.

cont. from page 148

● 1973: Gen. Mohammed Daoud Khan, cousin of the king, leads a military coup.

● 1978: Communist counter-coup topples Khan.

● 1979: Russia invades Afghanistan, joins Afghan army fighting the war against mujahadeen rebels. Osama bin Laden joins mujahedeen and forms al-Qaida.

● 1995: Taliban rises to power and takes over much of Afghanistan. Bin Laden and al-Qaida use Afghanistan for recruitment and training.

● September 11, 2001: World Trade Center bombings. The prime suspect, bin Laden, hides in Afghanistan.

● October 2001: US and UK attack Afghanistan, bombing Taliban targets.

● December 2001: Taliban is forced out of Afghanistan. Hamid Karzai takes over leadership of the temporary government.

● 2004: A new constitution is drafted calling for democracy and equality for women. The first presidential election is held, in which 10.5 million Afghans vote. Karzai is elected president by 55 percent of these votes.

● 2005: The first parliamentary elections are held, and Fawzia Koofi wins a seat.

HOW WILL YOU ROCK THE WORLD?

I will rock the world by discovering cures to diseases in impoverished countries. When I find cures, I will make them attainable to the citizens of those countries. I'll also help administer the cures and work with people to better their lives. Helping people in need will improve my life as I hope to improve theirs!

CLARA LUCZAK ⚛ AGE 13

Mindy Kaling

1979– ✦ COMEDIAN, ACTRESS, AND AUTHOR ✦ UNITED STATES

I have a personality defect where I sort of refuse to see myself as an underdog. . . . It's because of my parents. They raised me with the entitlement of a tall, blond, white man.

—MINDY KALING

Mindy and Mavis stared at the TV. Onscreen was an old woman in an ugly purple-and-blue dress and a grey wig, sitting in front of a stained-glass window. She spoke in a nasally voice, scolding and shaming her guests. At the end of the skit, she did an embarrassing dance around the stage like an oversized chicken fluffing its feathers.

The girls couldn't stop laughing. The Church Lady was their favorite, so they stayed up late on the weekends to watch her on *Saturday Night Live*. As they got ready for bed after the show, they were still laughing.

Mavis poked her toothbrush into Mindy's face and whined in the Church Lady voice, "How con-VEEN-ient!"

Mindy laughed so hard she sprayed water on the mirror. She pointed her own toothbrush back at Mavis and said, "Could it be . . . SATAN?!?"

Both girls busted into the Church Lady dance, strutting around the bathroom, laughing, and repeating the Church Lady's most famous catchphrase, "Well, isn't that SPE-CIAL?" over and over again.

Suddenly, Mindy's mom was standing in the doorway. "What in the world are you girls yelling about?" She was a doctor and had to get up early to go to the hospital. Looks like they'd woken her up with their silliness. It wasn't the first time.

The teens froze mid-dance. Then Mindy looked at her very serious mother and repeated (in her best Church Lady voice), "Hey Mom, isn't that SPE-CIAL?"

Her mother rolled her eyes and said, "Can you *please* stop saying 'Isn't that special?' in that strange voice. It is annoying to me and to others." This made Mindy and Mavis crack up even harder. They laughed so hard they couldn't breathe. Finally, Mindy's mom shook her head in disgust and went to bed.[1]

Today, Mindy Kaling is one of the funniest people on the planet, but she wasn't born a comedian. She didn't catch the comedy bug until high school, when she watched comedy shows obsessively with her BFF. She was born in Cambridge, Massachusetts, into a very normal house. Her mother, a doctor, and her father, an architect, had moved to America from India the year Mindy was born. They worked hard and sent Mindy to a private school. They expected she might grow up to be a doctor or lawyer—some respectable, serious career like theirs.

She was never the class clown. Quite the opposite—she was a model student who excelled in Latin. She was the nerd who sat *next* to the class clown and studied him. She also got teased a lot. Once, a group of bullies even called her a whale. At the time, it bothered her a lot, but not anymore. "If someone called me chubby, it would no longer be something that kept me up late at night. Being called fat is not like being called stupid or unfunny, which is the worst thing you could ever say to me."[2]

When she started high school, Mindy discovered her passion for comedy. She and Mavis spent hours and hours watching classic comedy shows like *Kids in the Hall*, *Saturday Night Live*, *Cheers*, and *Monty Python*. Soon, they were reenacting favorite sketches, which led to writing their own sketches; they video-taped the sketches so they could watch and critique them later. Mindy didn't know it, but she was teaching herself the skills she would need in her future career.

Mindy's parents had high expectations for her, so she spent a lot of time on home-work and studying for tests. She wasn't super popular, didn't star in any plays, and wasn't a cheerleader. She doesn't have any regrets about being the quiet, hard-working kid though: "What I've noticed is that almost no one who was a big star in high school is also a big star later in life. For us overlooked kids, it's so wonderfully *fair*."[3]

Mindy's nerdiness paid off. At the end of high school, she was accepted to Dartmouth, one of the top colleges in the country. At Dartmouth, Mindy began showing signs of the star she would one day become. During her four years there, Mindy was in an a cappella group—The Rockapellas—and the school improv group, The Dog Day Players. She wrote for the *Dartmouth Jack-o-Lantern*, the college humor magazine. She even wrote and illustrated a comic strip in the school newspaper called *Badly Drawn Girl*. Mindy was a very busy girl!

It was also during college that Mindy got her first showbiz break: she got a summer internship in New York City working for her comic idol, Conan O'Brien, on his talk show *Late Night with Conan O'Brien*. Mindy was a terrible intern, however. Instead of doing the menial tasks assigned to her, she just watched her hero in action, soaking up his comic genius.

After graduation, Mindy moved to New York City with two best friends from Dartmouth, thinking she'd rule the Big Apple the way

Mindy's real name is Vera Mindy Chokalingam. She shortened it when she was first doing stand-up in New York because emcees couldn't pronounce it. Her mother named her Mindy after the main character in the '70s TV sitcom *Mork and Mindy*.

To actors who don't fit the mold, Mindy has good advice: "Write your own part. It is the only way I've gotten anywhere. It is much harder work, but sometimes you have to take destiny into your own hands. It forces you to think about what your strengths really are, and once you find them, you can showcase them, and no one can stop you."[5]

〜〜〜

she'd ruled college. She was in for a shock. First, she tried writing for some TV shows, but she hated most of the ones that had openings and she wasn't very good at it. And she quickly discovered that there weren't many acting options for short, chubby Indian girls.

After a year or so of not getting anywhere with her dream career, Mindy felt like a total failure. Desperate, she took matters into her own hands and began doing what she'd done back in high school and college: she wrote her own shows and put in parts for herself.

In 2003, Mindy got her second big break: she cowrote and costarred in a play called *Matt and Ben* with her best friend and roommate, Brenda. It imagined life for actors Ben Affleck and Matt Damon before they became superstars, when they were just two friends hanging out. Mindy played Ben Affleck. The play was weird and funny, and audiences loved it. Every night sold out. The *New Yorker* called it "goofy, funny, and improbably believable."[4]

The show was such a hit that it traveled to Los Angeles. In the audience one night was LA producer Greg Daniels, who loved the play and invited Mindy to write with him on a new, unknown show he was developing called *The Office*. Mindy accepted, and at age twenty-four, she moved to LA and became the only woman writer on the show. She also acted on the show as Kelly Kapoor, a superficial, selfish, chatty customer-service rep. Later, she also moved into directing and producing the show. On *The Office*, Mindy got to do a bit of everything.

During one performance of *Matt and Ben*, Mindy accidentally broke Brenda's nose onstage. Even though Brenda was bleeding all over herself, they finished the show.

〜〜〜

Believe it or not, this beloved comedy wasn't an instant success. It started as a midseason replacement for a different show that got canceled. They only did six shows that first season, and early reviews weren't great. But *The Office* got picked up for a second season. Over its nine seasons and 201 episodes, *The Office* won tons of awards, earned stellar reviews, and became one of the most popular comedies on TV.

> Mindy also does a lot of great voice work in animated movies. She's voiced characters in favorites like *Despicable Me, Wreck-It Ralph,* and *Inside Out.*

Mindy loved working on *The Office*, but she longed for a new challenge. She wanted to be in charge—to make the big decisions about character, dialogue, and direction on a show. In short, she wanted to develop and star in her *own* TV show. So that's what she did. In 2012, Mindy left *The Office* to start *The Mindy Project*. Mindy wrote, produced, and starred in the romantic sitcom. On it, she played a doctor, like her mother.

Being the writer, producer, and star of her own show was not an easy job. A typical workday for Mindy started at 5 AM, she was in the studio by 6 AM to get her hair and makeup done, and then for the rest of the day, she shot the show and worked on writing episodes. In the evening, after filming and writing, she finished up in the editing room and got home around midnight. Mindy didn't mind the brutal schedule—she was used to hard work, and she finally had her dream job: "A lot of people ask how to get to where I am, and the single biggest thing, which is not profound, is that I work like a dog."[6]

All her hard work paid off. From the start, *The Mindy Project* received good reviews and award nominations. So far it's been nominated for a bunch of Emmys and NAACP Awards (which honor nonwhite artists), and it has won the Critics' Choice TV Award and some Gracie Awards (which honor female artists).

Mindy is changing TV. She was the first Indian American to write and star in her own network TV show, and she is showing Hollywood

Mindy has also written bestselling and funny (of course) memoirs: *Is Everyone Hanging Out without Me?* (2011) and *Why Not Me?* (2015). If you want to learn more about her life and career, check them out!

that actors don't have to be white and skinny for audiences to love them. But she isn't interested in her work being defined by her sex or her ethnicity: "I never want to be called the funniest Indian female comedian that exists. I feel like I can go head-to-head with the best white, male comedy writers that are out there. Why would I want to self-categorize myself into a smaller group than I'm able to compete in?"[7]

And Mindy is having no problem competing. She is already one of the most successful writers in Hollywood, male or female, and *Time* magazine recently put her on its 2013 list of "The 100 Most Influential People in the World." As the Church Lady would say, "Well, isn't that SPE-CIAL!"

If you've got it, flaunt it. If you don't got it? Flaunt it. 'Cause what are we even doing here if we're not flaunting it?

—MINDY KALING

HOW WILL YOU ROCK THE WORLD?

I'm going to rock the world by becoming a therapist. I will help people by listening to what they have to say and never judging them. I will help guide them down the right path. I think I will be good at it because I've been a mini therapist ever since I was able to talk.

TALULAH HENDERSON-BRAZIE ☼ AGE 12

Jhamak Ghimire

1980– ◦ AUTHOR ◦ NEPAL

*When I read [her book], I felt like I was talking to
Nepali Helen Keller of [the] literary world . . . It is . . .
evidence of her powerful writing.*

—HOM NATH SUBEDI, PRESIDENT OF THE INTERNATIONAL NEPALI LITERARY SOCIETY

Jhamak sat in the dusty courtyard outside her house. Her body curled over on itself, her useless hands tucked up under her chin, her head resting on one knee. She stretched her legs out in front of her. Her feet trembled, and sweat beaded on her brow.

I've almost got it, she thought, reaching her left foot a bit further. Almost . . . almost . . .

There! Her toes wrapped around a small bamboo twig. She gripped it like she'd seen her sister hold a pencil in her fingers.

Jhamak used all her willpower to command her foot. Slowly and painfully, she moved the twig across the dirt. First, she scratched a horizontal line, then a vertical line to make a T shape. Then, on either side of the vertical line, she drew two circles. The whole time, she struggled to balance her body and fought to keep the stick in her toe-grip. It took forever and she was exhausted when she finished, but she'd done it! Jhamak had written her first letter. It was the letter *Ka* and it looked like this:

Jhamak was so happy she squealed with delight. With her tired toes, she grabbed some dust and flung it in the air—her usual way of celebrating. The dust rained down, covering her from head to toe. Suddenly, her sister was there in the yard, a frown on her face.

"What are you making a fuss about?" she asked, not expecting an answer. She believed Jhamak's brain was as broken as her body. Jhamak wished she could answer her sister. She knew just what she would say: *I can write! Just like you!* But Jhamak's mouth couldn't form the words.

Her sister shook her head and walked away—right over the letter! Her footprints erased it! Jhamak was furious.

"Aaaargh!" she screamed. Her writing had been kicked aside, just as her own life was going by unnoticed and erased by everyone around her.

"What is the *matter* with you today, Saanpey?" said her sister.

Jhamak hated this nickname. They called her *Saanpey*, which meant "slithering snake," because she crawled across the ground. It was so unfair! It wasn't *her* fault her legs didn't work!

I will keep practicing, Jhamak vowed, *And someday I will be able to write whole words. Then I will tell her to stop calling me a snake!*

This unbelievably strong and determined girl *did* teach herself to write. She went on to write not just words but poems and stories and whole books. This "Helen Keller" from Nepal, a girl who couldn't talk or walk or use her hands, conquered her disabilities and has become one of the most celebrated writers in her country.

Jhamak was born in 1980 in the small village of Kachide in Nepal. Her parents and the other villagers were poor and uneducated. When Jhamak was born, her parents' first hope was that she would die. She was born severely disabled with cerebral palsy—she would never be able to speak, walk, or use her hands. Her family assumed her brain was equally damaged. At that time in Nepal, disabled people had no rights, protections, or services. Jhamak's family kept her alive but just barely.

Her grandmother was the only person who showed Jhamak any true love. For years, she carried her firstborn grandchild around on her back. She fed Jhamak by hand and brought her to sleep in her bed. The rest of the family ignored Jhamak at best or treated her like one of the animals at worst. She was beaten more times than she could count. Jhamak often overheard her grandmother worrying about her future: "I'm afraid this kid would also die when I'm no more."[1]

The fact that she needed help to do things that others could do for themselves bothered Jhamak. When she was hungry or thirsty, she had no way of telling anyone. When she had to go to the bathroom, she couldn't do it herself—she was entirely dependent on others. It made her feel like one of the animals penned up in her yard.

From a young age, she did everything in her power to become independent. She taught herself to crawl, pulling her body across the ground with her feet. When she was hungry and her grandmother wasn't around, she pulled bowls of rice onto the floor and used her toes to pick up the spilled grains and put them in her mouth. When her parents discovered Jhamak surrounded by spilled food, they beat her—they had no idea what she was trying to do. They thought she was just making a mess. "How I wished I could talk to people around me," Jhamak remembers, "but [I] was deprived of voice!"[2]

Her inability to communicate was so frustrating for Jhamak that she often rebelled. Sometimes she took the family bowls outside and filled them with dirt and sticks. Other times, when she dragged herself to the shed where her family kept a cow and goats, Jhamak felt such sympathy for the tethered animals that she burst into tears: "I had a feeling that my life was not much different from theirs."[3] Often, she would use a sickle to cut them free. And she was beaten for these small acts of defiance.

When Jhamak was just four years old, her worst fear came true: her grandmother died. With her only guardian and caretaker gone, she realized she had to learn to fend for herself. *Immediately*. When a person dies in Nepal, the Hindu custom says that close family members shouldn't see or touch each other for twelve days. Jhamak knew she would starve during that time, so she used the break from her family to teach herself to eat. She knocked food to the floor and learned to use her foot to scoop it into her mouth. No one beat her because they weren't allowed to touch her! Finally, after days of watching Jhamak make mess after mess, her family figured out what she was doing and left her in peace. By the end of twelve days, Jhamak could feed herself.

Next on her list was communicating. She couldn't talk, but maybe she could express herself another way. Each night, as her father held his younger daughter's hand, showing her how to write each letter, Jhamak scooted as close as she could to listen and learn too. When she was discovered, her father would shoo her away. "What's the use of your learning and reading?" he would ask.[4] But Jhamak didn't give up.

She began to practice writing letters, just like her sister. She practiced in the dirt with a stick of bamboo gripped between her toes. This method was difficult—the skin between her toes blistered and bled—but at least when she drew a letter, it stayed there. Until someone walked over it.

Today, Jhamak writes with her left foot. Just as you hold a pen using three fingers, she holds a pen clasped between three toes.

While her sister was at school and her parents at work, Jhamak took her sister's old notebooks filled with letters and copied them, using burnt-out cinders for a pencil. Day after day, she practiced until she heard someone approaching, then she hid the notebooks. If she was outside, she erased her writing with her foot. Writing with cinders or in the dirt was taboo in Nepal; people believed it would cause the family money problems. For the longest time, Jhamak's family had no inkling what she was up to.

Once Jhamak figured out the alphabet, she taught herself to read. She snuck her family's books while they were away and spent whole days reading. Eventually, the family discovered she could read and write, and while they didn't help or encourage her, they didn't stop her either. Friends and neighbors began bringing books for her to read. Jhamak loved them—especially the poetry—and read her books over and over again.

> The first word Jhamak wrote was *pen*, something she desperately wanted.
>
> ~~~

As she dove into reading, Jhamak thought, *How nice it would be if I also could learn to write similar stories and poems.*[5] First, she copied what was in the books into her notebooks. But eventually, she created poems of her own. Her parents were amazed. And so were the people of her village. When neighbors stopped by on an errand, they were astonished to see Jhamak writing with her toes. Word of this amazing girl spread, and soon their house was full of curious visitors.

These fans brought Jhamak gifts of paper, pens, and even money. Suddenly, she was earning an income. For the first time, she bought new clothes for herself and gifts for her siblings. When she was fourteen, the media discovered her. There were articles in the local newspapers. Everyone wanted to know about the girl who wrote with her toes. "I started seeing my life as a beautiful thing," Jhamak remembers.[6]

> Jhamak especially loved biographies: "When I would go through the biographies of some struggling or rebellious individuals, I would feel like following [in] their footsteps."[7]
>
> ~~~

In 1998, when Jhamak was eighteen, her first collection of poems was published, called *Sankalpa*. It was a big success, and the next year, she exploded onto the literary scene of her country. Collections of her poems, songs, journal entries, stories, and essays were published and her amazing life story was in the national newspapers. Even more people flocked to her tiny village just to meet her. Jhamak was the pride of Nepal.

Jhamak progressed from scrawling letters in the dirt to writing award-winning literature. She has published roughly a dozen books—everything from poetry to memoir—and writes a regular column for *Kantipur*, one of the most popular newspapers in Nepal. In 2011, she won the Madan Puraskar, the most respected literary award in Nepal. She was only the second woman to ever win it.

After years of abuse, Jhamak became the pride of her family as well. Products of a culture that didn't value or protect disabled citizens, Jhamak's parents realized the great gifts that were trapped inside their daughter. Jhamak taught them that everyone deserves a chance to live a full life and to be heard. And she is teaching these lessons to the rest of Nepal. Her writing is a political call to action expressing the struggles of many oppressed groups in her country (and everywhere)—the disabled, the poor, and women. Their challenges are Jhamak's challenges, and she encourages them to fight for their independence, as she did. "All our troubles are resolved if we remain self-dependent and self-sufficient," she writes.[8] Jhamak's extraordinary struggle is an inspiration to people not just in Nepal but around the world. And you can bet nobody calls her a slithering snake anymore.

HOW WILL YOU ROCK THE WORLD?

I will rock the world by becoming an artist, because I love to draw people and lots of animals. I love to draw lots of wonderful things.

GUADALUPE MUÑOZ ☼ AGE 10

Venus and Serena Williams

1980– (VENUS), 1981– (SERENA) ⊕ TENNIS PLAYERS ⊕
UNITED STATES

Venus and I really like it when people tell us that they have big dreams. One of the most important things you can do for yourself is envision a fantastic future. Dreams give you direction in life. Everyone who is successful started with one.

—SERENA WILLIAMS

*T*hwack! Richard hit a bright yellow tennis ball over the net. *Thwack!* His six-year-old daughter Venus returned it with a blazing forehand shot. *Thwack!* He managed to lob it back to his other daughter, four-year-old Serena.

Thwack! With her backhand, Serena fired it down the line. Richard dove and missed.

Man, these girls are getting good! he thought.

Venus and Serena were grinning from ear to ear. They loved beating their dad. And they loved playing tennis. They would play all day long if he let them. Luckily for him, the court had no lights, so when it got dark, they had to go home.

As he walked back to the shopping cart to get more balls, Richard glanced around. The court was falling apart. Its pavement was full of cracks, which made balls ricochet at unpredictable angles. The net was in tatters. Before they could play, they had to pick up the trash littering the ground. It wasn't an ideal place to teach your kids tennis.

Suddenly, they heard a gunshot.

"DUCK!" he yelled. Serena and Venus hit the pavement. They knew this tennis court was in gang territory. The Crips and the Bloods, two rival gangs, often fought over it. Sometimes Richard and the girls got caught in the middle.

After a few quiet minutes, they stood and brushed dirt off their clothes. *At least they're not messing with me anymore*, Richard thought. When he first started bringing the girls here, gang members tried to scare him away by beating him up. It didn't work. They came back every day. Recently, he'd worked out a deal: he paid gang members to "guard" the court while the girls practiced. It worked pretty well, but sometimes the troubles of the neighborhood still interfered with their tennis.

It will make them tough, thought Richard, stuffing his pockets with more balls to serve to Venus and Serena. He knew they would need all the toughness they could get to make it out of Compton and onto the courts of Wimbledon.

Thwack! It was time to get back to practice.[1]

—————

Venus Williams was born in 1980, and her little sister, Serena, was born a year later. Their family, which followed the faith of Jehovah's Witnesses, was very close. Venus and Serena lived with their three older sisters and their parents in a rough neighborhood called Compton, just outside Los

Angeles, California. Compton had a lot of violence, but it was also full of hardworking families just like theirs.

Their father, Richard, believed that growing up in Compton would be good for his children. He said, "The ghetto will make you rough, it'll make you tough, it'll make you strong."[2] Even before Venus and Serena were born, he had big plans for them. In the 1970s Richard watched a women's tennis tournament on TV and was surprised to see how much prize money they won—more than his yearly wages! He decided he would make his children tennis stars.

First, he taught himself how to play. He didn't take expensive lessons but, instead, read books and watched matches on TV. He bought a ball machine and practiced for hours. Then he taught his wife to play. He tried to teach his three older daughters, but they didn't like it. As soon as Venus and Serena were old enough to hold rackets, they fell in love with the game.

Venus began playing when she was four years old, and Serena started the next year. They went with their dad to the courts right after school and played until dinner, and then played after dinner until it got dark. Even though the courts they played on were in terrible shape and the neighborhood was dangerous, Richard and his daughters played every day, no matter what.

Richard believed in his daughters. When they were still very little, he told them they would one day win at Wimbledon, the most prestigious tennis tournament in the world. He was right—both girls won at Wimbledon (Venus five times, Serena seven times!).

The girls started competing in weekend tournaments when they were four and a half. First Venus and then Serena, when she got old enough. Both were amazing players. Serena won forty-six out of forty-nine tournaments she played in. Venus won all sixty-three of hers—she didn't lose a single game! The sisters were the top-ranked players in Southern California for their ages.

People told Richard that Venus should play more tournaments, get more experience. Agents offered the family cars, money, even houses!

But Richard didn't want his girls to play more tennis at such a young age. He wanted them to have normal childhoods with time for family and friends. In fact, the Williams family believes that God should come first, then family, then education. Tennis comes fourth.

When the girls were ten and eleven, a famous tennis coach named Rick Macci flew to Compton to watch them play. He was impressed with both girls but especially Venus. She reminded him of Michael Jordan, the world's best basketball player. He offered the Williams sisters full scholarships to live and train at his tennis school in Florida, so the whole family moved there.

The girls began a new daily routine: schoolwork for four hours and then tennis for six hours. For the next three years, Richard refused to let them play in any competitions at the junior level; he was worried they would feel too much pressure and burn out early. Instead, he had them train *only*, until they were old enough to play professionally.

Venus missed competing and wanted to go pro as soon as she possibly could, which was at age fourteen. Her parents thought that was too young, so she made them a deal: they had to let her turn pro *if* she got straight As in school that year. Her parents agreed. Venus got her straight As and in 1994, at age fourteen, she turned pro.

Her first professional competition was back in California. She easily won her first match against the player ranked fifty-ninth. Then she played the player ranked second and won the first game but lost the match. She did, however, show the tennis world that she was ready for the pros. And she earned $5,400 for the tournament—her first professional paycheck![3]

In 2007, Venus set the record for fastest serve by a woman at 130 miles per hour![4]

Bigger paychecks were coming. Soon after that first pro competition, Venus signed her first sponsorship deal. It was with Reebok for $12 million! As part of the contract, Richard got paid a consultant salary, and the family was able to move into a ten-acre estate in a fancy Florida neighborhood. They even had their own tennis court! It was a huge step up from the run-down court in Compton. Serena decided to go pro when she turned fourteen, too, and three years later, she signed her own deal with Puma, also worth $12 million! The family would never be poor again. Twelve million dollars may seem like a lot, but the Williams sisters were just getting started. Venus has endorsement deals with Wilson, Kraft, Ralph Lauren, and Tide and is worth a hefty $75 million. Serena has endorsement deals with Nike, Wilson, and Gatorade and is worth nearly $140 million!

> In 2016, Serena became the highest-paid female athlete in the world![6]
>
> ~~~

From the moment they turned pro, Venus and Serena began climbing their way to the top of the tennis world. In 1997, Venus made it to the US Open, America's top tennis tournament. Two years later, Serena *won* the US Open—the first of many Grand Slam titles for the sisters. In 2000, Venus won the US Open *and* Wimbledon and was the first African American to win Wimbledon in forty-three years. Also in 2000, the Williams sisters competed in their first Olympics, where Venus won gold in singles and they won gold together in doubles. That year, Venus renewed her Reebok deal for an astounding $40 million! It was the most money any female athlete had ever been paid![5]

> Venus and Serena have played against each other 28 times in tournaments.
>
> ~~~

The first time Venus and Serena played against each other for a championship was in 2001, at the US Open finals. Venus won . . . *that* time. In 2002, Venus was ranked the number-one women's player in the world and Serena was number two—the first time in history that sisters won the top two spots. Later that same year, Serena won the French Open, Wimbledon, and the US Open and took the number-one position from her sister. In 2010, they actually shared the number-one ranking in women's doubles.

In 2005, Venus won Wimbledon again, but she was frustrated because her prize money was smaller than what the men got when they

> Wimbledon is the oldest and most prestigious tennis tournament in the world. The US Open is the biggest tournament in America. These two, combined with the Australian Open and the French Open, make up the Grand Slam—the four most important tennis events of the year. They offer the most ranking points (to determine top players), prize money, and media attention.

won. She wrote a letter to the organizers, protesting this inequality. In 2007, when she won Wimbledon again, she became the first woman to earn equal prize money to male competitors.

For the next decade, Venus and Serena totally dominated tennis. Between the two of them, they have won twelve Wimbledon titles; Venus has won seven Grand Slam titles, and Serena has won a whopping twenty-two (the current Grand Slam men's leader has seventeen)![7] And they've each won four gold medals from three different Olympics.

While Serena and Venus have achieved all their tennis dreams, there have been difficulties too. In 2002, their parents got divorced. Then their oldest sister, Yetunde, was murdered in a drive-by gang shooting back in Compton in 2003. The girls were devastated. In 2011, Venus had to quit the US Open after being diagnosed with Sjögren's syndrome, an autoimmune disease that causes dry eyes and mouth, as well as joint pain and fatigue. Her tennis ranking has dropped since then, as Serena's continues to soar.

The sisters have also struggled against racism. When Venus and Serena started playing professional tennis, they entered an almost entirely white world. Many people were excited about this—but not *all*. Players and reporters sometimes said unkind things to and about them. In 2001, when Venus got injured and had to pull out of a semifinal at the Indian Wells tournament in California, the largely white crowd of thousands booed Serena through her entire match. They booed and jeered Venus and her father as they walked through the stands, and yelled out racial slurs, including the n-word. The family was shaken by such visible racism. Serena and Venus refused to play there again for fourteen years, in spite of stiff fines and penalties imposed by the WTA (Women's Tennis Association). Eventually, Serena decided to give Indian Wells a second chance. She felt enough time had gone by and wanted to heal the pain. Although she was nervous walking onto the court, this time, the crowd gave her a standing ovation.

Thanks to their father's continual insistence that the girls play less and live more, the Williams sisters have had time to explore other interests. In 2008, Serena opened a school in Kenya, and both sisters founded the Venus and Serena Williams Tennis Academy in Los Angeles, offering tennis classes to inner-city kids and helping them earn college scholarships through the sport. Venus and Serena also design their own unique tennis clothes. Both went to fashion school and both started their own fashion lines. Venus calls hers EleVen, and Serena's is Aneres (her name spelled backward).

The Williams sisters changed tennis forever. Not only have they helped to increase diversity in a very white sport, but they have demanded equal pay with male tennis stars. They have also forced their competitors to step it up. Women's tennis is a faster, more powerful, more exciting game than it was before Venus and Serena. "Both of them have done so much for the sport because they have brought it to another level on the court and because . . . of their story," said Serena's coach.[8] In a sport where pros are lucky if their career lasts ten years, the Williams sisters are still on top after more than twenty years. They are two of the greatest players the world of tennis has ever seen. More than that, they are two of the greatest athletes in history.

When Venus and Serena started, they were often the only African American players in the WTA's playing top 100 list. As of 2015, 15 players on that list were nonwhite. Tennis is expensive and some courts are better than others, making it hard for poor kids to compete. But the US Tennis Association is working to get low-cost and free equipment to kids who otherwise can't afford to play.[9]

ROCK ON!

LYDIA KO

Lydia Ko was born in Korea but immigrated to New Zealand as an infant, where she began playing golf at age five. She started competing in national tournaments at seven, and by the age of fourteen, she became the youngest person ever to win a pro golf event. Since then, she's become the youngest winner of a slew of golf contests. As of 2016, she is the number-one female pro golfer in the world, making her the youngest number-one player of either gender. Lydia, who currently practices golf thirty-five hours a week, hopes to find the time someday to go to college and study psychology.

Beyoncé

1981– ✦ SINGER ✦ UNITED STATES

Power's not given to you. You have to take it.

—BEYONCÉ

eyoncé and her friends waited for their cue. The twelve-year-old girls stood onstage at their marks, bathed in pink and purple lights. They were nervous but also confident they would win. After all, they'd been practicing for almost two years. And *Star Search* was a national TV show. Everyone they knew would be watching—rooting for them. If they won, they would get $100,000 and probably a record contract too. They would be famous!

This was their big break. They had to win.

When the defending champions, Skeleton Crew, finished their rock song, host Ed McMahon introduced the girls: "Your challenge is a young group from Houston. Welcome Beyoncé, LaTavia, Nina, Nikki, Kelly, and Ashley, the hip-hop-rappin' Girl's Tyme."[1] That was their cue!

The music started. All six girls did a high kick and launched into the routine they knew so well. Beyoncé, in a lime-green jacket, striped shorts, and sparkly high-tops, strutted to the front and belted out their song while the other five girls danced behind her. Her voice was strong and confident. She hit the high notes with ease and growled out fierce low notes.

At the end of the song, the girls huddled together, grins on their faces, while the audience clapped and hooted. *They loved us!* thought Beyoncé. *We're gonna win!*

It was time for the scoring. McMahon announced the results as both bands smiled at the audience. "The judges give champions Skeleton Crew four stars. A perfect score!"

Uh-oh. Beyoncé didn't think Skeleton Crew was *that* good. She did a quick prayer: *Please let us win, please let us win.*

"The challenger, Girl's Tyme, receives . . . three stars."

Beyoncé couldn't believe it. They had lost! After all their hard work.

She wanted to cry, but she couldn't. She had to keep smiling for the cameras.[2]

Other *Star Search* losers include Britney Spears, Justin Timberlake, and Christina Aguilera!

But this was a turning point for her. At age twelve, she realized for the first time that even if you work super hard and give it everything you've got, you can still lose. She decided then and there that she wouldn't give up until she was a star.

Beyoncé was born in 1981 in Houston, Texas. Her dad sold medical equipment and her mom was a hair stylist. She knew from a very early age that she wanted to sing and perform—she entered her first talent show when she was just seven years old. She sang John Lennon's "Imagine" against kids as old as sixteen—and she won!

When she was nine, she enrolled in a music school and she sang in the choir. She also auditioned for an all-girl group called Girl's Tyme. She made the cut, along with five other girls, and began singing and dancing at talent shows all over Houston. In 1992, the group appeared on *Star Search* (an early version of *American Idol* and *The Voice*) but lost in the first round. The next year, three girls left the group, a new girl joined, and they renamed themselves. Supergroup Destiny's Child was born.

When Beyoncé turned fourteen, the band became a family affair. Her dad quit his job to work as their manager, and her mom made the costumes and did their hair and makeup. The group began rehearsing every day, leaving Beyoncé little time for normal high school stuff, like having friends. They performed everywhere—churches, malls, and as openers for more popular bands.

Beyoncé was sixteen when Destiny's Child finally got their big break. They signed a recording contract with Columbia Records in 1997 and released their first album,

Divine intervention named the band. While searching for a new name, Beyoncé's mom opened her bible to where she had stuck in a picture of the band as a bookmark. Underneath the photo was the word "destiny." The group decided God was sending them a message: "Destiny" was their destiny.

Destiny's Child. Their song "Killing Time" made it onto the soundtrack for the blockbuster movie *Men in Black* starring Will Smith, and they won three Soul Train Awards that year, including Best R&B/Soul Album.

Over the next eight years, Destiny's Child grew to be hugely popular, with plenty of number-one hits like "Bills Bills Bills," "Say My Name," and "Bootylicious." They became the world's top-selling female vocal group, winning countless awards (including several Grammys), and *Billboard* magazine ranked them one of the greatest trios of all time. That magazine described *Destiny's Child* as "a combination of feisty female empowerment anthems, killer dance moves, and an enviable fashion sense."[3]

While still in the band, Beyoncé released her first solo album, *Dangerously in Love*, in 2003. With hits like "Crazy in Love" and "Baby Boy," the album went multiplatinum, selling millions of copies. Beyoncé won five Grammy Awards—the most of any artist that year—and Destiny's Child officially broke up two years later.

Beyoncé's solo career has been an even bigger success than her years with Destiny's Child. So far, she's released six albums, which have collectively sold over one hundred million records worldwide (that's *in addition* to the sixty million Destiny's Child albums), making her one of the bestselling music artists of all time. She has won twenty Grammy Awards and is the most nominated woman in Grammy history. *Forbes* named her one of "The Most Powerful Women in Entertainment 2015." And President Barack Obama asked her to sing at not one but two of his inauguration ceremonies.

> From 2000 to 2006, Destiny's Child won the NAACP Image Award for Outstanding Group a whopping five times! This award goes to artists who provide positive role models for African American kids.

In 2008, Beyoncé married rap mogul Jay Z in a super-secret wedding. The two have made many songs together, including "Crazy in Love, "That's How You Like It," and "Upgrade U." The two had a daughter in 2012 and named her Blue Ivy Carter. Blue Ivy should be all set for college: in 2014, her mom became the highest-paid black musician in history. In 2016, Beyoncé's net worth was estimated at $265 million, landing her on "*Forbes*' 2016 List of America's Richest Self-Made Women," right behind Oprah![4]

> Beyoncé's voice is an amazing instrument. She is a mezzo-soprano, meaning she can sing across three octaves. That's almost half the notes on a piano!

As if the singing talent and money aren't enough, Beyoncé is also a talented actress. Since her first role in 2001, she's starred in films like *Austin Powers: Goldmember*, *Dreamgirls*, and *Cadillac Records*. She also loves fashion and launched a clothing line with her mom in 2004 called House of Deréon. The brand is named for Beyoncé's grandmother, Agnez Deréon, who worked as a seamstress.

But even cooler than Beyoncé's creative and financial success is what she's doing to make the world a better place. As a modern-day feminist, she is showing girls how to be true to themselves and go after their dreams, like she did. From songs like "Flawless" to "Pretty Hurts" to "Formation," Beyoncé's lyrics are full of empowering messages for girls and women. At the 2014 MTV Video Music Awards, she performed in front of an enormous neon sign reading "FEMINIST." She is also part of the Ban Bossy campaign, which encourages girls to be leaders.

Beyoncé believes in giving back. She works with Feeding America, which stocks food banks for hungry kids and families; she has raised over $1 million for hubby Jay Z's Shawn Carter Foundation, which sends low-income kids to college; and after Hurricane Katrina destroyed New Orleans, she created the Survivor Foundation to provide housing for victims.

> Beyoncé created Sasha Fierce as a stage persona she puts on to help her overcome stage fright. When she's about to go on, "Sasha Fierce appears, and my posture and the way I speak and everything is different."[6]

Beyoncé may have lost on *Star Search*, but she won in the end. She didn't let that failure stop her and continued working hard until she achieved her dreams. She believes you shouldn't avoid failing, because failures can be the best teachers in life: "If everything was perfect, you would never learn and you would never grow."[5]

HOW WILL YOU ROCK THE WORLD?

I will rock the world with my voice, my creativity, and my taste. My passions are singing, making art, and baking, and I want all girls to be confident and pursue their dreams.

CHLOE JOHNPOLL ☼ AGE 13

Danica Patrick

1982– ☼ RACE CAR DRIVER ☼ UNITED STATES

I was brought up to be the fastest driver, not the fastest girl.

—DANICA PATRICK

Danica adjusted her helmet. Her hair, crammed inside it, was making her itch. She revved her engine and looked through her visor at her dad. He was standing at the starting line he'd drawn across the asphalt of the parking lot.

"On your marks, get set . . . go!" he yelled.

Danica stomped on the gas pedal and the go-kart her dad had built flew into action. *What a rush!* She'd never raced before, never even driven a go-kart. But from that first moment, ten-year-old Danica loved the feel of it—all that power in *her* hands.

Her tiny car flew down the straightaway of the track they'd made out of cans and bottles. As she entered the first turn, she lifted her foot off the gas and rotated the steering wheel carefully as the car drifted slightly to the outside, and then she accelerated again at the end of the turn. Perfect!

Another straightaway. Danica picked up speed until her go-kart was going twenty miles per hour. *It feels so fast!* she mused.

As she neared the second turn, she pushed the brake. Nothing. The go-kart didn't slow at all.

The brakes don't work! she thought in a panic.

Suddenly, she saw a concrete wall rushing toward her. She pumped the brakes over and over, trying to slow down . . .

CRASH!

The go-kart slammed into the wall and flipped over, trapping Danica beneath it.

Danica's father sprinted over and pulled her from the wreck. The go-kart was totaled. He yanked off her parka, which had caught fire on the hot muffler.

"Are you okay?" he asked, checking her for injuries, terrified he'd almost killed her on her very first time driving.

But Danica was grinning from ear to ear. She was ready to go again!

From that moment on, Danica was hooked on racing. She probably inherited that passion from her parents, who met at a snowmobile race. Her dad was a snowmobile racer and her mom was a mechanic. Danica's family had a serious need for speed.

Danica had an unusual Wisconsin childhood. While she did more traditional sports like baseball, basketball, volleyball, and cheerleading, her fascination with cars started early and quickly eclipsed her other interests. She spent hours and hours watching her dad race (snowmobiles, motocross, midget cars) and watching him tinker with race cars. "Thanks to him," she said, "I grew up thinking about things most other ten-year-old girls aren't even aware of, such as rpms."[1] ("Rpm" stands for revolutions per minute, which measures how quickly a car engine fires. The higher the rpm, the faster the car.)

When Danica was ten, her dad built go-karts for her and her sister. Danica loved racing from the very start, even after she crashed on her first day. They set up a race course made of paint cans in the parking lot of the family business, and Danica devoted herself to becoming the best. "After four or five weeks, Danica was really picking it up," her dad remembered. "I'd been around racing my whole life, and I knew she was different. She instinctively understood what to do."[2]

Danica had found her calling. The first year she raced, she broke the record at the local go-kart track, Sugar River Raceway. At thirteen, she begged her family to move to California so she could race year-round. They said no but began flying her west to compete in races. Soon, she was winning races all over the country; in her five years of go-kart racing, she won the World Karting Association Grand National championship three times!

The Indy 500 is the nickname for the 500-mile race held on the Indianapolis Motor Speedway each year. When it began in 1911, women weren't allowed anywhere but the spectator stands. In 1956, the first female reporter was allowed to cover the event, and it wasn't until 1977 that a woman finally raced on the track. Only 10 women, including Danica, ever have.[3]

⎯⎯⎯⎯

At age sixteen, Danica made a decision that changed her life. She wanted to become a race car driver, but she couldn't do that at home. When she got invited to train and race real cars in England, at the world's top training facility for rookies, she dropped out of high school, left friends and family behind, and moved to a country where she didn't know a soul. It was hard and Danica was homesick, but she got the training and experience she needed. She raced in England for four years, turning heads in the year 2000 when she finished second in the prestigious Formula Ford Festival. It was the best finish ever for an American—male or female!

That's when eighteen-year-old Danica's career went into overdrive. Race car champ and Indy 500 winner Bobby Rahal invited her back to the States to drive for his team, Rahal Letterman Racing (co-owned by David Letterman), and she began competing in the Indy Racing League (IRL). Finally, she was a professional race car driver! And she raced well for the team, earning herself a spot in the 2005 Indy 500. The race is one of America's most famous car events— five hundred miles driven in two hundred laps by thirty-three drivers.

At just twenty-three, Danica was young—a complete rookie. She was also the only woman in the race and just the fourth woman ever to compete in it. Interest in Danica drew thousands more viewers to watch the race that year, and media coverage was intense. It was a lot of pressure for young Danica, but she showed everyone that she deserved to be there. During practice, she had the fastest speed of all the drivers, reaching 229.880 miles per hour, and the fourth-fastest qualifying time.[4]

Due to her strong qualifying time, Danica started the race in the fourth position. Then, in lap fifty-seven, Danica surprised everyone and flew ahead into first place—the first time a woman had ever done so in the Indy 500! She remained in first place, off and on, for much of the race. Near the end, her car ran low on gas so she had to slow down to avoid running out entirely. In her first Indy 500 race, Danica took fourth place—the best-ever finish for a woman. She was also the first woman to ever take the lead in the race for not just one but nineteen laps![5] It was a historic, record-breaking race that made Danica a star of the racing world.

In 2007, Danica switched teams to Andretti Green Racing, and a year after that, she took first place in the Indy Japan 300 (another IRL race, like the Indy 500), making her the first female winner in IRL history.

Fans at the 2005 Indy 500 had Danica fever! Retailers sold more Danica merchandise than they had for any other racer in the track's 94-year history. A week later, Danica graced the cover of *Sports Illustrated*, the first Indy car driver to receive that honor in 20 years.[6]

After she won the Indy race in Japan, her home state of Illinois named April 26, 2008, Danica Patrick Day.

> Danica is one of a select few who have led a race in both the Daytona 500 and the Indy 500. Only 14 drivers have ever achieved it, and of course, Danica is the only female driver to have done it.[9]
>
> ᨬᨬ

Danica continues to improve as a driver, year after year. During her time in the IRL, she consistently finished in the top ten. In 2009, she bested her earlier Indy 500 finish by coming in third. In 2011, she switched to racing much heavier stock cars in the more popular NASCAR (National Association of Stock Car Auto Racing) league. That same year, she finished fourth in a Las Vegas NASCAR race, the highest finish for any female racer. And she's gotten better and better since then, working her way again to the front of the pack. As of 2013, she was the fastest woman ever to race NASCAR. But that's not good enough for Danica. She won't be satisfied until she's the *best* NASCAR racer. Period.

Like other world-class athletes, Danica is in high demand for ads and product sponsorships. But what's most important to her is being a role model for girls who want to break into the male-dominated sport of car racing. More girls than ever are competing in go-karting, and Danica is their hero. Lyn St. James, the first woman to race in the Indy 500 and Danica's mentor, said, "Somewhere between 15 and 20 percent of all young kids racing today are girls. Danica's victory is so empowering to them."[7]

> Danica has appeared in fourteen Super Bowl commercials—more than any other celebrity![10]
>
> ᨬᨬ

Danica Patrick chose a path rarely taken by girls. She's had to work hard and fight to be successful and earn respect on that path. Today, she wants all kids to find their own unique path: "I try to encourage kids to embrace what's different about them. In the end, what makes you valuable . . . is what's different about you."[8]

HOW WILL YOU ROCK THE WORLD?

I'm going to rock the world by becoming an Olympic athlete in track and field. Right now, I run the 100, 200, and relays, and I do high jump, long jump, and pole vault. Last year, I made it to districts. I plan to donate a percentage of my track earnings to cancer research. My mom had leukemia when I was six years old, so I have a soft spot in my heart for families who are going through cancer. I hope that someday I can help find a cure.

HANIA HALVERSON AGE 12

Misty Copeland

1982– ◎ BALLET DANCER ◎ UNITED STATES

My body is very different from most of those I dance with. But I didn't let that stop me.

—MISTY COPELAND

Misty pulled on her gym shorts. They were huge—almost to her knees. She stood in the empty locker room gathering her courage.

I can do this, right? she thought. *It's going to be fine.* But she wasn't so sure.

She walked out of the locker room and onto the Boys & Girls Club basketball court. Across the room, the other students were lined up along the wall, holding on to some kind of rail as they bent their knees, kicked up their legs, raised their arms. They were all dressed in pretty matching leotards and tights. On their feet were delicate slippers.

Misty looked down at what she was wearing: too-baggy shorts, a grubby gym shirt, and ratty socks.

Maybe this wasn't such a good idea . . . she thought, nearly turning back to the locker room.

"I've seen you sitting here every day," called a voice. It was the teacher, and she was looking right at Misty. "Are you going to join us?"

Misty thought about the kind of dancing she was good at—drill-squad dancing to hip-hop and pop music. Ballet seemed like another world entirely. Not her world.

This was her coach's idea. She'd told Misty that she should check out the class—that she had the perfect physique and natural ability for ballet. Misty checked out the other students again; she didn't look like any of them. What if her coach was wrong?

"I don't have a leotard or tights," she mumbled.

"Don't worry about that," the coach said, pulling Misty into the group.

What if I make a fool of myself? she worried as she began imitating the warm-up movements. *What will these kids think of me? What will my coach think?*

Then she had an even scarier thought: *What if my brothers find out I'm doing ballet?* They'd never let her live it down. Ballet was for rich white kids.[1]

But as Misty laid her hand on the barre for the very first time, her body took over. She bent her legs into *pliés*, stretched her arms into *ports de bras*, kicked up her foot for *grand battements* . . . Every movement felt right. Made sense. Misty felt like she was finally home.

It took Misty Copeland much longer than most ballet dancers to find her calling. While most professional ballerinas begin training at six or seven, Misty was thirteen when she took this first class at the Boys & Girls Club. But with her natural gift and a great deal of hard work, Misty quickly became one of the top ballet dancers in the United States. And one of the only black ballerinas in the world.

Certainly, no one expected Misty to become a prima ballerina when she was born in Missouri in 1982. When she was two years old, her mother left her father, loading Misty and her three siblings onto a Greyhound bus bound for somewhere new. She didn't see her father again until she was twenty-two. Her mother married and divorced several more times, and as a result, Misty's childhood was chaotic, with the family moving all the time. Mostly, she lived in San Pedro, a beach neighborhood of Los Angeles, California.

Misty was five years old when she made her stage debut in a school talent show. She and her siblings sang and danced to "Please Mr. Postman." They were a hit, especially with their mom. "I felt so special that night," Misty remembered. "I felt for once that I'd stood out from the crowd of little Copelands, that Mommy's attention was focused solely on me."[2] When she was seven, Misty watched a TV special about Olympic gold medalist Nadia Comanici, the first gymnast to score a perfect ten. She watched the recording over and over and began teaching herself gymnastics. In no time—and with no lessons—Misty could do difficult gymnastics moves, like backbend walkovers, handstands, and the splits. Misty could instantly do things with her body that it took others months to learn: "I didn't question why . . . my arms and legs had the elasticity of a rubber band. They just did, and I just knew."[3]

> Misty was a big worrier as a child. In one instance, she begged her mom to take her to school on the last day of summer so she could walk her class route—so she knew where to go and wouldn't be late. And Misty never was late, not once, all the way through high school.
>
> —www—

As her gymnastics obsession evolved into a dance obsession, Misty figured out something about herself: when she was dancing, she wasn't worrying about her mom's new boyfriend, or where they would be living in a month, or whether they had enough money for groceries that week. When she was dancing, she felt free. Misty spent hours choreographing routines to her favorite singers, like Mariah Carey, New Edition, and Tupac. She practiced all the time. In sixth grade, when she tried out for her school's award-winning dance team, not only did she make it, but they made her the team captain.

In spite of her physical gifts, however, Misty was nervous and insecure. She never felt like she fit in, and she worried about everything. But she had plenty to worry about in middle school. In seventh grade, Misty's mom divorced again, and then lost her job. The family hit rock bottom. Misty and her five siblings moved into the Sunset Inn Motel—all six kids sleeping on one couch and on the floor. They often had no money for food and had to go on food stamps. Misty remembers this hard time: "We were pretty much homeless and we were living in a motel, trying to scrape up enough money just to go to the corner store and get 'cup of noodle' soup to eat. It was probably just the worst time in my childhood when ballet found me."[4]

Misty didn't know anything about ballet—she'd never even seen one—but when her dance coach encouraged her to try it out, she started going to the free weekly classes at the Boys & Girls Club. And she loved it from the very start. Ballet was an escape from her chaotic, scary life. She loved its structure, its rules, its beauty and dignity—all elements that were missing from Misty's home life.

The ballet teacher, Cynthia Bradley, also recognized Misty's amazing gift and invited her to take more challenging classes at her ballet school. At first, Misty said no because her mother didn't have a car to drive her there and was working twelve to fourteen hours a day. Only when Cynthia offered to pick up Misty after school and drive her to the classes did she accept. After just three months of lessons, Misty was dancing *en pointe* (up on her toes), a milestone that takes a typical ballet dancer years of training to achieve.

Misty's mother was never very enthusiastic about ballet—the class was too far away and it took up too much of Misty's time. She told Misty she had to quit. But when her teacher Cynthia heard, she offered to let Misty live with her to make it easier to continue her training. Misty's mother let her go. Misty left the motel and moved in with the Bradley family. On weekends, she visited her own family.

Once Misty committed to her path, the ballet world began calling her a prodigy. After only eight months of lessons, fourteen-year-old Misty won a national ballet contest and drew two thousand people to San Pedro High School to watch her dance the lead in *The Nutcracker*.[5] At fifteen, she won first place in the Los Angeles Music Center Spotlight Awards, for which she won scholarship money. That summer, she got a full ride to attend a summer program at the San Francisco Ballet School, one of the top ballet schools in the country. Misty was a rising star.

The rise wasn't easy, however. After the summer in San Francisco, Misty returned to the motel, where she and her mother battled. The Bradleys had given her a lot when she lived with them, including more attention than her mother could with five other children. For her mother's part, she felt like the Bradleys were taking over Misty's life; she wanted Misty to quit training with them. Misty was terrified her mother wanted her to stop dancing altogether, so she filed for "emancipation," which meant she could legally live on her own and make her own decisions. She ran away from home while the papers were delivered to her mother. Once Misty's mom reassured her that she would always let her dance, Misty dropped the suit and moved back in with her family.

Misty's other struggle was with the prejudices of the ballet world. Not only did Misty begin her training late but most elite ballerinas are much taller, skinnier, and more flat chested than Misty. They are also nearly all white. After finishing high school, Misty applied to the top ballet companies and received some harsh rejections. She summarized the nature of their complaints in an Under Armour ad she starred in: "Dear Candidate, thank you for your application to our ballet academy. Unfortunately, you have not been accepted. You lack the right feet, Achilles tendons, turnout, torso length, and bust. You have the wrong body for ballet."[6]

> Misty was the first ballet dancer to star in an Under Armour ad campaign. The ad, which has a young girl reciting the ballet academy rejection letter as Misty dances up a storm, went viral. It has racked up 9 million views to date.[7] Check it out on Misty's website: mistycopeland .com/misty-under -armour-ad-goes-viral/.

Misty didn't let other people's image of what the perfect ballerina looks like stop her; she just kept dancing. In 2000, after only four years of ballet classes and one summer program, Misty was selected to join the American Ballet

Theatre (ABT) in New York City. It's considered one of the top three ballet companies in America. For more than ten years, she was their only black ballerina, and in 2007, she made history by becoming their first African American soloist.

To those who thought audiences only wanted to see tall, skinny, white ballerinas, Misty's ever-growing success and popularity was a complete surprise. Her unique look and incredible talent brought packed houses and tons of media attention. In June 2015, after fourteen years with ABT, Misty was promoted to principal dancer. She is the first African American to earn this position in ABT's seventy-five-year history.

While at ABT, Misty has danced many famous ballet roles, including the leads in *Swan Lake*, *Romeo and Juliet*, and *The Firebird*. She is one of the top ballerinas in the world—a dream she's had since she was thirteen and living in a motel—yet Misty keeps stretching herself and stretching how people view ballet: she danced with pop god Prince on his 2009 concert tour of Europe, she debuted on Broadway dancing *and singing* in the musical *On the Town*, and she was on the cover of *Time* magazine as one of "The 100 Most Influential People" of 2015.

While ballet's audiences have been shrinking over the years, Misty gets more popular every day. She's fighting to expand ballet's audience, to make it more inclusive, and to change who dances in it. She's launched a program with ABT called Project Plié, whose goal is to recruit diverse students. Misty is also attracting diverse audiences to her shows: "To see all the little brown girls out there in the audience supporting me . . . is the start of change and the direction of where ballet should be going."[8]

Misty speaks out about healthy and positive body image too (not always a strong suit of ballet). She believes that anyone who wants to be a part of ballet and is willing to put in the work should be able to, no matter what kind of body they have. "The ballet world has been a certain way for forever," she says, "which has been very exclusive and not completely open to people that look different. Not just for your skin type but for the body types that are allowed in. My belief is that if you understand how to train your body . . . how to nurture it and feed it, it can become anything you want it to be."[9]

Misty Copeland, who knew nothing about ballet, not only rose to the top of the field but is changing it dramatically. Because of Misty, people who have never been interested in ballet—in watching it *or* dancing it—are now fascinated. Her struggle and triumph, and her mesmerizing stage presence, have changed everything. Who knows where ballet will go now that Misty is their star . . .

> I never dreamed at thirteen years old, living in a motel, that I'd be in this position and be able to bring in so many people that never felt like they belonged in the Metropolitan Opera House.
>
> —MISTY COPELAND

HOW WILL YOU ROCK THE WORLD?

I will rock the world by being the first person in my family to play professional sports. I will be in the WNBA and become the next Candace Parker. I will achieve this by continuing to attend training camps and working hard on and off the court. My plans include Texas Tech University, where I will be part of the basketball program. I believe I can make it with determination and hard work.

KIYAN WILLIAMS · AGE 16

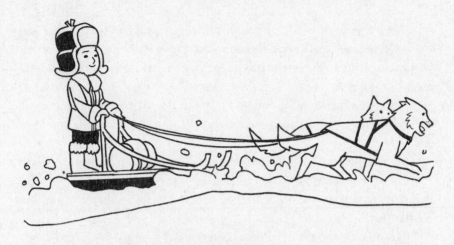

SaRah McNaiR-LandRy

1986– ◦ ADVENTURER AND CINEMATOGRAPHER ◦ CANADA

I love wide open spaces, nature's beauty, and the Arctic's vast regions covered with snow through most of the year.

—SARAH MCNAIR-LANDRY

The icy winds howled and shrieked around her. *Must be blowing fifty miles an hour*, thought Sarah. *Feels like forty below.* She tugged her scarf higher on her face so just her eyes peeked out. Bits of flying snow pricked her skin and tiny icicles covered her eyelashes. Sarah couldn't hear the *snick-snick* of her cross-country skis over the wind.

Sarah turned to look at the team running beside her: twelve Canadian Inuit huskies, the best dogs in the world for sledding across the harsh Arctic plains. They seemed fine. They were pulling her hand-built sled uphill into the fierce winds, following her partner, Boomer. She and Boomer were both on skis to keep the sled light for their long journey.

The trip was supposed to take 120 days for them to travel 2,500 miles around the edge of Baffin Island in the Canadian Arctic. They were only four days in and already they'd been hit by a storm.

Sarah knew it wouldn't be easy. Her parents had done the same trip twenty-five years earlier, and growing up, Sarah had heard stories about windstorms, melted ice, unruly dogs, and frozen body parts. She was ready for anything.

Suddenly, the team slowed and the lead dog turned toward her.

What's he doing? Sarah wondered, *Oh no . . . he's leading the team back downhill!*

"Whoa!" she yelled. "Whoa!" But her command was lost in the wind.

Or maybe the dogs weren't listening—maybe they'd had enough. As they raced past her, a line looped around Sarah's leg and jerked her off her feet.

Sarah's foot caught in the line, and she was dragged backward down the hill.

"Put the dogs down!" she screamed to Boomer, hoping he could hear her and stop the team.[1]

Sarah tried to free her foot but couldn't reach it. She was terrified that at any moment she would hit a rock, smashing her skull or breaking a leg.

"Put the dogs down!" she screamed again. *Where was Boomer?*

Again she stretched to reach the line. As she did, she noticed the sled, heavy with all their gear, was picking up speed. It was sliding right toward her, faster than the dogs were running. In seconds she would be under it.

Sarah's life of ice, dogs, and adventure began in 1986 in the tiny town of Iqaluit, Canada. She grew up in the Canadian Arctic on Baffin Island, just a stone's throw from Greenland and the North Pole. As a girl, Sarah had the Arctic Ocean for a playground and a pack of huskies for friends.

Her parents were Arctic guides who owned and operated an adventure tourism company. Sarah grew up sledding, camping, hunting, and taking care of the dog team. She learned early on how to travel and survive in the extreme cold. She took her first overnight trip without grown-ups when she was just eight years old. She and her ten-year-old brother did an overnight hiking trip up one river and down another: "My parents made us practice camping on the back porch, putting up the tent, and lighting stoves before we were able to head out on our own."[2] After that, the siblings went out into the wilderness together quite often.

Sarah's first big expedition was a month-long dogsledding and kite-skiing journey across the Greenland Ice Cap with her brother—they were the first brother-sister team to do it. It's 1,500 miles across, which is like going from Boston to Miami on a sled! During that trip, she fell in love with polar expeditions and started thinking about even bigger trips.

When she was eighteen, she joined an expedition to the South Pole, and at nineteen, she dogsledded to the North Pole. These two trips made her the youngest person, male or female, to reach both poles. Even as a teen, Sarah had an endurance and mind-set beyond her years. As one travel partner described, "Sarah grew up out on the ice, running dogs and living out of tents in the extreme cold, and because of that, our system is second nature to her. She is also very driven to keep traveling, but keeps a fun attitude the whole time."[3]

Since her groundbreaking teenage expeditions, it's been nonstop adventure for Sarah. She's continued exploring frozen lands, returning to the North and South Poles as a guide. In 2014, Sarah and her boyfriend, Erik Boomer, spent 120 days circumnavigating Baffin Island by dog team, retracing the trip her parents had done years before. Sarah

What is an "adventurer," exactly? According to Sarah, "I explore places that are new to me. Some routes I have taken have never been done before; other expeditions retrace past routes."[4] To earn money, she writes, takes photos, and guides other groups.

A life of adventure keeps you in great shape. During one trip to the North Pole, Sarah got hit by a storm and fell behind schedule. To make up time, she cross-country skied for 15 hours a day!

survived getting tangled in the dog lines and being dragged along with her sled, but it was no easy trip.

Sarah doesn't limit her adventures to just the frozen places. In 2009, she crossed the Gobi Desert in a kite buggy. She had never traveled in the desert before, which presented some new and unusual challenges for her: "We encountered a lot of dust devils—small tornadoes of sand blowing across the desert. When they hit you, within seconds you would be lifted out of your buggy and crash down on the ground."[5] She followed that up with a canoe trip on the lakes of Mongolia and a camel trek across Egypt's Sahara Desert.

Although she's young, Sarah is already a leader in her field. She's been nominated for *National Geographic*'s Adventurer of the Year, was named one of *Adventure Magazine*'s top ten women in adventure, and has won the Outdoor Idol Award. She's a talented photographer and filmmaker as well; she takes photos on all her trips, which she later posts and sells to magazines and websites. She has also directed several documentaries, the most recent being one about the problem of garbage in northern Canada and another showcasing an Inuit artist.

> On her Arctic expeditions, Sarah must bring all the food for herself and her dogs. For the dogs, it's dried food with lots of fat, plus fresh seal meat when they can get it. For Sarah, the menu is granola for breakfast; chocolate, nuts, soup, and dried fish for lunch; and dehydrated meals for dinner. Fortunately, she has access to all the water she needs—by melting snow!

Why is Sarah drawn to these extreme, often dangerous environments? Her answer is "the challenge, the adventure, and the fun. Once you have learnt how to travel comfortably in the Arctic, you then notice the beauty of the areas you're traveling through."[6] She also hopes to inspire young people to get outside, explore their world, and be active. "Exploration doesn't need to be multi-month expeditions; I just want to encourage youth to get outside and explore their backyard, or the park down the road."[7]

HOW WILL YOU ROCK THE WORLD?

My swimming heroes are Missy Franklin and Michael Phelps, and I hope that someday I can be a combination of both of them. I started swimming when I was nine, and now I practice fifteen hours a week. Even though there are days when I'm in pain from a hard practice and from pushing myself, I know it's making me stronger and faster. I can see how much I've improved with this hard work. I've gone to state championships four times and made it into regionals this spring. I hope someday I'll go to the Olympic trials and get to swim in the Olympics, just like my heroes.

SIENA GEREN ☼ AGE 14

Nadia Nadim

1988– ❀ SOCCER PLAYER ❀ AFGHANISTAN AND DENMARK

I'm grateful I'm here and alive. And playing soccer, which I love.
—NADIA NADIM

Nadia was tired of being inside the back of the truck. She and her four sisters and their mother were packed inside a dark, window-less metal container with a bunch of other refugees, bouncing around like loose cargo. Eleven-year-old Nadia was exhausted and sore and hungry—their food was long gone.

How much longer?

When they paid the driver their money back in Italy, he told them it would take about twenty-four hours to get to London. They had family there who would take them in and help them find a place to live and work. But it felt like they had been on the road for days now.

Every time the truck slowed down, Nadia held her breath, worrying that they were being stopped, that they would be caught and sent back. Even though she missed her home, she did not ever want to go back to Afghanistan. Girls there were treated like animals. In Kabul,

Nadia couldn't go to school or even leave the house without a man by her side. And she certainly couldn't play soccer—at least not in public.

Plus, the Taliban had murdered her father. If she and her family were sent back, they would probably be killed too. Suddenly, the truck slowed to a stop. Nadia's thoughts raced around in a panic.

Is this it? Are we in London or are we caught? Will the police arrest us and send us home?

The doors to the back of the container swung open and light poured in.

"Get out," said the driver. "We are here."

Nadia shielded her eyes from the blinding sunlight. She couldn't see anything for a minute, but when her vision returned, what she saw surprised her: it was a small village. There were cute little houses—some brick, some painted in bright pastel colors—lining narrow, deserted streets. The countryside around them was completely flat—so different from the mountains of Nadia's homeland.

Where were the skyscrapers? Where were the busy streets and all the people?

The only person out on the street was a man walking his dog.

"Where are we?" Nadia's mother asked him in English.

"You're in Denmark," he answered. "Randers, Denmark."

Nadia was confused. They didn't know anyone in Denmark and didn't speak the language. But at the same time, she wasn't too worried. After the long, hard journey and years of living in fear in Afghanistan, she finally felt safe. And as long and she and her family were together, it didn't matter where they were.[1]

Although young Nadia had to start from scratch as a refugee in a new, unknown country, she would one day become one of the top female soccer players in the world and the pride of Denmark, her adopted home.

—ᵐᵐ—

Nadia Nadim was born in 1988, in Herat, Afghanistan. Her father, Rabani, loved sports, especially soccer. But he had five daughters and no sons, and in Afghanistan, girls weren't allowed to play soccer in public.

Rabani, however, believed that girls should have the same opportunities as boys, so he secretly taught his daughters inside the garden walls of their Kabul home.

Nadia's father was a high-ranking general in the Afghan National Army. In the early 1990s, an Islamic militia called the Taliban rose to power in the country. The Taliban cracked down on anyone who opposed them, including the Afghan army. (To learn more about the Taliban and what they did in Afghanistan, check out Malala's and Fawzia's chapters.)

When Nadia was ten years old, the Taliban called her father in for a "meeting." The family never saw him again. Six months later, they discovered the truth: the Taliban had murdered him. Nadia's mother, Hamida, realized she and her five daughters had to leave Afghanistan immediately—the Taliban could kill them at any time. But even if they didn't, Hamida didn't want her daughters growing up in a country where they had no freedom and no chance for an education. Nadia remembers her life then: "Basically, if you are a woman, you are not a full person. My mom knew that if we stayed there we would not have any life."[2]

So they fled. In 2000, with forged papers and passports, Hamida and her five daughters (ages three to thirteen) snuck first into Pakistan. From there, they flew to Italy and then traveled by truck to Denmark. Nadia was eleven when they arrived in their accidental new home. Danish police took Nadia's family to a refugee camp in Copenhagen, where they lived for six months while their asylum request was processed.

> Nadia speaks five languages: English, Danish, German, Persian, and Urdu.
>
> ⌒⌒⌒

Next to the refugee camp was a soccer club. Nadia and her sisters studied English and Danish in the mornings, but their afternoons were free, so Nadia played soccer for hours and hours every day. "That was the first time I saw girls and ladies playing soccer," she remembers. "And I was like, 'Wow, you can also do that!'"[3]

Eventually, Denmark agreed to let Nadia's family stay in the country. They got an apartment, and the girls started school. Nadia also began playing on a girls' soccer team called *Gug Boldklub*. From the start, it was obvious she was a gifted player. Fast, nimble, and fearless, she rose quickly through the ranks of Danish women's soccer. In 2005, seventeen-year-old Nadia began playing professionally on Danish teams. By the time Nadia turned twenty, Denmark gave her citizenship *and* asked her to play for the their national team.

After Nadia played pro soccer in Denmark for ten years, the National Women's Soccer League (NWSL) recruited her to play in America. In 2014, she joined Sky Blue FC (football club) in New Jersey, where she became an immediate sensation by scoring seven goals in six games. Sky Blue coach Jim Gabarra called Nadia a "once-in-a-generation" player.[4]

They didn't get to keep her for long, however. In 2016, the top team in the league, the Portland Thorns, stole her away. Nadia is their striker, which means she's on the team to score goals. "Goal scorers are really hard to find," said her Sky Blue coach. "She just has this pure love of the game that comes out when she is playing."[5] During her season and a half at Sky Blue, she scored thirteen goals, and she's scored twelve goals for her Danish national team (so far).[6] While she's still new to the Thorns, she is one of the top scorers on the team.

Her coaches and teammates have high praise for Nadia and what she's overcome. Thorns midfielder Dagny Brynjarsdóttir said, "You can sometimes tell, when Nadia's playing, what she's been through. There's so much passion; she works so hard and gives everything."[7]

Nadia couldn't apply for Danish citizenship until she was 18. When she was granted citizenship two years later, Denmark called her up to play for their national team. She was blocked from playing, however, because the international soccer rules stated she needed to be a citizen for five years. The Danish Football Association challenged the rule, and an exception was made for her; she got to play for Denmark just one year after becoming a citizen.

Nadia is just as determined off the field as she is on it. For six years, Nadia attended medical school in Denmark. She was one of the few elite athletes in the world going to medical school while also training and competing at a professional level. Every day, she practiced up to seven hours with the Thorns and then hit the books when practice was over. Of her brutal routine, Nadia said, "Obviously it's not easy. It takes a lot of time. You really have to want it. I want both from the bottom of my heart."[8]

> The Portland Thorns, Nadia's current team, regularly have a crowd of 17,000 cheering for them, where Nadia's old team, Sky Blue FC, has 2,000 fans on average. Average attendance for NWSL games is 5,558.[11]

Nadia is also passionate about education, especially for refugees. She supports From Street to School, a Danish group that works to send Afghani street children back to school. By succeeding in both soccer and medicine, Nadia wants to send a message that girls and refugees can do anything if they are just given a chance: "It is important to see someone you can relate to. And to see 'Okay, she has done this, it's not impossible.' If someone has done it, it makes it more possible, more realistic. . . . I know that will help people in the same situation."[9]

Nadia is proof that anything is possible. She went from playing soccer in secret, in a country where it was illegal, to being one of the best female soccer players in the world. And today, she is inspiring kids—especially refugee kids who are struggling through terrible life-and-death situations—to not give up.[10]

From Street to School gives financial support to Afghan children who are homeless due to war or poverty by helping them to get an education and stay off the streets. Ten dollars gives a street child one week of school, food, and clothing. Fifty dollars pays for a month! To find out how you can get involved, go to FSTS.dk.

HOW WILL YOU ROCK THE WORLD?

I am going to rock the world by fighting for equal pay for women. When the US men's soccer team got eliminated in the first round of the 2014 World Cup, they got paid $8 million; yet when the women's team won the 2015 Women's World Cup, they got just $2 million. The top five players on the men's team make six times as much as the top five players on the women's team. It's not fair, and it needs to change.

LUCI DOHERTY ⚛ AGE 15

Adele

1988– ❀ SINGER AND SONGWRITER ❀ ENGLAND

I didn't make music to become a sex symbol. I make music to inspire people and make a good record... To me, the image isn't part of music. Music is in your ears, not on your eyes.

—ADELE

Two teens waited outside a London tube station. Adele felt nervous. She was meeting Nick Huggett for the first time. He was the supposed A&R man from XL Recordings, and he wanted to offer her a recording contract. He said he could make her dreams come true!

But Adele wasn't sure she believed he *really* worked for a record company. He had contacted her through her MySpace page, where a friend had posted three songs she wrote and recorded for her high school graduation project.

Who gets discovered on MySpace?

This Nick Huggett was probably just some pervert—that's why she brought her friend Ben along. For protection. Just in case. Even though Ben was tiny and wouldn't scare a flea, at least she wouldn't be alone.

It's funny to think of Adele as being nervous about anything. But she was only eighteen years old—had just graduated from high school—and she was about to take the biggest leap toward her dream of being a singer. Of course we now know that Nick Huggett really was with a record label and Adele really *did* get that deal. And she went on to become one of the most popular and famous singers of her generation.

mm

Adele Laurie Blue Adkins was born in 1988, not far from that tube station, in a working-class neighborhood of London. She was the only child of young parents whose marriage didn't last. When Adele was four, her father moved back to Wales, where he was from, and after that, she was raised by her "artsy" mom.

Adele began singing at age four. Growing up, she sang all the time: alone in the shower, riding in the car, private concerts for her mom, school talent shows, with her friends. Adele always loved to sing, but she never took it seriously.

As a preteen, she loved the same pop music as her peers—the Spice Girls, Lauren Hill, Destiny's Child—but as a teen, she had two experiences that changed her view of music and of her own singing. At thirteen, she went to a Pink concert, which she described like this: "I had never heard...someone sing like that live. I remember sort of feeling like I was in a wind tunnel, her voice just hitting me."[1] And when she was fifteen, she discovered Etta James and Ella Fitzgerald at a local record store. These two American blues singers from the 1940s blew her away: "Chart music was all I ever knew. So when I listened to the Ettas and the Ellas, . . . it was like an awakening."[2] You can certainly hear these blues legends in Adele's singing today.

Although they were usually broke, Adele's mom always managed to scrape up enough money to pay for Adele's piano and guitar lessons. At age fourteen, Adele, who hated regular school and was never a strong student, had an epiphany while giving a concert for her mom: "As soon as I got the microphone in my hand, I realized I wanted to do this."[3]

She told her mom she was done with regular school and wanted to be a singer, so her mom enrolled her in the BRIT School for Performing Arts & Technology, which was the right price—free!

Adele isn't the only famous BRIT alum. Amy Winehouse also graduated from the school.

Like the school from the *Fame* movie, BRIT is full of dancers and singers and artists of every stripe—all trying to make their mark. For the first time in her life, Adele was happy in school: "It was inspiring to be around a bunch of kids who were trying to be something."[4] But even at BRIT, Adele still didn't believe in her talent. She planned to work for a record label in A&R (artists and repertoire) when she graduated, discovering *other* talents (just like Mr. Huggett). But the universe had other plans for Adele.

For university, Adele wanted to stay close to home, but her mom wanted her to leave London and stretch her wings a bit. After the two fought about it, Adele stormed off and wrote "Hometown Glory" in ten minutes. The song was about her love of London and her neighborhood in particular. "I played it as a protest song to my mother," she explained. "It basically said, 'This is why I'm staying.'"[5]

Believe it or not, this world-famous singer has terrible stage fright. Adele has confessed that before performing she sometimes has panic attacks and throws up backstage!

In order to graduate from BRIT, Adele had to make a demo tape of three songs she'd written. She recorded "Hometown Glory" and two others, and agreed to let a classmate post them on MySpace just for the fun of it. "I figured the best that might come out of it was that I might get a job as an intern," she remembers.[6]

Almost immediately, record labels came knocking. Adele was so surprised by the attention that she didn't actually believe it: "I'd never heard of those labels; I thought they were just some internet perverts. So I didn't call them back."[7]

But Nick Huggett didn't give up. "She had the most amazing voice I had ever come across," he said.[8] Nick finally got lucky that day at the tube station and convinced Adele to sign with his label. XL Recordings was home to tons of popular indie groups like The White Stripes and Radiohead, and they loved Adele's honest, unique sound. They weren't the only ones—Adele's star shot up from there.

In 2008, she released her first album, *19* (her age), which included her high school song "Hometown Glory." The album went platinum in both the United Kingdom and the United States and sold over seven million copies.[9] Critics raved about Adele's voice. *People* magazine said, "With a knockout voice that's rich and supple, robust and sultry, it's hard to believe that this singer-songwriter is barely out of her teens."[10] The following year, she won Grammys for Best New Artist and Best Female Pop Vocal Performance.

Her next album, *21*, did even better. Released in 2011, it has sold seventeen million copies and became the UK's fourth-bestselling album of all time.[11] Adele won six Grammys for it, including Album of the Year.[12] In 2012, she released "Skyfall," a song for a James Bond movie of the same name, which won an Oscar, a Grammy, and a Golden Globe for Best Original Song. In 2015, her album *25* dropped, quickly becoming the year's best-selling album. It seems like everything Adele records turns to gold.

In addition to her amazing pipes, Adele is also admired for her body-positive attitude. In an industry that puts too much value on being

> Adele is so successful she's made Guinness World Records more than once! She's the first woman to have two singles and two albums in the UK Top five at the same time (the Beatles did it in 1963). And with three million copies sold in one year, *21* broke records as the first album in UK chart history to ever do this. That album also set records for the most consecutive and the most cumulative weeks for a number-one UK album (solo female).[13] Not bad for a girl who never thought she'd make it as a singer!

skinny and showing off women's bodies in super-skimpy outfits, Adele is something entirely different. She describes her feelings about body image this way: "I've never had a problem with the way I look. I'd rather have lunch with my friends than go to a gym."[14] Adele is elegant and hip, and she sets fashion trends with her timeless style. She has become an unintentional icon for girls of all shapes and sizes.

Adele never planned to become rich and famous—she never dreamed it could happen to her. But she's accepted her role as top diva with grace and humor. *Time* magazine has named her one of the most influential people in the world, and her albums have sold more than one hundred million copies, making her one of the bestselling artists in the world.[15] The young girl who thought she would grow up to discover other singers ended up discovering herself.

ROCK ON!

LORDE

New Zealand pop star Lorde began her career in school talent shows, winning her first at age thirteen. At fourteen, she began writing her own songs, and a few years later, she released her first album through SoundCloud. After it was downloaded sixty thousand times, record company UMG signed Lorde and released the album. Her song "Royals" flew to number one on charts around the world, and the eighteen-year-old became the youngest solo artist with a number-one US single in almost twenty years. She went on to win two Grammy Awards—Best Pop Solo Performance and Song of the Year—and she recorded songs for the blockbuster movie series *The Hunger Games*.

Emma Watson

1990– ⚜ ACTRESS AND ACTIVIST ⚜ ENGLAND

I don't want other people to decide who I am.
I want to decide that for myself.

—EMMA WATSON

Emma ran through the lines in her head. She knew this scene backward and forward. She had been practicing for weeks, videotaping herself reading lines and watching her deliveries over and over again, figuring out where she could do better. She began at nine in the morning and didn't stop until dinnertime.

Sitting on either side of her at this final audition were Daniel and Rupert. She'd only met them a few times, but they seemed nice enough. Both were very funny. She hoped they all got parts, but mostly she hoped she would get to play Hermione.

As the director got the lights and cameras ready to record their first screen test, Emma allowed herself to think about her competition. Hundreds and hundreds of girls were trying out for the first Harry Potter movie, and every one of them wanted the lead role. Emma should have been

An avid reader, Emma is also part of the London-based organization Books on the Underground, where members secretly plant books around underground transit centers. The Day after Donald Trump won the presidential election in November 2016, Emma shared her favorite titles throughout New York's 23rd Street C and E line stations while being interviewed by Vanity Fair. Her idea was to "spread a little bit of love."

nervous—her parents certainly were—but she felt calm.

"Scene eight, take four. Mark!" a crewmember called, and *snap* went the clapperboard.[1]

The three children began. It was a Hermione-centered scene. She read from a history of magic book, looking for clues about Nicholas Flamel and the Philosopher's Stone, as Rupert and Daniel mostly sat and listened. Emma delivered each line perfectly, enunciating each word—never stumbling. Her eyes sparked with mischief, and her mouth twitched in an almost grin. She looked like a girl who knows way more than everyone around her. She looked like Hermione.

Out of the hundreds of girls trying out, Emma knew from the very first audition that she would get the part. She could just feel it.

Emma Watson had to come back for *eight* different auditions! But she was right—she did get that part. And the rest is history. At just nine years old, Emma would bring one of the most beloved heroines in all of literature to the big screen: brilliant Muggle-born witch Hermione Granger. And her outstanding performance would win her the hearts of millions of fans around the world for decades to come.

Emma Watson, one of the most famous British actresses, was actually born in Paris, France, in 1990. When she was five, her parents divorced and the family moved back to England, where Emma lived with her mother and visited her dad on the weekends. Emma's parents were lawyers, and she went to a fancy private school in Oxford. She was an excellent student. "I always loved school," she says. "I was a proper, proper nerd."[2] She also discovered that she loved acting. She took acting classes and was soon getting the leads in school plays. "Whenever there was a part at school, I went for it," she remembers.[3] Very early, by age seven, Emma knew she wanted to be an actress.

In 1999, casting directors scoured all of England looking for the perfect children to play the lead roles in the soon-to-be biggest movie franchise of all time: Harry Potter. The books were already hugely popular, and nine-year-old Emma was a big fan. She believed she was perfect for Hermione and desperately wanted the part. But thousands of girls auditioned. Emma's parents tried to keep her hopes in check—they didn't think she'd get it. But Emma knew: "I just felt like that part belonged to me. I know it sounds crazy, but from that first audition, I always knew."[4]

She was right, of course. Emma had to worry through eight auditions, but eventually, everyone realized what she already knew: Emma was Hermione, through and through.

Of course, the movies were huge. Harry Potter is the second-highest-grossing film series ever, earning $7.7 *billion* worldwide.[5] Emma also earned great reviews for her performance. A reviewer at epinions.com wrote of the first movie, "I was especially impressed by young Emma Watson's masterful portrayal of Hermione Granger. I have trouble believing that *Harry Potter* is her first film, and I suspect she is destined for a

> While Emma was auditioning for Harry Potter, her father cooked a chicken dinner and gave her the wishbone. Even though she was confident she would get it, Emma wished to play Hermione. That lucky wishbone is still in Emma's jewelry box.
> ⟿

> Emma once confessed that the most difficult scenes she ever had to film were the ones where she had to kiss Daniel or Rupert.
> ⟿

In 2010, Emma was the highest-paid actress in Hollywood! She earned $15 million each for the last two Harry Potter movies. By her early twenties, she had already earned a $70 million fortune![8]

~~~

great career."[6] Maybe this reviewer had some magical divination skills?

Filming the movies wasn't easy, however. For ten years, Emma worked eleven months out of twelve. She woke up every day around six in the morning and got home around nine at night. On set, they tried to keep life as normal as possible for the kid actors—they had "school" for five hours a day with a tutor. Emma's costars Daniel and Rupert became like brothers to her. And thank goodness they got along, because they filmed eight consecutive movies together—over the course of practically their entire childhoods.

Over those ten years, Emma got better and better at acting, winning more and more awards. But she definitely gave up a lot of normal life. She couldn't do sleepovers or sports. Paparazzi mobbed her whenever she went out. In 2007, when she was supposed to renew her contract for the sixth movie, *Harry Potter and the Half-Blood Prince*, Emma nearly quit the films entirely. She wanted to go to college and explore other passions. Emma wanted a normal life again. In the end, however, she couldn't stand the thought of someone else playing Hermione. She made a deal with the studio:

she would film the last three movies *if* they gave her time off to go to college and experience some normalcy. Of course they agreed.

In 2009, Emma headed to America to attend Brown University, an Ivy League school. She was nervous that students there would treat her like a movie star and that she'd have to deal with paparazzi. To her happy surprise, people treated her like any other freshman, and she made great friends who didn't care that she was Hermione. She lived in a dorm, she went to parties, and she even

While Emma was at Brown, she took acting classes! She was worried that after so many years of playing one character, she wouldn't know how to play any others.

~~~

wore her pajamas to class sometimes—just like any other college student. Emma finally had her normal life back. She graduated in 2014 with a degree in English literature.

Since she had to attend so many premiers and Hollywood events as a child, Emma developed an early interest in fashion. At fifteen, she became the youngest person to ever do a cover shoot for *Teen Vogue*. She made an effort to wear clothes by new, unknown British designers. "I thought, *If people are going to write about what I'm wearing, then I would wear young British designers who need the publicity*," she says.[7] At nineteen, she became the face of Burberry, a high-fashion British label. She also designed a teen clothing line for People Tree, a fair-trade company (they pay all their workers a living wage) that helps poor people in developing countries by teaching them work skills while also protecting the environment.

> Believe it or not, the multitalented Emma is trained and certified to teach yoga and meditation. As part of her training, she did a meditation retreat where she couldn't speak out loud for a week.

But Emma's focus on fashion doesn't mean she's stopped making movies. In 2011, she starred in *The Perks of Being a Wallflower*, and *The Bling Ring* the year after that. Her 2017 film, *Beauty and the Beast*, had the biggest opening weekend for a PG movie, Emma has many passions and talents, but doing these movies reminded her how much she loves acting and wants to keep doing it.

Emma also devotes a big chunk of time to fighting for women's rights and education for girls around the world. In 2014, she was chosen as a UN (United Nations) Women goodwill ambassador, helping promote global empowerment for women. That year, Emma

> While filming *The Perks of Being a Wallflower*, Emma and her costars, Logan Lerman and Ezra Miller, formed a band called Octopus Jam, with Emma as lead singer.

delivered a speech at the UN to launch their new campaign, HeforShe, calling for *men* to stand up for gender equality. Emma also explained her belief that "feminism" means that men and women should have equal rights and opportunities. Within hours of giving the speech, Emma received threats online, but her response was unwavering: "It made me so angry . . . If they were trying to put me off, it did the opposite."[9]

As a UN ambassador, Emma travels the world speaking about gender equality in countries where women are oppressed. For this work, the Ms. Foundation for Women named Emma their Feminist Celebrity of 2014. And at age twenty-five, she made *Time* magazine's "The 100 Most Influential People" list. In 2016 Emma started a feminist book club on Goodreads called "Our Shared Shelf" (check it out!) to share ideas and spark discussion.

Emma certainly didn't have a normal childhood, but when asked if she has any regrets about spending it on the Harry Potter set, she answered that she "wouldn't swap it in a million years."[10] Who knows what her future holds? More movies for sure. But Emma is smart, talented, and passionate—she could do anything. One thing she will *always* do is keep pushing herself: "I have so much to learn, and I couldn't be more excited about that."[11]

If you truly pour your heart into what you believe in—even if it makes you vulnerable—amazing things can and will happen.

—EMMA WATSON

HOW WILL YOU ROCK THE WORLD?

I will rock the world as a realtor and make affordable housing more accessible. I also love cosmetology, so I will help the world by introducing more eco-friendly cosmetics.

MAYA TODD AGE 12

Hou Yifan

1994– ◈ CHESS GRANDMASTER ◈ CHINA

Titles don't really matter anyway—it's your chess rating that matters. Whatever you are or not, it is more important to show your skill than to have a fancy title.

—HOU YIFAN

Yifan stared into the case, her hands pressed against the glass. She loved looking at the figurines inside—they fascinated her. Her father brought her to this bookstore nearly every night after dinner, so she had many chances to study them.

There was a gleaming black horse, a stately castle, and a mildly scary man in a pointy hat. But her favorites were the tallest figurines wearing crowns. The ebony pieces were so beautiful, lined up across each side of the checkered board.

What do they do? Yifan wondered.

The next day, her father handed Yifan a gift. It wasn't her birthday—she wouldn't turn four until the winter. *So what's the gift for?* she wondered.

Her father explained that they wanted to give her something to broaden her mind. Yifan wasn't sure what that meant, but she couldn't wait to open it. Inside was a box with a tiny latch on one side. She opened it, and the box unfolded. Tucked inside was a set of the figurines just like the ones in the bookstore.

"For me?" she shouted gleefully.

"For you," said her mother, a smile on her face. Yifan's parents knew that chess wasn't a typical game for Chinese girls, but Yifan had already beat an older neighbor at checkers after just one game. Maybe Yifan would have a knack for strategy games. She certainly loved the chess pieces, so why not?

Within a few weeks, three-year-old Yifan could beat her father *and* her grandmother at the game. In just a few years, she would beat the top chess players in all of China—and then around the world!

—————

When Yifan was a little girl, her first dream was to be a detective! Now she sees the similarities between detecting and chess: "Both need theoretical thinking... You need to think very far away in [the] future and then step by step go back to the current [time] to see what kind of things you need to do."[2]

—————

This astounding chess prodigy was born in 1994 in the city of Xinghua, on the outskirts of Shanghai, China. When Yifan was three years old, her parents wanted to introduce her to some kind of "brain game," like Chinese checkers, Go, or chess. Yifan always stared at the chess pieces at a local bookstore, so that's the game they picked.

It turned out to be a game that suited Yifan perfectly.

From a young age, Yifan was *obsessed* with chess. She would go to school during the day, come home and do her homework, and then at 5:00 PM, she would leave to go play chess for five to six hours.[1] For Yifan, it never felt like too much: "I had such an interest in the game, a passion . . . that meant I

never got bored with it. I never tried to get out of playing. . . . I always wanted to keep playing, to keep learning more."[3] Her parents didn't push her; they just wanted her to do what made her happy. The drive came from Yifan. "My parents always gave me a choice about playing," she says.[4]

When Yifan was five, her parents realized she had a rare talent and hired a private chess coach to tutor her. But by the age of seven, there was no one left at her town's local chess club who Yifan couldn't beat. Her family moved to Shandong province so she could play at a larger club, where she would have more competition. Yifan's mother rearranged her job as a nurse, taking night shifts so she could drive Yifan to chess practice and tournaments.

At nine years old, Yifan came to the attention of China's national chess team coach, Grandmaster Ye Jiangchuan. When he played the young girl, she immediately recognized and exploited his weak moves better than most players on his national team. He could see she was a prodigy: "She had wisdom beyond her years. She was . . . an aggressive and fearless player. It was clear to me then that she was a very rare talent."[5] After that first meeting, Yifan began training with Ye Jiangchuan and the national team in Beijing.

Yifan was eleven when she competed in her first tournaments; just one year later, she was already ranked as one of the top ten female players in the world! At age thirteen, she became the youngest-ever Chinese women's champion, and at fourteen, she became the youngest female ever to become a grandmaster—earlier than even her hero,

> The grandmaster title is awarded to chess players by FIDE, the World Chess Federation. A grandmaster must demonstrate in competitions an advanced understanding of chess. Apart from world champion, grandmaster is the highest title a chess player can get; once awarded, it is their title for life.

chess legend Bobby Fischer. In 2010, sixteen-year-old Yifan conquered the world to become the youngest-ever Women's World Chess Champion, eventually gaining the nickname "Queen of Chess."

In addition to winning, Yifan enjoys the human interaction of chess. While some players like to practice against a computer, she prefers the real thing: "When you play chess with a real person, you're not just playing a game—you're having a conversation with someone. Chess is like life."[6] Life for Yifan isn't just about chess, however; she has other interests too. She likes to swim, listen to music, read books, and travel. Her favorite place she's visited in her many travels for chess is Paris. In 2016, she graduated from the University of Beijing, one of China's top colleges, where she majored in international relations. "An education in other areas is very important too," she said.[7] The degree should be helpful in her life as a world traveler.

As a young chess prodigy, Yifan was sometimes teased for her lack of fashion sense. Eventually, she learned about style from the older players. Now she's considered quite glamorous—not what most people think of when they think of chess champions!

Graduating from university was a major goal for Yifan, and now she has her sights set on other goals. While many chess experts predict she will one day be the greatest female chess player in history, Yifan wants to take on the greatest male players as well. She is already in the top one hundred players in the world

Yifan has certainly ruffled some chess feathers. After winning four Women's World Chess Championships in a row, she refused to defend her title in the 2016 championship, instead choosing to focus her energy on beating the top 100 chess players in the world—men. Another scandal erupted at a 2017 tournament when Yifan intentionally lost the final game in just five baffling moves. She threw the match to protest the fact that she'd been paired up against seven women and just three men. She wanted the chance to compete against her peers and felt she wasn't getting that chance. Her public outcry stunned the chess world.

(one of just three women to make that list), and her coach thinks her chances of climbing that list are good: "Yifan has the potential to rival the best men . . . You need to have a strong, aggressive desire, but [Yifan] has that. Now only time and hard work will tell."[8]

With Yifan's work ethic and determination to win, chances are good that she'll achieve her newest dream. Not bad for a little girl who got into the game simply because she liked how the pieces looked!

ROCK ON!

ABBY WAMBACH

With 184 international goals—the most of *any* soccer player in the world, male or female—Abby Wambach is the reigning Queen of Soccer. The youngest of seven, she began playing with her siblings at age four. When she joined a team at age five, she scored twenty-seven goals in the first three games! The coaches had to move her to a boys' team! She went pro in 2002 and has since won US Soccer Athlete of the Year six times and Olympic gold twice. She played on the national team for twelve years, and after her fourth World Cup tourney in 2015 (which the United States won), Abby retired. While US women's soccer gets stronger every year, Abby's are some big cleats to fill.

Lizzy Clark

1994– ❖ ACTRESS AND ACTIVIST ❖ ENGLAND

*I don't see my Asperger's syndrome as a problem;
that's just other people's ignorance.... Hopefully I'm helping to
bring understanding of the condition to more people.*

—LIZZY CLARK

"Are you ready, Lizzy?" asked the director. Lizzy was distracted by the crew moving around behind the cameras and by the bright lights glaring in her eyes. But this was what she wanted—to be an actress. She wouldn't let her Asperger's syndrome stop her. She took a deep breath and nodded.

You can do it, Lizzy, she told herself.

"Okay then. Actors to your marks," said the director. Lizzy and Dakota walked onto the set, the interior of the Fairdale Residential School. Lizzy couldn't believe how real it looked once they were standing in it.

This was the scene where her character, Poppy, first meets Dakota's character, April. They would become good friends later in the movie, but in this early scene, they are strangers. Lizzy knew her lines, but she was still nervous. Dakota was a famous actress—everyone in England knew her. She had been acting for years and knew exactly what to do. This was Lizzy's very first acting job.

"Lights?" asked the director. "Camera?"

The crew quieted and took their places.

Dakota leaned over and whispered to Lizzy, "Don't worry, you're going to be great." She gave Lizzy a big, friendly smile.

Lizzy smiled back. She *could* do it—she was sure of it.

"And . . . action!"

Lizzy Clark was born in 1994 in Shrewsbury, England. She knew about acting because her mother was an actress, but it wasn't something she knew she would do. Early in life, she was diagnosed with Asperger's syndrome, a developmental disorder related to autism. People with Asperger's (or Aspies, as some like to be called) have higher-than-average intelligence, weaker social abilities, and a desire to focus on just a few same interests and activities, over and over again. Acting is not a common career path for people with Asperger's—you can count the famous autistic actors on one hand.

Lizzy's disability was subtle, so many people didn't know she was autistic. "They see me as someone who's a bit strange and not very easy to get on with, although I do have lots of friends who love me and support me."[1] When Lizzy was fourteen, her actress mom, Nicky, saw an ad on an autism website. The BBC was holding auditions for a TV movie based on the children's book *Dustbin Baby*. Lizzy tried out and got the part of Poppy, a teenager with Asperger's syndrome. Lizzy's mother said, "I think it's incredibly positive that the BBC chose to find an actress who has the same condition as the character."[2]

> There are a few other famous actors with Asperger's syndrome or other autism spectrum disorders, including Dan Ackroyd (*Saturday Night Live, The Blues Brothers, Ghostbusters*) and Daryl Hannah (*Splash, Bladerunner*).[3]

Lizzy, who had never acted before, described the challenges: "My Asperger's made some things on the film set difficult at first, like dealing with the sudden noise of the storyboard, but I was soon so focused on acting that I didn't notice anything else."[4] She was also intimidated by working with the more experienced and famous actors on set, but she soon got used to it and just enjoyed herself. It was a huge boost to her self-esteem. "It was lovely for Lizzy; it was lovely for people with autism . . . to show that anything is achievable," said her mother.[5]

Lizzy's performance was watched by 2.3 million viewers when it was broadcast in 2008.[6] The movie got great reviews. The *Telegraph* called it "a rare treat this Christmas: something teenagers and parents can watch together."[7] And the praise did not go unnoticed: the movie won two Kidscreen Awards, a BAFTA Award (the British Oscars), and an International Emmy Award.

When the movie wrapped, Lizzy was eager to play new parts . . . but there weren't any. It's not that there aren't disabled characters on TV and in movies; it's just that nondisabled actors almost always play them. This trend isn't fair, so Lizzy and her mother have decided to do something about it. They started the "Don't Play Me, Pay Me" campaign. The campaign encourages disabled people to follow their chosen creative-career path; it urges actors to stop "playing disabled," asks directors and producers to hire more disabled actors, and encourages theater schools to recruit more disabled students.

Discrimination is just as bad in American showbiz. While people with disabilities make up almost 20 percent of the US population, a recent study showed that able-bodied actors play 95 percent of characters with disabilities on the top 10 TV shows! Only four actors with disabilities were cast in the top shows, which is less than 2 percent of all actors on the screen. The study concluded there is "unjust and troubling discrimination of actors with disabilities in Hollywood."[8]

Lizzy is passionate about her cause:

It is not just mentally disabled actors who lose out when nondisabled people are employed to act them. Audiences think they are getting an authentic portrayal of a mentally disabled person, but they're not . . . You can't understand what it is like to have a mental disability unless you've really lived with it. When nondisabled people try to portray us, they tend to fall back on stereotypes that have done our community so much harm in the past.[9]

Viewers agree. A study by the Independent Television Commission found that 79 percent of TV watchers would be happy to see a disabled person host the evening news, and 60 percent think disabled actors should appear in a wider variety of roles.[10] Lizzy's advocacy is making a difference. In 2010, the BBC—the largest media company in England—held a nationwide search for disabled actors in an effort to increase their representation on its shows. Hollywood is also slowly waking up to the problem. Hopefully, there will be more parts for Lizzy and other disabled actors coming soon.

HOW WILL YOU ROCK THE WORLD?

I will rock the world by bringing positivity and confidence to others. Everyone needs that person they can talk to—a friend or mentor. I will be a mentor for kids one day, to thank those who have mentored me.

AnaMarie Lopez ☼ Age 17

Bethany Mota

1995– ◦ YOUTUBE VLOGGER AND FASHION DESIGNER ◦
UNITED STATES

I do talk about beauty and fashion...Some people might see it
as kind of superficial, but in the end, my main goal for what I do
is to...promote self-love and self-confidence, and taking a bad
situation and making it into something amazing.

—BETHANY MOTA

ethany was *super* nervous. She didn't have a tripod, so she set the
video camera on a stack of boxes and books. It was a little wobbly,
but it would have to do.

Do I really want to do this? Bethany wondered. *What if everyone hates
me? What if they write mean things in the comments?*

Bethany had reason to worry. A group of seventh graders had been
cyberbullying her—they had posted ugly pictures of her along with mean
comments.

It was mortifying.

Bethany never wanted to go to school again. In fact, she didn't want to do anything anymore, so she just stayed in her room all the time. At least she had the internet. She spent hours watching YouTube videos—mostly of girls doing makeup and fashion tutorials. Bethany loved how positive and happy these girls seemed. They posted nice comments on each other's videos and were really supportive of each other.

Bethany was inspired: if those other girls could make videos, why not her? She didn't even have to leave her room.

Bethany took a deep breath and switched on the camera. She leaned back in her chair, looked straight at the lens, and smiled.

"Hey guys . . . This is going to be my first video."[1]

She felt unsure at the start. As she tried to remember what she wanted to say, she looked at the ceiling and walls and talked quietly. Old worries came back—the need to look perfect, sound perfect, be perfect.

Bethany took another deep breath and reminded herself, *Hey, I'm alone in my bedroom. Probably no one will even watch this. Don't be perfect, be yourself!*

She looked at the camera again and smiled—*big* this time. "I'm going to be starting a lot of tutorials and hauls and reviews and things," she said. "So if you guys have any requests, just let me know in a message or a comment. So . . . yeah . . . let's get started."[2]

For the next seven minutes, Bethany relaxed and smiled and laughed while showing makeup products she'd bought from MAC and Sephora.

It wasn't the best video Bethany Mota would ever make, but that wasn't important. What was important was that she'd done it—Bethany had put herself out there and tried to do something creative. Even so, the video would go on to be watched by *four million* viewers, launching shy Bethany into a career in the spotlight.[3]

Bethany made her first video in 2009, when she was just thirteen years old. By the time she was eighteen, she was a millionaire, with more YouTube subscribers than Lady Gaga and more Instagram followers than all the top fashion magazines combined! Bethany Mota is a certified social-media tycoon!

Bethany was born in a small town in California to a family of Mexican and Portuguese descent. Her mom homeschooled her until third grade, and for a while, she loved going to school and being with other kids. Then middle school happened. Up until then, she had been outgoing; had a lot of friends; did school plays; and took dance, acting, and voice lessons. Middle school, however, was the worst experience of Bethany's life.

Girls she thought were her friends began cyberbullying her. They set up a fake MySpace page in her name and filled it with pictures of Bethany, along with nasty comments. "The captions were written to sound like I was making fun of myself, like, 'Oh my God, I'm so ugly.'"[4] Bethany was hurt and humiliated. She didn't know who to trust and lost most of her "friends."

The bullying led to depression and anxiety. "It got to me," she remembers. "I didn't want to hang out with my friends or go anywhere. I wasn't eating a lot, like, maybe one meal a day."[5] Bethany quit her dance and acting classes, and she went back to being homeschooled. But once her schoolwork was done, she stayed in bed the rest of the day, crying much of the time. Her parents were worried sick.

Then one day, Bethany discovered YouTube. She loved watching the beauty and style videos, especially those made by girls like her. "It was so cool seeing girls being positive and spreading happiness," she said.[6] In 2009, she filmed her very first haul video (a video of stuff she'd purchased) on her channel Macbarbie07. "[YouTube] was kind of an outlet for me to be myself and not really worry about what anyone thought."[7] She began making videos regularly to escape her stress and anxiety and launched a second channel, BethanysLife, in 2010. In her videos, Bethany shows off her hauls, models outfit ideas, gives makeup and hair lessons, tests recipes, makes do-it-yourself projects, and shows how to decorate your room ("room tours"). Teen fans flocked to

> Bethany's millions of diehard fans are called "Motavators."

her channel, and it quickly became one of the most popular YouTube channels in the world!

"At first . . . I'd try to act perfect," Bethany remembered. "But then I realized it might be more fun if I was just myself. So I showed my silly side and kept in the bloopers."[8] The girls watching appreciated that Bethany seemed normal—like them—and not like some fashion superstar. As of 2016, Bethany had nearly ten million YouTube subscribers (plus six million followers on Instagram and three million on Twitter)![9]

Bethany's fans wanted even *more* of her style, so she started her own fashion and room décor lines for Aéropostale. She gets inspiration from her fans and hopes to inspire them as well: "So many of [my followers] have told me that my style gives them ideas, but they do just the same for me. I love being engaged with my audience because they are all so unique and creative. Whenever I need some help designing, I love just sending a tweet out, asking my viewers what they want."[10]

The year 2014 was busy for Bethany. She launched a perfume, xoxo Beth, and she was a guest judge on *Project Runway* and a contestant on *Dancing with the Stars*. She was also honored with Teen Choice and Streamy Awards and was ranked sixth on *Time* magazine's "The 25 Most Influential Teens of 2014" list.[11] That year, she also branched into the music biz when she released her first single, "Need You Right Now," which hit number four on the iTunes charts.[12]

> Bethany was the most Googled fashion designer in 2014![14]

But Bethany hasn't forgotten how it all started. She speaks out against bullying everywhere she goes. In 2015, she joined with PACER, a national bullying prevention group that encourages kids to fight bullying in their schools and where they live. Her success on social media has given her a lot of wisdom on the topic of bullying: "I've really learned the importance of not worrying about other people's opinions."[13]

Bethany's career shows no signs of slowing down. Her fan base just keeps growing, as do requests for her star power. When she's not filming her videos, she's traveling the world, talking to people about her story and inspiring girls. Recently, YouTube recruited her to interview President Barack Obama!

The lonely thirteen-year-old who was too anxious to leave her room has grown up into a successful business mogul with confidence to spare. "I'm my own boss," she says. "My biggest thing to overcome has been not being afraid to be different. It's safer to do what everyone else is doing, but it pays off way more to be yourself."[15] Bethany quit worrying about what the bullies thought and started being herself—and look where it got her!

> Did you know that one in four students is bullied? If you or someone you know is being bullied, or if you just want to find out how to get involved, check out PACER's National Bullying Prevention Center at pacer.org/bullying.

Sometimes, the things that we're afraid of are the things that can change our lives and make us stronger.

—BETHANY MOTA

HOW WILL YOU ROCK THE WORLD?

I am going to rock the world by being the first person in my family to own my very own business. I will make this happen not only to help create jobs for people but because I believe in and value myself. I will keep education first, keep volunteering in areas to help others, and learn as much as I can on my journey to becoming the best entrepreneur the world has ever seen.

DAPHNE VARMAH ✺ AGE 13

Tavi Gevinson

1996– ❖ AUTHOR, EDITOR, AND ACTRESS ❖ UNITED STATES

Feminism to me means fighting. It's a very nuanced, complex thing; but at the very core of it, I'm a feminist because I don't think being a girl limits me in any way.

—TAVI GEVINSON

Up on the runway, Chanel models paraded by, wearing gray, silver, black, and white. Frilly dresses, sleek pantsuits, and gaudy hair bows made of tulle and silk, beads and leather—everything in that icy palette. Tavi perched on the edge of a silver couch—it was her first time at Paris's Fashion Week and she didn't want to miss a thing.

In honor of the show's theme, Tavi was decked out in a swirling silver dress, a baggy black sweater, and a black pillbox hat atop her silver-dyed hair. In her signature big glasses, Tavi looked more like a little old lady than a fourteen-year-old. That was fine by Tavi; she had her own style and didn't care what other people thought.

She had been flown to Paris to work, reporting for a fashion TV show. After the last model sashayed off the stage, Tavi waited to meet the designer: a man with a white ponytail, wearing a charcoal-gray suit, skinny silver tie, and matching silver biker gloves.

When it was Tavi's turn, they shook hands and chatted for a few minutes. "She has a fresh eye," the designer told the camera. "She's not ruined by zillions of bad collections."

"Thank you very much," said Tavi.

"I like your hair color," he added, touching her locks. "Normally, children—young people—don't have this hair color. It's great to have it."[1]

After they said their good-byes, Tavi smiled as she walked away, the camera crew hustling after her.

Karl Lagerfeld, world-famous head designer for Chanel, liked her hair color! Tavi couldn't wait to write about it in her blog.

Tavi Gevinson wasn't just any teen blogger. By the ripe old age of fourteen, she was a fashion prodigy and a style icon, especially for young style makers. And she would eventually move beyond fashion into pop culture, politics, and feminism, becoming a voice for her entire generation.

Tavi was born in Chicago, Illinois, and grew up in the suburb Oak Park. Her father was a high school English teacher, and her mother was a weaver who had immigrated from Norway. Tavi's parents raised the family in the Jewish faith and encouraged their three daughters to be creative. Tavi, their youngest, was always working on some creative project, whether it was a collage, a sculpture, or an outfit. She remembers that, as a child, she liked "the theatrical idea of fashion—that you can make up different characters."[2] She filled binders with clippings from fashion magazines and created her own unusual ensembles from clothes she got at Goodwill.

When she was eleven, she started a fashion blog called *Style Rookie*. She posted photos of herself modeling unusual outfits and she commented on fashion trends. Tavi impressed readers with her incredible knowledge of fashion history combined with her eloquent but funny, down-to-earth tone. Fans also loved the experimental style of her outfits.

At first, just a few kids read the blog. But word spread fast, and soon, *Style Rookie* had fifty thousand readers a day![3] Tavi's parents had *no* idea it was so popular until one day when Tavi asked them for permission to be interviewed by the *New York Times*, which was doing an article on teen bloggers. Suddenly, Tavi was getting invitations to Fashion Week in New York and Paris; top fashion designers were flying her around the world to see their latest lines; and she was fielding offers to write for magazines, to give talks, to star in commercials, and even to design her own line of clothing!

Tavi was psyched that people loved her blog, but she didn't like the backlash. Some in the fashion community and media complained that she wasn't experienced enough. A few even claimed that Tavi's mom or older sisters must be writing the blogs—no kid could be that good. It bothered Tavi enough that she sometimes cried herself to sleep. "A lot of people on the internet have a problem with a young person doing well," she said of that time.[4]

Tavi owns a pair of leather gloves once owned by world-famous style icon and actress Audrey Hepburn. They were given to Tavi by another famous style icon: '90s actress Winona Ryder. Audrey gave them to Winona when Winona turned eighteen, and Winona gave them to Tavi when Tavi turned eighteen.[5]

In Tavi's 100th *Style Rookie* blog post, she announced her fashion manifesto: "In my opinion, the most interesting fashion is the Anti-Fashion. No rules, no restrictions, no normalcy, no *pleasing anyone*... I'm twelve! I have no one to impress and I'm not concerned about wearing something flattering to my body. I will dress as ugly and crazy as I want as long as I'm still young enough to get away with it. Suckersss."[6]

Eventually, Tavi quit letting the haters get to her. Her fresh voice and honest opinions were a magnet not just for teens but for jaded fashion "experts" as well. Amy Astley, the former editor of *Teen Vogue*, said, "Sometimes I say to my staff, 'Wow, I had more fun reading the blog of this teenager than reading professional copy that we wrote.'"[7]

After four years of writing *Style Rookie*, Tavi was ready for something new. At age fifteen, she founded *Rookie*, a web magazine written by teen girls (including Tavi) that focuses on issues impacting other teen girls. Tavi, *Rookie's* editor in chief, wanted it to be the anti-*Seventeen*: a smart magazine for girls all about self-expression. Tavi and others wrote about fashion but also pop culture, politics, and feminism. *Rookie* passed one million page views in its first week!

> Tavi's favorite *Rookie* interviews were the ones she did with Lorde, Emma Watson, Sky Ferreira, Miley Cyrus, and David Hildebrand Wilson (whose name you may not recognize, but he's the co-founder of LA's quirky Museum of Jurassic Technology). Check them out at rookiemag.com.

Tavi had another runaway hit on her hands, and she used her platform to speak out on a variety of issues. In 2012, she spoke at TEDxTeen on how women are represented in pop culture, and then again at the *Economist's* World in 2012 Festival. Tavi has twice made *Forbes* magazine's "30 Under 30: Media" list, and she was on *Time* magazine's list of "The 25 Most Influential Teens of 2014."

Tavi conquered fashion when she was a tween, and magazine publishing in her teens. What's next for this creative force? Recently, she has branched out into acting. Her first movie was *First Bass* in 2008, and since then, she's been in several more, including the 2012 award-winning *Enough Said*. She has also starred in Broadway plays, including *This Is Our Youth*, with Michael Cera and Kieran Culkin.

Tavi has this motto on her wall: "There is not enough time for hating [yourself]. Too many things to make. Go."[8]

In 2016, Tavi enrolled at New York University. When asked what she wanted to do when she grows up, Tavi responded in a blog post titled

"Dreams": "I wish I was a cat. I would have a life to fulfill my fashion dreams, one to fulfill my acting dreams, one for guitar, one for writing, one for movie directing, one for fine arts, one for a normal life, and one for teaching. . . . Also I could poop in a box."[9]

With all she's done already, there's little doubt that Tavi will have her nine lives. And she will rock each one.

ROCK ON!

LILLY SINGH

Like other social media stars, Lilly Singh began making YouTube videos to help cope with her feelings. In college, she made videos about her depression and did comedy sketches under the name "IISuperwomanII." Since 2010, her videos have gotten more than 1.5 billion views, and she has over ten million subscribers. She's one of the most successful YouTube stars of all time—in 2016, *Forbes* magazine ranked her the eighth-highest-paid YouTuber in the world! Proud and vocal about her Indian heritage, Lilly was the first South Asian comedian on the channel, and now there's no stopping her. She's expanded her empire into movies, comedy tours, books, and music! Need a laugh? Check out Lilly's YouTube comedy channel: IISuperwomanII.

Simone Biles

1997– ◦ GYMNAST ◦ UNITED STATES

*I'm not the next Usain Bolt or Michael Phelps.
I'm the first Simone Biles.*

—SIMONE BILES

Simone looked out across the room. To her left, kids walked gracefully across a balance beam. To her right, they jumped over some tall obstacle. *What did they call it?* She tried to remember. *A vault?*

Straight ahead, on the sea of blue mats, girls and boys were running and tumbling and doing crazy flips. Simone held her breath. *She* could do some of those flips too—she'd been practicing at home. She could even do a backflip off her mailbox.

"Do you want to try it?" someone asked, breaking Simone out of her trance. It was one of the teachers. "You can, if you want."

Simone *did* want to try it. More than anything.

She spent another minute watching a group of older girls practicing their floor routine. She was pretty sure she could copy what they were doing. She nodded and stepped out onto the mats.

First, Simone did some cartwheels across the mat, and then a hand-stand into a forward roll. Next, she ran and leaped into the air, her legs snapping into the splits.

This is awesome!

Next, she did a handstand, dropping her legs behind her until she was in a backbend. When she popped out of the backbend, she raced across the mat a final time and then launched into a roundoff, finishing off with a back handspring—just like she'd practiced at home. When she was done, Simone froze and held her hands high in the air, as she'd seen the other girls do.

When Simone looked back at the teacher, she saw that several teachers and parents were gathered at the edge of the mats watching her. Some were clapping, but most just stood there with their mouths hanging open.

What? Did I do something wrong? Am I in trouble? she wondered.

The teacher approached her and asked, "Have you ever taken a gymnastics class before?"

"No," answered the six-year-old.

The teacher scribbled something on a piece of paper and handed it to Simone.

"Give this to your mom when you get home, okay?"

Simone couldn't read what it said, but that night, her mother told her the note was asking if they would sign up Simone for gymnastics classes.

"They say you've got some natural talent. I could have told them that," said her mother, giving her a proud hug.[1]

Natural talent indeed! Just ten years later, Simone would surprise everyone by becoming the best gymnast in the world.

———

Simone Biles was born in 1997 in Columbus, Ohio, into very difficult circumstances. Her biological father abandoned the family, and her biological mother struggled with drug and alcohol addiction. Simone and her three siblings were taken away from their biological mother because she couldn't care for them, and they went into foster homes. When Simone was three, a social worker called Ron, her grandfather on her mother's side, and told him the situation. Ron said, "Send them to me."[2]

The situation was supposed to be temporary. Simone and her sister lived with Ron and his second wife, Nellie, for two years before being sent back to their mother. But Simone's mother had not overcome her drug addiction. The social worker called Ron and told him that the children were being put up for adoption. Ron and Nellie were nearly retired and had already raised two grown sons. They had a big decision to make.

They chose to adopt five-year-old Simone and her three-year-old sister, while Simone's great-aunt adopted her two brothers. On the very first day that the girls moved back in with their biological grandfather, Simone asked Nellie if she could call her "Mom." Nellie and Ron have been Simone's parents ever since. When an Olympic commentator repeatedly called them her "grandparents," Simone responded, "My parents are my parents, and that's it."[3]

Through her mom, Nellie, Simone is a dual citizen of Belize and the United States. During Simone's Olympic events, the First Lady of Belize held viewing parties for Belizeans to cheer her on!

Simone grew into a restless, energetic girl, always running around the house, jumping, and flipping off furniture. Her mom was grateful when Simone discovered gymnastics at age six—it was a great focus for her endless energy. Within two years, Simone was already mastering the sport and began training with Aimee Boorman, who has been her coach ever since. Aimee knew Simone was special, but she had never coached an elite gymnast before. Just like Simone, Aimee didn't let her lack of experience hold her back. Simone says, "I think that's what helped us both, because we were both kind of clueless about it."[4]

Simone and Aimee's teamwork paid off, and in 2011, when Simone was fourteen, she began competing at the junior elite level. Her first major competition was the American Classic in Houston, where she did pretty well. She placed third all-around, first on vault and balance beam, eighth on uneven bars, and fourth on floor exercise. At the US Classic in Chicago later that year, she came in twentieth all-around. This wasn't a terrible start to her career, but Simone knew she could do better.

The next year, Simone begged her parents to let her homeschool so she could have more time for training. She went from practicing gymnastics twenty hours to thirty-two hours a week.[5] The difference was *astounding*. In national competitions that year, she began taking first place in all-around and got higher marks in all her other events. Her improved performances got her invited to the USA Gymnastics National Championships and eventually earned her a spot on the US Gymnastics Junior National Team.

In 2013, when Simone was sixteen, she began competing internationally on the junior national team. At her first big-time, elite competition, however, Simone struggled. The crowd was huge, and she was constantly distracted by the noise and yelling around the arena. "She couldn't get focused," said her mom.[6] She fell several times, and her coach pulled her from the vault after she hurt her ankle during her floor-exercise routine. The stress of the higher-level competition really got to her, so her mom found a sport psychologist for Simone to talk to. It helped a lot.

At her next competition, the 2013 USA Gymnastics National Championships, Simone ignored the distractions, conquered

Simone is an incredibly hard worker. In all her years of gymnastics, she has never once missed a day of training, even when she was sick or injured.[7]

Simone discovered she has attention deficit hyperactivity disorder (ADHD), which makes it challenging for her to focus or stay still without medication. When Russian hackers exposed her medical records in an attempt to discredit her Olympic wins, Simone spoke out proudly: "Having ADHD and taking medicine for it is nothing to be ashamed of, nothing that I'm afraid to let people know."[8]

her anxiety, and claimed her first world title. She was crowned national all-around champ and took silver in her four individual events. She hasn't lost an all-around competition since. At that year's world championships, she won gold in all-around and floor, plus a silver in vault and a bronze in balance beam.

That earned her a spot on the senior national team and the world championship team. At the 2014 World Championships in China, Simone completely dominated. She won gold in four competitions: team, balance beam, floor exercise, and all-around. She also took silver in vault. She became the first female gymnast to win three world all-around titles in a row, and the first African American gymnast to become the world all-around champion. Suddenly, Simone was in the spotlight at the top of the gymnastics world. Soon, she would become a household name.

Even in her teens, Simone is tiny—four foot eight inches tall, to be exact (the same height as your average fifth grader).[9] But she's also incredibly strong and unbelievably agile. She is known for her mastery of the floor routine. She is so good at it that her third pass (most gymnasts' easiest move) is as difficult as her competitors' first pass (their hardest). This means Simone starts with a move as hard as her competitor's most difficult, and then she'll do two more after that that are even harder! Simone is such a floor-routine goddess, she invented her own move that no one else can do, called "The Biles": two backflips followed by a half twist in a straight body position. At the 2016 Olympics, The Biles brought down the house.

At the 2016 Olympic games in Rio, Simone was the star. She led the US team to victory over their closest competitor—Russia. The United States (and Simone) won a team gold medal, and Simone won three individual

> In spite of her gymnastics superpowers, Simone is a regular teenager in many ways. She loves pizza and ice cream, her four dogs, and experimenting with eye makeup. She's also scared of bees! After getting her gold medal at the 2014 World Championships, Simone jumped off the podium to escape one buzzing around her bouquet.

gold medals as well—in vault, floor exercise, and all-around—plus a bronze in balance beam. With her fourteen world championship medals, that brings Simone's medal count up to nineteen, making her *the most decorated female gymnast of all time.* Team USA also chose Simone as the flag bearer for the closing ceremonies—and she was the first American female gymnast to win that honor.

Simone is tiny but tough. At four foot eight inches, she was the shortest athlete at the 2016 Rio Olympics.

As for the future, Simone plans to go to UCLA for college and is hoping to compete on *Dancing with the Stars.* She should certainly be back for the 2020 Olympics—she will only be twenty-three years old, after all. Simone once said, "Surround yourself with the dreamers, the doers, the believers and thinkers; but most of all, surround yourself with those who see greatness within you even when you don't see it yourself."[10]

Simone surrounded herself with people who believed in her and showed the world that having a rocky start in life doesn't mean you can't rock the world!

HOW WILL YOU ROCK THE WORLD?

I am going to rock the world by starting the first African American gymnastics company in my community before I turn twenty years old. To accomplish this, I will keep my grades up and learn how to run a strong business. I'm going to teach my students not only how to do backflips and front flips but also how to reach their goals, just like I will.

CARRINGTON TERRY　AGE 11

Malala Yousafzai

1997– ◦ ACTIVIST ◦ AFGHANISTAN

When the whole world is silent, even one voice becomes powerful.
—MALALA YOUSAFZAI

Malala sat squeezed between two friends on the bus. The bus was crowded with friends and teachers from her school, everybody laughing and chatting on the way home. Malala was happy. Last night, she'd studied hard for a test, and today, she'd done well on it.

Suddenly, the bus jerked to a stop. A man got on at the back. He was young and had a beard. He looked nervous.

"Which one of you is Malala?" he yelled over the noise.

The teen's heart skipped a beat. Was he Taliban? She couldn't tell—most men in Mingora wore beards these days. The Taliban forced them to. And most Pakistanis knew her name; she'd been in all the papers and on TV for months now.

No one answered the question.

"Speak up, otherwise I will shoot you all!" he yelled, pulling a gun from his jacket and waving it around.[1] People screamed, and Malala squeezed her best friend Moniba's hand. A few girls glanced at Malala. The gunman saw them looking—that was all it took.

The man walked up to her seat and glared at her. She was the only girl on the bus whose face was uncovered. He looked in Malala's eyes and knew it was her. He raised the gun and pointed it at her face.

Then he fired three shots.

mm

Malala was born fifteen years earlier in Mingora, Pakistan, into a Pashtun family of the Sunni Muslim faith. Her father was a teacher who had founded her school and others in their city. But Malala's birth wasn't an entirely happy one: "When I was born, some relatives came to our house and told my mother, 'Don't worry, next time you will have a son.'"[2] In Pakistan, parents wanted sons who would take care of them when they got old and could carry on the family name. Girls were seen as a burden.

Malala's father, however, didn't see it that way. He and his wife were happy to have a girl, and they named her after a legendary Pashtun poet and warrior girl. They believed Malala could achieve great things, just like a boy. Though all girls in her city did not get to go to school, Malala did—she went to the coed school where her father taught. She loved learning and was an excellent student, always at the top of her class.

Her family encouraged her intellectual curiosity and let her stay up late listening to her father and other men talk politics after her younger brothers were sent to bed. The political talk soon turned to Afghanistan, where a violent religious group called the Taliban had taken over the country. They'd enacted laws severely restricting the rights

The Pashtuns are an ethnic group who live in Afghanistan and northwest Pakistan. They are a tough people who live primarily in the mountains. Throughout history, they've fought off many enemies to keep their own traditions and way of life. They are named for the Pashto language they speak.

mm

of women. Girls and women couldn't leave the house without a male relative; they had to wear a *burqa*, a garment that covered them from head to toe with only their eyes showing; and girls could no longer go to school. Women who disobeyed these new laws were beaten or killed, and there was talk that the Taliban were headed to Pakistan next.

> Malala was a pretty normal kid. When she lived in Afghanistan, her favorite book was *Twilight*, her favorite TV show was *Ugly Betty*, her favorite singer was Justin Bieber, and her favorite color was pink.

In 2007, when Malala was seven, the Taliban invaded the Mingora. Just like in Afghanistan, they changed life for everyone—but especially for women and girls. Women could no longer vote, have jobs, or even go to a doctor or the hospital! All girls' schools would soon be closed. If any teachers tried to continue teaching girls, they would be severely punished, and if any girls' schools stayed open, they would be destroyed.

The Pakistan army arrived to fight the Taliban, and Mingora turned into a war zone. There was shooting in the streets and bombs dropping day and night. Most kids quit going to school—both girls and boys. But Malala's father refused to close his school, and Malala refused to stop going. She wanted to do something to help fight against the Taliban, so she gave a speech called "How Dare the Taliban Take Away My Basic Right to Education?" at a local club for reporters. Newspapers all over Pakistan printed what she had to say.

When the British Broadcasting Corporation (BBC) came to Mingora looking for a student or teacher to write about what the Taliban was doing to schools there, no one volunteered; they thought it was too dangerous. Malala desperately wanted her normal life back—she wanted to do something. Using a fake name, Malala took the job and began writing blogs for the BBC Urdu website. Her father thought she would be okay because she was only a seventh grader. He didn't think anyone would dare to hurt a child.

The BBC website published a series of Malala's writings, called "Diary of a Pakistani Schoolgirl." She had to work like a spy to not get caught—

she handwrote notes and passed them to a reporter who scanned and emailed them to the website. Malala wrote about what it was like to live through the battles in her city, how fewer and fewer girls came to school, and finally, how the Taliban stopped her from going to school completely. In January 2009, the Taliban officially made it illegal for girls to go to school, and they blew up nearly 150 girls' schools.

Soon, Malala's diary was read all over Pakistan and in other countries as well. "She had a huge audience, both local and international," said Aamer Ahmed Khan, former head of BBC Urdu.[3] At the same time, Malala and her father were interviewed in a *New York Times* documentary film, on a Pakistani talk show, and in several large newspapers. They became the face and voice of the Pakistanis who opposed the Taliban.

By the summer of 2009, the Pakistan army had pushed the Taliban out of Mingora and into the hills surrounding the city. The fighters didn't leave the area, but they no longer controlled Pakistani lives. Girls went back to school, and life returned to almost normal.

In 2011, Malala was nominated for the International Children's Peace Prize for her "courageous or otherwise remarkable acts and thoughts . . ."[4] Pakistan's prime minister awarded her the country's first National Youth Peace Prize (later renamed the National Malala Peace Prize). Malala was a celebrity! Everyone in Pakistan knew who she was and was proud of her bravery.

The Taliban *also* knew who Malala was. They had seen her on TV and knew what she looked like. On October 9, 2012, fifteen-year-old Malala was riding a bus home from school when a Taliban fighter got

> As of 2016, there are still more than 130 million girls in the world who aren't able to go to school. The reasons for this are sometimes war, poverty, natural disasters, child marriage, or child labor; but often, it is just because they are girls who live in a place that bans girls' education. There are more than 20 countries that still discriminate against girls by preventing them from learning.[5]

on and fired three shots at her, at point-blank range. The first hit her in the head and the other two hit the girls next to her. The shooter left Malala for dead.

But she wasn't dead. The bullet had entered her left eye socket, traveled down the inside of her face, and then exited into her left shoulder. She was still alive—but barely. The other two girls survived as well. A helicoptor took Malala to a military hospital in Peshawar, Pakistan, where surgeons saved her life. The five-hour operation was a success, but Malala got very sick afterward and went into a coma. To get her the best care possible, Pakistan flew her to a hospital in Birmingham, England, that specialized in war injuries like hers. Malala was in the hospital for three months and had several more surgeries, but she came out of her coma and miraculously had no brain damage. It took her many more months of physical therapy to recover her ability to talk and walk.

> Malala's activism has improved education for people around the world but also close to home. After Malala's shooting, her own mother, who had never been taught to read or write, went to school for the first time. She learned to read and write and studied English. Malala helped her with her homework.

Before the shooting, Malala was well-known in Pakistan. After the shooting, she was famous around the world. Her courage made a huge impact. The United Nations (UN) declared July 12, 2013 (her sixteenth birthday), Malala Day at the UN, and she was invited to come speak to the United Nations Youth Assembly to tell them what could be done to help Pakistani children.

It had taken nine months for Malala to recover, but she was eager to resume her fight—to speak out again. She wanted to show the world that a terrorist with a gun would not stop her. Malala flew to New York City and gave her speech on Malala Day. She said, "They thought that the bullets would silence us, but they failed. And then, out of that silence came thousands of voices. The terrorists thought that they would change our aims and stop our ambitions, but nothing changed in my life except this: weakness, fear, and hopelessness died. Strength, power, and courage was born."[6]

Malala continued to spread her message to a global audience. Three months after her UN speech, she published a memoir, *I Am Malala*, which became a worldwide bestseller. Her courage also led to real change in the world. In Pakistan, thousands of people protested the shooting, and two million people signed the Right to Education petition, which was then ratified into Pakistan's first Right to Education Bill. And in 2013, the UN launched an initiative in Malala's name, demanding that all children around the world be in school by the end of 2015.

Then, in 2014, Malala won the Nobel Peace Prize, which is awarded to people who work to make the world a better place. At just seventeen years old, Malala was the youngest person ever to receive it.

Since she recovered from the shooting, Malala has been going to school in England. Once again, she is a straight-A student. But she isn't finished fighting for girls who aren't able to get the education they deserve. She continues to speak out and raise money for her cause. At her Nobel Prize acceptance speech she said, "I am those sixty-six million girls who are deprived of education. And today I am not raising my voice; it is the voice of those sixty-six million girls."[7]

As long as there are girls who are being denied an education, Malala will continue raising her voice.

> Malala also published a version of her memoir just for kids called *I Am Malala: How One Girl Stood Up for Education and Changed the World.* If you're interested in Malala's life, you should definitely read it.
>
> ᗢᗢᗢ

> Malala donated the Nobel Prize money—half a million dollars—to her foundation, the Malala Fund. It helps children around the world to get an education, it builds and repairs schools, and it helps girls speak up for their right to go to school. To learn more and to get involved, check out Malala.org.
>
> ᗢᗢᗢ

It feels like this life is not my life. It's a second life.
People have prayed to God to spare me,
and I was spared for a reason—to use my life for helping people.

—MALALA YOUSAFZAI

ROCK ON!

SALMA KAKAR

Taliban repression led to plenty of Afghani girls fighting to change their world. One such rebel is sixteen-year-old Salma Kakar, lead rider on the new Afghan National Cycling Team. In a country where girls couldn't leave the house without a male escort and their bodies covered, riding a bike was unthinkable. But a bike means freedom of movement, and Salma is fighting for girls and women to have that freedom. Her team of thirteen must train in hidden locations and sometimes at night. And while they wear long pants and sleeves, and head scarves under their helmets, they still get harassed on the streets and receive death threats. Salma won't let that stop her. She dreams of one day waving the Afghan flag in the Olympics as part of her country's first female biking team.

BiNdi IRWiN

1998– ◌ CONSERVATIONIST AND ACTRESS ◌ AUSTRALIA

Every time we lose an animal species, it's like losing a brick from the house. Pretty soon, the house just falls down.

—BINDI IRWIN

indi watched as the zoology students unrolled the long mesh tube along the river's edge. They cut sticks and pounded them into the ground along each side of the fifteen-foot trap, anchoring it. Then they lifted the top edge and tied it to the sticks, forming a tunnel. Through the mesh at the entrance, they wove a rope, creating the drawstring, and then tied the other end to a sturdy tree. Finally, they set the bait a few feet inside the tunnel and scattered mud and leaves around the entrance.[1]

"All set," a student called to Bindi's father.

"Let's check it," he called back.

He turned to his five-year-old daughter. "You reckon this trap will work all right?"

Bindi nodded. She was so excited she could barely speak. She'd heard her mother and father talk about trapping crocs a million times, but this was the first time she got to go along.

She sure hoped they caught one. In fact, she hoped they caught *all* the crocodiles. They had a bunch to trap and move. It wasn't safe here for the crocs anymore. In the old days, property owners would just shoot crocodiles that came on their land. But Bindi's family had been rescuing and moving crocs to safety for years now—it's what they did.

The trap worked! While they reset it, Bindi grabbed a sandwich. All this waiting for crocs was making her hungry.

"Here comes a big one!" yelled another student. Bindi could see an enormous female lumbering toward the trap—she was twice as big as Bindi's father. Bindi thought she was beautiful, but she stayed quiet and didn't move, so she wouldn't scare the croc away.

The croc stuck her nose in the trap and sniffed the bait. *Would she go in?* Bindi worried. She held her breath . . .

The croc waddled farther into the tube . . . and . . .

Zzzzzept!

The students hauled on the rope and the entrance zipped closed. The giant croc thrashed, knocking down the sticks and collapsing the tube around her like a sleeping bag. Bindi clapped her hands—it had worked just how her father designed it, so the crocodile wouldn't get hurt.

As they held the ropes tight, Bindi's father wrestled the alligator and slipped a noose around her snout so she couldn't bite.

"Bindi!" her father called, "I could use your help."

She leaped up and ran to the group. "What can I do, Daddy?"

"I need someone to hold the tail while we load her in the truck. Can you do that?"

"Of course!" said Bindi, taking another bite of her sandwich.

"Can you eat your sandwich *and* hang on to that tail?" he asked with a grin.

Bindi stuffed the rest in her mouth. "Yeah," she said, reaching through the mesh and grabbing the crocodile's tail. It was warm and soft, just like her pet pythons at home.

Bindi smiled. She knew she would love crocodiles just as much as she loved her snakes. She could feel it.[2]

~~~

Bindi Sue Irwin was just five years old when she had her first wild-crocodile encounter, but protecting animals was something she was born into. In 1998, Bindi was born in Queensland, Australia. Her parents, Steve and Terri, were conservationists who ran the Australia Zoo together. Bindi was homeschooled with her younger brother and grew up at the zoo, surrounded by animals. She had her own pet Burmese pythons before she was two years old. "I really love snakes and crocodiles, but my favorite animal is my pet rat," she said.[3]

Bindi's family always knew that the best way to protect and save animals is to educate humans. They wanted to educate as many people as possible, so her father starred in a popular nature show called *The Crocodile Hunter*. Bindi first appeared on his show when she was just a few weeks old.

Like her parents, Bindi wanted to be a conservationist too. She took care of animals at the zoo, helped her parents on crocodile rescue missions, and appeared on TV with her family. When she was just eight years old, she launched her own TV show, *Bindi: The Jungle Girl*. The show was set in a huge tree house, and in each episode, Bindi would teach kids about a different wild animal.

Even Bindi's name comes from animals. She was named for her dad's favorite crocodile, Bindi, which is an Australian aboriginal word meaning "young girl." Her middle name came from the family dog.

~~~

Later that year, the family suffered a terrible tragedy: Bindi's father died after being stung by a stingray while snorkeling in Australia's Great Barrier Reef. Bindi was devastated. Her father was famous around the world, and the world mourned his death along with her.

Five thousand people attended Steve's memorial, including Australia's prime minister, and three hundred million more watched it on television.[4]

Eight-year-old Bindi delivered a eulogy to the crowd that she wrote herself. In it, she said, "I don't want Daddy's passion to ever end. I want to help endangered wildlife just like he did. I had the best daddy in the whole world, and I will miss him every day."[5] The crowd gave her a standing ovation and a TV Week poll voted her speech "Television Moment of the Year."[6]

From then on, young Bindi took over spreading her family's message of conservation. In 2007, she starred in a TV documentary *My Daddy the Crocodile Hunter*, and she talked about animals and how to help them on dozens of talk shows, including *Oprah*, *Ellen*, *Larry King Live*, and *Late Night with David Letterman*. That year, she was also appointed Australia's tourism ambassador.

> Wildlife Warriors does research and helps animals around the world. There are projects to help crocodiles, Cambodian elephants, whales and nurse sharks, Tasmanian devils, black rhinoceros, Sumatran tigers, and cheetahs. Learn more about the important work Bindi's group is doing and how you can help at WildlifeWarriors.com.

Bindi donates money from her earnings to Wildlife Warriors, an organization she cofounded with her parents. And Bindi has plenty of projects earning money for conservation. She did an exercise video called *Bindi Kidfitness* and designed Bindi Wear, an eco-friendly clothing line for kids. She performed with the popular Australian children's band the Wiggles, hosted a game show called *Bindi's Bootcamp*, and wrote a series of children's books, Bindi Wildlife Adventures, based on her life growing up at the zoo. You can even buy a talking Bindi Irwin doll or her hip-hop album *Trouble in the Jungle*!

In recent years, Bindi has explored new passions. She starred in the movies *Free Willy: Escape from Pirate's Cove* and *Return to Nim's Island*. Both her characters were on missions to protect wildlife. And in 2014, Bindi competed on the popular TV show *Dancing with the Stars*—and won! How many girls can wrestle crocodiles *and* dance the rhumba?

Like her father, Bindi has been recognized for her many contributions. She won a Logie (Australian TV award) for Most Popular New Female Talent and was the youngest person ever to win a Daytime Emmy Award for Outstanding Performer in a Children's Series. She also won two Kids' Choice Awards and a Biggest Greenie Award from Nickelodeon. And the one her father would be most proud of: Australian Geographic Society's Young Conservationist of the Year in 2014.

Bindi is using her fame to help educate the next generation of conservationists. "I do not think of myself as a celebrity, but I do think I am a teacher," she said. "It's not about 'look at me, I'm so great,' I don't think like that at all. It's about getting people to take responsibility for keeping our animals safe and protected."[7]

> I think it's so important to empower kids because we are the next voters. We are the next decision makers, and we are the next generation making a difference on our planet.
>
> —BINDI IRWIN

HOW WILL YOU ROCK THE WORLD?

I will rock the world as a marine biologist. I hope to bring awareness to many endangered sea creatures, like the blue whale. I want to make the world a better place for all animals of the oceans.

SOPHIA GARVEY ⚛ AGE 13

Amandla Stenberg

1998– ◦ ACTRESS AND ACTIVIST ◦ UNITED STATES

*I don't feel afraid to talk about racism or to talk
about sexism or the gender binary.*

—AMANDLA STENBERG

mandla paced nervously outside the audition room. She *had* to get this part! *The Hunger Games* was one of her favorite books of all time—she'd already read the series three or four times—and this role was *perfect* for her. Rue, a tribute from District 11, was small and musical, just like Amandla. Rue was also one of the most important parts in the movie—the heart of the story. It's Rue's death that motivates Katniss to fight back against the Capital.

It also happened to be one of the best parts for an African American actress Amandla had seen in a long time. She'd begged her agent to get her this audition.

Amandla wanted the part so badly that she'd even enlisted her mom's help. Her mom took some Rue-style clothes—old khakis and a T-shirt—and rolled them around in the dirt. When Amandla was dressed in the stained clothes, her mom put twigs in her hair and leaves all over her body. Finally, Amandla tucked a tiny flower wreath into her pocket—a good-luck charm Rue might have carried.

Suddenly, the door opened and an assistant called Amandla's name. Her mom gave her hand a squeeze for reassurance, and then the twelve-year-old actress strode into the room.

Inside sat the director, Gary Ross. He smiled at Amandla's getup and said, "I see you have your own makeup and hair department."[1] Amandla grinned, and the director grinned back. As she performed her Rue scene, she thought maybe he could see what she felt inside—the role was hers.

Amandla was right, of course. She beat out all the other actresses and got the part of Rue. Many months later, in thousands of movie theaters across America, audiences watched her brave and cunning Rue and fell in love. The young actress was a movie star in the biggest blockbuster of the year!

―――

Amandla Stenberg was born in Los Angeles, California, to an African American mother and a Danish father. On her father's side, she also has Greenlandic Inuit ancestry, and her name means "power" in Zulu. Little did her parents know how much power their daughter's words and actions would someday have.

She got started in the entertainment industry when she was very young. At age four, she began modeling for Disney, and then appeared in commercials for such brand giants as McDonald's and Walmart.

In 2011, she starred in her first movie, *Columbiana*, as the younger version of the lead character played by Zoe Saldana. Critics loved her from the start. A reviewer posted on *ScreenAnarchy*, "A star is born! Amandla Stenberg steals the entire film, which isn't bad considering she's only ten years old and is onscreen for only the opening fifteen minutes."[2]

Soon after, when Amandla heard that they were casting for *The Hunger Games*, she desperately wanted to be the one to portray Rue's powerful story: "I called my agent repeatedly, saying, 'Please, please, please get

> Amandla's wise words (on growing up black): "I think that as a black girl you grow up internalizing all these messages that say you shouldn't accept your hair or your skin tone or your natural features, or that you shouldn't have a voice, or that you aren't smart. I feel like the only way to fight that is to just be yourself on the most genuine level."[7]

me an audition.'"[3] And all her preparation and hard work (and maybe that good-luck charm) paid off!

The four-month shoot wasn't easy—there was a ton of running and tree climbing for the young teen. But Amandla gave it her all, and in the end, she was one of the most popular characters in the movie. Again, she got great reviews, but this time, she also won an NAACP Image Award and a Teen Choice Award.[4] Fans loved Amandla and the movie, which was an enormous block-buster. It set records for opening day gross ($67.3 million) and had the third-largest opening weekend gross of any movie in North America ($152.5 million).[5]

Amandla followed her gargantuan screen success with smaller movie roles, plus a regular gig on TV's *Sleepy Hollow*. Currently, she has more movies in the works, but she is also a talented musician who plays the violin, drums, and gui-tar. Her folk/rock duo, called Honeywater, recorded an album in 2015.

That same year, she also began cowriting the comic book series *Niobe: She Is Life*, about a black elf girl. Her inspiration, Amandla says, came in her childhood:

> *I was always super into fantasy and* The Lord of the Rings *and* Game of Thrones *and all of that, but I could never find black char-acters whom I really liked. . . . I think [*Niobe *is] officially the first comic book to be written by a black girl, starring a black girl, and illustrated by a black girl.*[6]

In addition to her movie career, Amandla has become famous for her social activism and for speaking her mind on social media. A Tumblr video she made for school entitled "Don't Cash Crop on My Cornrows" went viral in 2015. In it she criticized white actresses and pop stars who adopt black culture and fashion for personal profit, without any acknowledgment or respect for where it came from (called "cultural appropriation").

She is also passionate about feminism. When she interviewed feminist leader Gloria Steinem, Amandla said: "I'm learning now that a feminist does not look like one certain thing. I used to think it just meant fighting for women's rights, but . . . it's so much more than that. It's about dismantling this entire wack system."[8]

At age seventeen, Amandla came out publicly as bisexual. She also identifies as nonbinary, which means she doesn't identify as exclusively male or female: "My identity exists without the labels; it's already there. A label is just a name for it."[9]

For her social activism, *Dazed* magazine called her "one of the most incendiary voices of her generation"[10] and *Time* magazine named her one of the 30 most influential teens of 2015 and 2016.[11]

So, keep your eye on Amandla Stenberg. She's still making her mark all over the place.

Amandla's wise words (on the power of social media): "In the past you could look only to movies or TV or music or celebrities in order to feel like you had representation. Now you can go on Instagram and you can see a girl who looks like you who is killing the game and expressing herself. Just being able to see that is so affirming."[12]

Amandla has many causes she cares about, but she volunteers her time as a youth ambassador for No Kid Hungry, which aims to end child hunger in the United States, and for the Ubuntu Education Fund in South Africa.

ROCK ON!

MIKAILA ULMER

After getting stung twice in one year, four-year-old Mikaila Ulmer was both terrified of and fascinated by bees. She studied them for a school assignment and
discovered honeybees could soon be extinct! This could cause a lot of problems
for humans, since most of our food crops need bees for pollination. Mikaila
decided to do something about it. She pulled out her great-grandmother's 1940
lemonade recipe, which uses honey for sweetener, and started a business, Me
& the Bees Lemonade. Mikaila's business boomed. At age ten, she was on
ABC's *Shark Tank* and won $60,000 to grow her business. A year later, she
signed an $11 million deal with Whole Foods to carry her lemonade. She even
served some to President Obama! Mikaila now gives workshops on how to save
the honeybees and donates part of her profits to the cause.

Chloe Kim

2000– ◉ SNOWBOARDER ◉ UNITED STATES

*I just go into a contest looking to put down a good run.
As long as I feel like I've done what I came to do and
I'm happy with my riding, where I end up doesn't matter
that much to me.*

—CHLOE KIM

Chloe stood at the top of the drop-in hill, contemplating the half-pipe. It was a perfect day at the US Snowboarding Grand Prix. Blue skies and fast snow. The fifteen-year-old prodigy had already clinched the gold medal in her earlier run. With her nearly perfect first run, she had beaten her idol and the reining American champ, Kelly Clark. Now it was time to take it easy. Nothing crazy, just get through the pipe and don't get hurt.

But Chloe didn't feel like playing it safe.

Why not? she thought. She hadn't worked on the trick in practice and hadn't been planning to do it here in Park City, Utah. But she felt a little crazy.

She went into a tuck, bouncing on her toes and gaining speed as she hit the deck. Over the lip and down into the pipe she flew. Then up the right wall, and—

"Look at the *size* of that backside air!" yelled an announcer.[1]

Hovering in the air, Chloe grabbed the back of her board and then soared back down into the pipe. More speed. She hit the left wall fast, and at the lip, she threw her body into a frontside spin.

One. Two. Three times around . . . And *boom!* She landed it perfectly. A 1080.

"She's setting the standard for women to follow," a second announcer crowed.[2]

Back down into the pipe, picking up speed again. Could she do it? Should she do it? Chloe hit the lip and her body decided for her, twisting into a backside spin.

One. Two. Three times around! She landed a second 1080!

"Whoa-ho-ho!!!" The announcers at Park City whooped excitedly.

"Oh my goodness, back to back! Are you kidding me?" yelled one.

"Ladies and gentlemen, you have just witnessed history!" cried another. "That has never been done before!"[3]

At the finish line, Chloe laughed and gasped for breath. She'd done it! She was the first female to hit back-to-back 1080s! Kelly Clark, the best female snowboarder in history, was the first to wrap her arms around Chloe in a congratulatory hug.

"That was insane," she said quietly. Chloe just laughed.[4]

"Insane" is right. Fifteen-year-old Chloe not only landed a nearly impossible trick but also earned a perfect score of one hundred for the run. Another first for women. Sean White is the only other snowboarder to earn a perfect score *ever*, and he's twice Chloe's age! The girl dubbed "The Future of Women's Snowboarding" is claiming her spot at the top of the sport.

———

Believe it or not, Chloe Kim didn't really like snowboarding at first. Her parents immigrated to southern California from Korea. When Chloe was four, her father took her snowboarding for the first time. "My dad pretty much dragged me into it," she remembers.[5] But it was a way to spend time with him, and after a few years, Chloe grew to love it.

She was just six when she started competing, and by age ten, she realized she wanted to be a professional snowboarder. That's when she began training and competing more seriously. Chloe joined the US Snowboarding team at thirteen.

Chloe's been racking up wins and setting records ever since. Her first year on the team, she won her first X Games medal (silver), and over the next three years, she won three gold medals. She is the only X Games athlete in history to win three gold medals before the age of sixteen.[6] And in 2016, as the youngest member of the US Snowboarding team, she not only won gold in the X Games but she became the first woman to land back-to-back 1080s and to score a perfect hundred.[7] That same year, at the Winter Youth Olympics, she was the first snowboarder to be the Team USA flag bearer, the first American woman to win a gold medal in snowboarding, and the winner of the highest snowboarding score in Youth Olympic history.[8] Not a bad year for Chloe Kim!

Her coach for the US Snowboarding team, Ricky Bower, is confident about her future: "She rides with a tremendous amount of amplitude and carries a lot more speed than any other female in the half-pipe. She's in a whole different league. There's really no one that can ride like that."[9]

> An early snowboard model was dubbed a *snurfer*, combining the words *snow* and *surfer*.
>
> ⎯⏛⎯

> Although snowboarding takes up most of her time, Chloe does have other interests. She is fluent in French, English, and Korean, she plays guitar, and she loves animals and "tranny skating" (or transitional skating, which involves doing tricks with a skateboard).
>
> ⎯⏛⎯

At the time of printing, Chloe is only seventeen years old. She has a full career ahead of her, and the heights of her achievements on the slopes are anyone's guess. But most experts are betting that Chloe is the new American (and possibly world) champion of snowboarding. No doubt, she's got a long and glorious ride ahead of her.

It's always important to work hard, but never forget to have fun. I think that in snowboarding...when I stop having fun and I take things a little too seriously, that's when I don't really enjoy it as much. And I just have to take a step back and realize... how much I love snowboarding...That's when I learn so much more and I progress more when I'm having fun.

—CHLOE KIM

ROCK ON!

KATIE LEDECKY

Katie Ledecky began swimming at age six, when she followed her older brother to swim practice, and before long, she was beating him! At age fifteen, at the 2012 Olympics, she surprised everyone at by winning gold in the women's 800-meter freestyle. Four years later, she became the most decorated female athlete at the Rio Olympics, winning four golds, one silver, and two world records! Still a teenager, Katie is the undisputed world champ: she has won the world championship a whopping nine times and is the current world record holder in the women's 400-, 800-, and 1500-meter freestyle. She's won twenty medals in international competitions (nineteen gold, one silver) and has broken thirteen world records. Watch out Michael Phelps, Katie's coming for your record!

Jazz Jennings

2000– ⚬ ACTIVIST ⚬ UNITED STATES

*Being transgender is not just a medical transition, [it's]
discovering who you are, living your life authentically, loving
yourself, and spreading that love towards other people
and accepting one another.*

—JAZZ JENNINGS

"Mommy, will you put pigtails in my hair?" Jazz asked. As her mother brushed her short locks, trying to gather enough of it into two hair ties, Jazz closed her eyes. She was finally allowed to grow her hair long, and she loved it when her mother brushed it. She also loved looking like her big sister, Ari. Today, she was wearing one of Ari's old dresses. It was pink—her favorite color. Soon, she'd be able to wear dresses to school, just like Ari. Her preschool was finally going to let her wear what she wanted to wear.

Jazz couldn't wait.

"There. All done," said her mother.

Jazz opened her eyes and looked in the mirror. Her chin-length hair stuck out from the sides of her head like mini trumpets. Her mother wrapped an arm around her shoulders, and together, they looked at the reflection. "You are a very pretty girl," said her mother.

Jazz couldn't believe it! Her mother had just called her a *girl* for the first time ever! Finally, she understood.

"I love you," said Jazz, dancing giddily around the room. "And I love my hair!"

Jazz froze midtwirl. She was thinking about her brothers and how they'd just taught her how to play soccer, a game that Jazz loved.

"Can girls still play sports?" she asked, worry lines wrinkling her forehead.

Her mother smiled. "Girls can do anything they want."[1]

〜〜

Jazz Jennings was born in 2000 with a boy's body and a boy's name—Jaron—but she knew from the start that she was really a girl. When asked about how old she was when she first realized it, Jazz said, "Ever since I could form coherent thoughts, I knew I was a girl trapped inside a boy's body."[2] Jazz is transgender, and as soon as she could speak, around age two, she began telling her parents all about it. When her mom called her a good boy, she would reply, "I'm a good *girl*."[3] Once, she asked her mom, "When is the good fairy going to come and change my penis into a vagina?"[4]

In fact, Jazz was a total girly girl. She loved dolls, princesses, mermaids, and everything pink. And she always wanted to wear her older sister's dresses, skirts, and heels. Her parents let her wear whatever she wanted at home, but when she left the house, they

> "Transgender" describes a person whose sense of self—of who they are—does not match the gender of the body they were born into. The number of transgender kids in America is unclear, but there are 1.4 million adults who identify that way.[5]
>
> 〜〜

insisted that she wear "boy" clothes (plain shorts and a T-shirt—no pink and no princesses). Jazz hated it and threw massive fits. She explained how it felt: "Imagine a young boy who is super into trucks and cars and playing in the mud. Then imagine that every time his parents take him out in public, they parade him around in a pink frilly dress with a parasol. The humiliation he'd feel is exactly the same humiliation I felt."[6]

It took a little while for her parents to understand transgender kids and how Jazz was feeling. Before Jazz, there was almost no information on transgender people that young. But at age five, while Jazz was still in preschool, her parents decided to let her be who she wanted to be. She began wearing skirts and princess T-shirts in public. It wasn't so easy to convince her preschool, however. They had a strict dress code, and at first, they didn't want Jazz dressing like a girl or growing her hair long. Jazz kept fighting to express who she was inside.

> Jazz's obsession with mermaids never faded. In middle school, she launched a company, Purple Rainbow Mermaid Tails, for which she designs and manufactures extremely realistic silicone mermaid tails. Check it out on YouTube, youtu.be /YnQxrO7edDY.

Jazz's parents registered her as a girl for kindergarten. This school was fine with Jazz dressing as a girl—but they wouldn't allow her to use the girls' restroom. Her only option was to use a bathroom in the nurse's office or in her classroom. But the nurse's office was crowded with sick kids, and the bathroom was where they went to barf. The bathroom in the classroom was no better—it had no lock (so Jazz got walked in on many times), and every time she peed, the entire class could hear her! Frustrated by her lack of options, Jazz quit using the bathroom and wet her pants a lot. When she did sneak into the girls' bathroom, she often got caught and got in trouble. It wasn't until she was in fifth grade that the school board changed their policy, finally letting Jazz use the girls' bathroom.

Also while in kindergarten, Jazz took a big step into the public eye. World-famous journalist Barbara Walters interviewed her for *20/20*, a

The battle for transgender bathroom rights is being fought right now, probably at a school near you (maybe even yours!). In May 2016, the Obama administration directed US public schools to let transgender students use bathrooms and locker rooms of their chosen gender identity. Schools that didn't comply risked losing their federal funding. Twelve states fought back, asking the courts to overrule the president. When North Carolina enacted its own state law requiring people to use public bathrooms that correspond with the sex on their birth certificate, the Justice Department sued, and people around the world boycotted the state in protest.[8]

national TV show. Jazz and her family thought it would be good to help other families who might be struggling to understand their own transgender kids. After the show, they were flooded with letters thanking Jazz for her courage in speaking out publicly. Some transgenders confessed that before seeing the show, they had been suicidal or were attacked for being transgender. At age six, Jazz already began to see that she could be an inspiration for other young transgender people.

Throughout Jazz's childhood, she was always honest about who she was. Her parents didn't let her go to another kid's house unless they knew she was transgender. And people had different reactions when they found out. Some kids teased her and wouldn't play with her, while others shrugged and said, "Oh, you're transgender? That's cool. Let's go get pizza."[7] Like most girls her age, Jazz had sleepovers, went to parties, and had several BFFs. She even had her first boyfriend in the fifth grade.

When Jazz did face ignorance and bullying, she worked hard to keep a positive attitude. In sixth grade, a group of new friends ditched her after discovering she was transgender (one even called her a "chick with a dick"), which made her sad for a while, but then she moved on. "It would have been easy for me to stay really bummed out and wallow in misery," she remembers, "but . . . I'm genuinely proud of who I am, and someone who can't see a person's soul beyond their body isn't worth getting upset about."⁹ She also stood up for herself, calling out bullies for their ignorant behavior or comments.

Another area where Jazz had to fight back and defend herself was on the soccer field. Jazz always loved the sport, and she was good. While in the rec league, she'd always played on a girls' team. But when she moved up to club soccer, the state soccer league said she could no longer play with the girls—they considered her boy body an unfair advantage (even though she was the smallest player on the girls' team!). Some teams threatened to sit out games in protest. Jazz tried playing on a boys' team but was miserable without her girlfriends.

Jazz and her parents appealed the state ruling and continued to fight until finally, when Jazz was eleven, the US Soccer Federation (the governing body for the sport nationwide) changed its policy and ruled that Jazz *could* compete as a girl on girls' teams. In fact, they went even further and created a new policy to include transgender players—a policy that had to be followed by *all* the states. Finally, Jazz could play with her friends. And even better, other transgender kids could play soccer on a team that matched their gender identity. Jazz was amazed that by fighting for her own rights, she changed things for everyone in the United States.

It's hard being a transgender kid. Transgender youth are much more likely than their peers to be depressed (50 percent vs. 20 percent), have anxiety (27 percent vs. 10 percent), engage in self-harm (17 percent vs. 4 percent), and attempt suicide (17 percent vs. 6 percent).¹⁰ If you or someone you know is struggling with being LGBTQ and needs someone to talk to, call The Trevor Project hotline: 866-488-7386 (TheTrevorProject.org).

Jazz decided that she wanted to speak out more, to help more transgender kids, so in 2007, she and her parents founded TransKids Purple Rainbow Foundation to do just that. Her organization fights bullying and helps transgender kids advocate for their rights in school. It also collects money for research, for financial aid for homeless transyouth, and for scholarships to trans-friendly camps. Jazz also began speaking at conferences, talking to kids and families about her experience.

When Jazz was eleven, the Oprah Winfrey Network filmed a documentary about her life and family, called *I Am Jazz: A Family in Transition*. That same year, she became the youngest person to win the Youth Courage Award, which is given to "remarkable young people who refuse to be silenced by societal norms and demonstrate profound courage in the face of hardship, intolerance, and bigotry. . ."[11] When Jazz gave her acceptance speech in front of hundreds of people, she realized for the first time that speaking out was what she was meant to do with her life.

Jazz has continued speaking out in different ways, reaching a larger and larger audience. She published a picture book about her childhood called *I Am Jazz* and a memoir for teens called *Being Jazz: My Life as a (Transgender) Teen*. In addition, she is a social media star, with a YouTube channel boasting millions of views, as well as hundreds of thousands of followers on Instagram, Twitter, and Facebook.[12] In 2015, she was honored with an invitation to the White House, where she met President Barack Obama. And the honors keep pouring in. *Time* magazine named her one of "The 25 Most Influential Teens of 2014," and *Out* magazine made her the youngest person ever profiled on their "OUT100" list.

In some cultures, transgender people have been celebrated for a long time. The indigenous people of Alaska use the word *Aranu'tiq* to describe someone with both a male and female spirit. *Aranu'tiq* people are highly respected because they view the world in a different way. Other Native American groups have a similar concept—"two spirit"—and a similar respect for different ways of being.[13]

Jazz and her family are now starring in the award-winning reality series *I Am Jazz*, which began airing in 2015. *Time* magazine praised it as "an engaging story of a teen girl who has transitioned. But it is also the story of everyone else, transitioning."[14]

Through her advocacy, outreach, and philanthropy, this teenager has changed the world for transgender kids and teens. And she's only seventeen! Surely Jazz Jennings will be rocking the world for many years to come.

HOW WILL YOU ROCK THE WORLD?

I'm going to rock the world by creating an app called "Safe House." It will create a safe environment for young adults to express the way they feel anonymously. This will be a good way to connect and find people going through the same things as you.

ELENA SIEKMANN AGE 13

Ashima Shiraishi

2001– ✦ ROCK CLIMBER ✦ UNITED STATES

In climbing, gender really doesn't matter. You're just facing the wall. Even if you're bigger or smaller than someone, you're tackling the same thing. It's just your determination and focus and dedication, and that's what makes you stronger.

—ASHIMA SHIRAISHI

Ashima raced ahead of her father. She could see the baseball fields on her left, so she knew the playground was just up ahead. Suddenly, a dark shape caught her eye. A giant slab of gray rock jutted out of the ground to her right. She'd seen the baseball-diamond-size rock before, but she'd never really noticed it. She'd heard her parents call it Rat Rock because the rats of Central Park swarm around it at night. *Gross!*

She didn't see any rats there today, just a few grown-ups climbing it. *That looks fun*, thought Ashima, heading for the rock. The climbers waiting their turn on a wall smiled at the adorable six-year-old.

"Don't you use ropes?" asked Ashima.

"Not for bouldering," said one. "It's only fifteen feet up, so not too dangerous." To tiny Ashima, Rat Rock looked enormous. It towered over her like a Manhattan skyscraper.

Her father caught up to her. "Why'd you stop here?" he asked.

"I want to climb it," Ashima said, pointing at the rock. "Can I?"

"Sure," he said, "Just be careful."

Ashima stretched her arm up and grabbed hold of a crack, found a tiny ledge for her toes, and pulled herself up onto the rock. She looked up, searching for more ledges and cracks she could hold on to. As she climbed the rock face, Ashima mapped out her next moves in her head. She could picture a route laid out in front of her.

Down below, Ashima's father and the other climbers watched in amazement. She looked like a monkey scrambling up the granite wall. It wasn't an easy climb—especially for a kid who'd never done it before—but in a minute, Ashima reached the summit. She did a little happy dance as the grown-ups below applauded.

Ashima didn't make it to the playground that day. She climbed Rat Rock over and over again, trying different routes and finding new, harder climbs. She was hooked![1]

In the years since Ashima Shiraishi's first climb, she has traveled the world, tackling some of the most difficult climbing routes any human has ever tried. In just ten years, she's gone from being a "gumby" (a novice climber) to one of the greatest climbers in the world. And she's still a teenager!

Ashima was born in New York City to parents who immigrated from Japan. When she first scaled Central Park's Rat Rock, Ashima's father, a trained dancer, immediately recognized her gift. From that first climb, Ashima fell in love with the sport and climbed as often as she could.

Within two years of that first climb, Ashima was breaking records in bouldering, which is free climbing without ropes or harnesses. When she was eight, she climbed her first V10, called Power of Silence. A year later,

Bouldering and rock climbing have different rating systems. Bouldering routes go from V0 (easiest) to V16 (hardest), and rock-climbing routes go from 5.0 (easiest) to 5.15a (hardest). The most difficult bouldering route ever climbed was a V15, and for sport climbing, it was a 5.15a. Ashima has done both.

~~~

she conquered the V11s and V12s, and at age ten, she got the world's attention when she successfully climbed Italy's Crown of Aragorn, a V13. She became the youngest person—and one of very few females—to ever climb a V13. But she didn't stop there. At thirteen, she tackled her first V14, becoming just the second female to "send" it (in rock-climbing lingo, to do something difficult with style). And in 2016, at Mount Hiei in Japan, Ashima became the first female to complete a V15 boulder climb. There are only a handful of V15 boulder climbs in the world, and only a few male climbers have climbed them. Climb designer Garrett Koeppicus is in awe of her: "She's like Spider-Woman. She's just crazy good."[2]

When she was eleven, Ashima began sport climbing, which uses anchors fixed to the rock, plus ropes and harnesses, and quickly dominated there as well. She became the youngest person to climb a 5.14c when she topped Kentucky's Red River Gorge. At thirteen, Ashima went to Spain and climbed Ciudad de Dios, making her the youngest climber, male or female, to complete a 5.15a. Only six other climbers have completed the route. *Ever!*

To excel in climbing, Ashima needs many abilities. First is sheer strength: she has to support her body weight with just her fingertips or her toes and be able to hang by one hand as she swings her body across the rock. Endurance is another, for longer climbs. She is also a gymnast, stretching her limbs, pretzeling her body into impossible positions, and launching herself into space to get to out-of-reach holds (a move called a *dyno*). Most important, Ashima needs mental strength. She has to figure out the best route up the rock and problem solve quickly as she climbs. To prepare for climbs, Ashima does a ritual her father taught her to achieve "a deep, quiet and strong mind and soul."[3]

The ritual must be working—Ashima is unbeatable! In 2015, she won the World Youth Championships for both lead climbing and bouldering in the female youth category. She also won the Sport Climbing National Championships. *Climbing* magazine named her 2015's Climber of the Year and *Time* magazine put her on their list of "The 30 Most Influential Teens of 2015." She has many sponsors, including well-known brands like The North Face and Clif Bar.

Being one of the best rock climbers in the world isn't easy, however. Ashima trains hard year-round and has to sacrifice some of the fun normal teenagers take for granted. "I have a pretty hard time balancing school and rock climbing," she says. "I get out of school around 3:00 PM, then I go to the climbing gym for three hours or more. I get home, I do homework, and I'm usually asleep by 1:00 AM. Then I'm up again at 6:30 AM."[4] And then there's the ever-present risk of falling and getting hurt.

Ashima thinks the risks and sacrifices are worth it, especially if she gets to compete in the Olympics. Climbing is being considered as a new sport in the 2020 Olympics, and when asked about it, Ashima says, "That would be a dream come true. Since I began climbing, my dream was to have it in the Olympics and . . . to be there competing."[5] Whether climbing becomes an Olympic event or not, Ashima will surely keep smashing records. "My goal is to keep on pushing myself as far as I can in rock climbing," she says.[6]

Many fans (including other climbers) wonder how much she'll improve once she's graduated from high school and can climb all day, year-round, like the rest of the pros. "Ashima is unstoppable right now . . . Imagine what would be possible if [she] devoted weeks, months, or years to climbing

> In 2016, Ashima took the biggest fall of her career. At a climbing gym in Georgia, while her dad belayed her (supported her with safety ropes as she climbed), he accidentally squeezed the brake release lever, causing her to drop 45 feet to the padded floor. She was rushed to the hospital and, fortunately, had no serious injuries. She was able to compete again later that week.

something at her absolute limit,"[7] said top female climber Angie Payne. Having conquered both a 5.15a sport climb and a V15 boulder climb, Ashima is the first young woman to join a small, elite group of climbers who've managed that milestone.

Ashima has the potential to do more than just dominate the sport; she might completely change it. "I think Ashima could be the biggest game changer in high-end climbing," said filmmaker Josh Lowell. "When you watch her climb it's like a different sport than what everyone else is doing. Somehow the same laws of gravity don't apply."[8]

Just think of what Ashima has left to accomplish! This teenager is already the greatest female rock climber in the world. And with time, many believe she will become the best climber—man or woman—in history.

> Climbing isn't easy. Much of the time, you keep falling.
> It's repetitive falling. But once you stand up,
> you're that much closer to getting to the top.
>
> —ASHIMA SHIRAISHI

ROCK ON!

MO'NE DAVIS

In 2014, Mo'ne Davis did what no girl had ever done before: with her seventy-mile-per-hour fastball and wicked curveball, she pitched a shutout game (which means the other team didn't score any runs), and her team won the Little League World Series. She was also the first African American girl to play in the series. For her trailblazing success, she earned another first: she was the first little leaguer to make the cover of *Sports Illustrated*. Now Mo'ne has set her sights on a new sport: basketball. She loves hoops even more than baseball and is working to make it into the Women's National Basketball Association (WNBA). You can bet a determined athlete like Mo'ne will keep at it until her dreams are a reality.

Acknowledgments

Thank you to all the amazing women in my family who have encouraged me through the writing of this book and other books, and through every milestone of my life: my mom, Kathy; my stepmom, Joy; my aunt Patty; my sisters, Jamie and Charlotte; and my sister-cousins, Jody and Jenny. I am part of a family of serious butt-kicking women—from Gramma Dottie on down the line. It makes me fiercely proud.

The men in my family are pretty awesome too. My dad, Jim, and my stepdad, Jeff—thanks for always believing in me. And to Ivo—the best brother-in-law in the world—and my three rock-star nephews, Lukas, Oliver, and Simon: you're not girls, but I love you anyway!

Thank you to my other family, the McCanns, who are always supportive fans: Viv, who was a smart, strong, funny woman who raised an amazing family; Tom, who loves encouraging his many brilliant granddaughters and great-granddaughters; and the rest of my sisters- and brothers-in-law and their kids. And to Chuck: thank you for all you gave to our family and all you taught us. I miss you—we *all* do.

Thank you to my husband, Jerry, who was supportive and encouraging even during his hardest times. What would I do without you? And to my kids, Ronan and Fiona, for putting up with my nonstop jabbering about each new girl I wrote about. I love you, McCann Clan!

Thank you to my fabulous girlfriends, many of whom saved me during the writing of this book and the family tragedy that coincided with it. To my college BFFs, Karen Kerr, Bridget Carpenter, Kristin Thielking, and Kristin Hurdle: you are amazing, world-rocking women who inspire me in all that you do. Heifers unite! My Oregon girlfriends—Kristin Doherty (thank you for Nadia), Kenan Smith, Lissa Kaufman, Kelly Burke-Doyle, Marcela Villagran (who even translated some obscure Nicaraguan Spanish for me!), and Beth Nelson—thank you for the meals, the hugs, the daily support and encouragement. You are my Village. I am blessed.

Thank you to the wonderful team (and my "work family") at Beyond Words Publishing for giving me the chance to flex my writing muscles again, and for the brilliant editing, design, and marketing of the book: Richard Cohn, Michele Ashtiani, Lindsay Easterbrooks-Brown, Emmalisa Sparrow Wood, Devon Smith, Jackie Hooper, and Whitney Diffenderfer. And thank you to the stellar folks at Simon & Schuster who have done such a wonderful job of publicizing and selling this series. And a *huge* thanks to Jen Weaver-Neist, editor extraordinaire, for your careful combing and thoughtful suggestions, for catching all my stupid mistakes, and for making my writing so much better. Thank God for editors!

And my final thanks goes to Emily Einolander, my writing assistant. Emily worked tirelessly and passionately on this book with me. She found great resources—books, articles, and videos—and then helped me wade through them to find the juicy bits. She was my first reader and editor for every word on these pages. Thanks to Emily, this book is something I'm really proud of. There is no way I could have finished it without you, Emily. I am eternally grateful.

Recommended Resources

Here is a list of resources I used to research the incredible girls profiled in this book, along with some additional materials you can check out if you want to know more. I've listed them by profile for easy referencing. A few of the websites are not in English, but if you paste the URL into Google Translate, Google will (roughly) translate the whole site for you.

ESTHER

Here are some excellent picture books about Esther, but to read the original story, you should read the Bible, where there is a whole book about her. I used the New American Standard Bible, but any Bible will have the story.

The Story of Esther: A Purim Tale by Eric A. Kimmel (Holiday House, 2011)

Queen Esther Saves Her People by Rita Golden Gelman (Scholastic, Inc., 1998)

You might also like to watch this movie about Queen Esther:

One Night with the King directed by Michael O. Sajbel (2006)

And if you want to learn more about the Jewish holiday Purim, its ties to Esther, and how it's celebrated today, check out Chabad.org.

"What Is Purim?," Chabad.org website, www.chabad.org/holidays /purim/article_cdo/aid/645309/jewish/What-Is-Purim.htm

CLEOPATRA

There are many good books on Cleopatra, but I liked these two the best. Schiff's biography is for adults but is utterly fascinating. Blackaby's biography is for kids and gives a concise, clear explanation of her life and times.

Cleopatra: A Life by Stacy Schiff (Little, Brown and Company, 2010)

Cleopatra: Egypt's Last and Greatest Queen by Susan Blackaby (Sterling Publishing, 2009)

You might also enjoy watching the famous Liz Taylor movie about the queen.

Cleopatra directed by Joseph L. Mankiewicz (1963)

GRACE O'MALLEY

The Pirate Queen by Emily Arnold McCully (Putnam Juvenile, 1995)

The Pirate Queen: In Search of Grace O'Malley and Other Legendary Women of the Sea by Barbara Sjoholm (Seal Press, 2004)

NAYA NUKI

The factual information in this chapter (dates, locations, and so forth) I took from Lewis and Clark's account in their journal of the Sacagawea and Naya Nuki reunion. For inspiration, I also used Thomasma's thoroughly researched historical fiction account of what Naya Nuki's journey might have been like. It is a great read for kids.

The Journals of the Lewis and Clark Expedition: July 28–November 1, 1805 by Meriwether Lewis and William Clark (University of Nebraska Press, 1988)

Naya Nuki: Shoshoni Girl Who Ran by Kenneth Thomasma (Grandview Publishing, 2011)

MARY WOLLSTONECRAFT SHELLEY

Mary Shelley led a tumultuous life. I liked Garrett's biography best because it didn't shy away from her darker sides. If you're curious, you should read Mary's *Frankenstein* novel—it is likely quite different from the versions you've heard.

> *Frankenstein* by Mary Wollstonecraft Shelley (Dover Publications, 1994)
>
> *Mary Shelley* by Martin Garrett (Oxford University Press, 2002)

There are also several movies based on Mary's book. My favorites are the original 1931 version and the Abbot and Costello comedy classic.

> *Abbot and Costello Meet Frankenstein* directed by Charles Barton (1948)
>
> *Frankenstein* directed by James Whale (1931)

ADA BYRON LOVELACE

Wallmark's picture book is a great overview of Ada's life. The graphic novel by Sydney Padua, however, was one of the most fun, absorbing books I read in all my research. If you want to know more and you like graphic novels, check it out!

> *Ada Byron Lovelace and the Thinking Machine* by Laurie Wallmark (Creston Books, 2015)
>
> *The Thrilling Adventures of Lovelace and Babbage: The (Mostly) True Story of the First Computer* by Sydney Padua (Pantheon Books, 2015)

And if you'd like to see what Babbage's Difference Engine looked like, the Computer History Museum website has a great photo and description.

> "The Babbage Engine," Computer History Museum, www.computerhistory.org/babbage

ANNIE OAKLEY

> *Bull's-Eye: A Photobiography of Annie Oakley* by Sue Macy (National Geographic Children's Books, 2006)

Who Was Annie Oakley? by Stephanie Spinner (Grosset & Dunlap, 2002)

While the books tell a truer story of Annie's life, there is a wonderful musical loosely based on her called *Annie Get Your Gun*. You can see it onstage or rent the movie.

Annie Get Your Gun directed by George Sidney (1950)

Nellie Bly

The Daring Nellie Bly: America's Star Reporter by Bonnie Christensen (Dragonfly Books, 2009)

Ten Days a Madwoman: The Daring Life and Turbulent Times of the Original "Girl" Reporter, Nellie Bly by Deborah Noyes (Puffin Books, 2017)

Eleanor Roosevelt

Russell Freedman is one of the great biographers of our time and his book about Eleanor is wonderful. You can also read Eleanor's popular newspaper columns in the collection below.

Eleanor Roosevelt: Life of Discovery by Russell Freedman (Clarion Books, 1993)

My Day: The Best of Eleanor Roosevelt's Acclaimed Newspaper Columns, 1936–1962 by Eleanor Roosevelt (Da Capo Press, 2001)

Dora Thewlis

There isn't a ton of information on Dora—she was a mystery even in her own time. There are a few newspaper accounts from the time, but just one book: a historical fiction imagining of her life. It's well researched and thoroughly enjoyable.

Give Us the Vote! (My True Stories) by Sue Reid (Scholastic, 2011)

If you want to learn more about the suffragettes, check out this award-winning movie:

Suffragette directed by Sarah Gavron (2015)

JOSEPHINE BAKER

Powell's picture book is as beautifully written as it is gorgeous to look at. Caravantes's book goes in depth about all the phases of her entrancing life.

Josephine: The Dazzling Life of Josephine Baker by Patricia Hruby Powell (Chronicle Books, 2014)

The Many Faces of Josephine Baker: Dancer, Singer, Activist, Spy (Women of Action) by Peggy Caravantes (Chicago Review Press, 2015)

GRACE MURRAY HOPPER

Headstrong: 52 Women Who Changed Science—and the World by Rachel Swaby (Broadway Books, 2015)

Technology: Cool Women Who Code by Andi Diehn (Nomad Press, 2015)

MARY LOU WILLIAMS

The Little Piano Girl: The Story of Mary Lou Williams, Jazz Legend by Ann Ingalls (Houghton Mifflin Harcourt, 2010)

If you'd like to see Mary Lou jamming on the piano, check out this amazing clip from a 1973 episode of *Mr. Rogers' Neighborhood*. She rocks! Mr. Rogers interviews her too.

"Mr. Rogers Neighborhood - Mary Lou Williams (Piano) and Milton Suggs (Bass) 1973," YouTube, youtu.be/gjM63eZmsao

BEVERLY CLEARY

The best way to learn about Beverly is to read her autobiographies. They are funny and fascinating, just like her fiction.

A Girl from Yamhill: A Memoir by Beverly Cleary (Avon Books, 1999)

My Own Two Feet: A Memoir by Beverly Cleary (HarperCollins, 2009)

If you're lucky enough to live in or visit Portland, Oregon, where many of Beverly's books are set, you can also do a walking tour with this awesome book:

Walking With Ramona: Exploring Beverly Cleary's Portland by Laura O. Foster (Microcosm Publishing, 2016)

Ruth Bader Ginsburg

I Dissent: Ruth Bader Ginsburg Makes Her Mark by Debbie Levy (Simon & Schuster Books for Young Readers, 2016)
Ruth Bader Ginsburg: Iconic Supreme Court Justice (Gateway Biographies) by James Roland (Lerner Publications, 2016)

In this mesmerizing radio interview Ruth tells the story of seeing the "No dogs or Jews allowed" sign and discusses other major events of her life:

"A Conversation with Justice Ruth Bader Ginsburg: Her Life as a Woman, a Jew and a Judge," Only in America, www.only inamerica.cc/ginsburg.shtml

Julie Andrews

As with Beverly Cleary, the best book about Julie is this one she wrote herself:

Home: A Memoir of My Early Years by Julie Andrews (Hachette Books, 2009)

Here's an amazing recording of twelve-year-old Julie singing the Polonaise, which I wrote about in my introductory scene—check out those pipes!

"12-Year-Old Julie Andrews-Polonaise; Je suis Titaniã = Mignon," YouTube, youtu.be/iV2-YGGn0y4

And if you haven't seen them already, you should definitely watch her beloved movies. Here are a few to start:

Mary Poppins directed by Robert Stevenson (1964)
The Princess Diaries directed by Garry Marshall (2001)
The Sound of Music directed by Robert Wise (1965)

Wangari Maathai

Unbowed: A Memoir by Wangari Maathai (Anchor Books, 2007)
Wangari Maathai: The Woman Who Planted Millions of Trees by Franck Prévot (Charlesbridge Publishing, 2015)

Aretha Franklin

Aretha Franklin: Motown Superstar by Silvia Anne Sheafer (Enslow
Publishers, 1996)
Respect: The Life of Aretha Franklin by David Ritz (Little, Brown
and Company, 2014)

And if you want to have your mind completely blown, watch these two
videos! In the first, a very young and groovy Aretha sings her new hit
"(You Make Me Feel Like) A Natural Woman." In the second, a much
older Aretha brings down the house with the same song at a 2015 Kennedy
Center performance. Watch President Obama cry!

"Aretha Franklin - (You Make Me Feel Like) A Natural Woman,"
YouTube, youtu.be/q9nSU2hAqK4
"Aretha Franklin - You Make Me Feel (Like a Natural Woman) -
Kennedy Center Honors 2015," YouTube, youtu.be/c7
D5y_5lM5Q

Hillary Rodham Clinton

There are several excellent books for kids about Hillary, including those
listed here. Hillary's memoir, *Living History*, is excellent reading as well.

Hillary Rodham Clinton: Do All the Good You Can by Cynthia
Levinson (Balzer + Bray, 2016)
Hillary Rodham Clinton: Some Girls Are Born to Lead by Michelle
Markel (Balzer + Bray, 2016)
Living History by Hillary Rodham Clinton (Scribner, 2004)

Here you can listen to young Hillary's passionate commencement speech
at her graduation from Wellesley College:

"Hillary Rodham Clinton's Student Speech," YouTube, youtu.be
/2CAUOa5m5nY

Sheila Sri Prakash

There aren't any books about Sheila, but there are plenty of fascinating
interviews online, including this one:

"Architect Shelia Sri Prakash, Shilpa Architects Planners Designers," Modern Green Structures and Architecture, www.mgsarchitecture .in/architects/453-architect-sheila-sri-prakash-shilpa-archi tects-planners-designers.html

In this video Sheila talks about her childhood, the challenges of becoming an architect, and her design philosophy:

"Ms. Sheila Sri Prakash-Architect and Urban Designer=Chenai= India = Speaker, IWC 2014," YouTube, youtu.be/WskgTcaty_Y

Explore the incredible buildings and projects Sheila has designed at her architecture firm's website.

Shilpa Architects, www.shilpaarchitects.com

Arlen Siu Bermúdez

There is almost nothing written in English about Arlen Siu. She is well-known in Nicaragua and much of Central America, but not elsewhere. Here are links to a Spanish article and blog that I used for research:

"Vida y muerte de Arlen Siu, la mariposa clandestina," La Prensa, www.laprensa.com.ni/2016/09/18/suplemento/la-prensa -domingo/2101994-vida-y-muerte-de-arlen-siu-la-mariposa -clandestina

"Arlen Siu Bermudez," *Agaton* (blog), carlosagaton.blogspot.com /2014/02/arlen-siu-bermudez.html

And here you can also listen to a performance of Arlen's beautiful song "Maria Rural":

"'Maria Rural' Escrita por Alren Siu," YouTube, youtu.be/d-Xb faJpbJY

Björk

Sadly, there aren't any kids' books about Björk. Here are a couple of books for adults that are intriguing and easy to read:

Björk: An Illustrated Biography by Mick St. Michael (Omnibus Press, 1996)

Björk: There's More to Life Than This (Stories behind Every Song)
   by Ian Gittins (Thunder's Mouth Press, 2002)

Björk is definitely best experienced aurally, so give her a listen. Included here are videos of her at ten years old singing "I Love to Love," at seventeen years old singing with the band "Tappi Tíkarrass," and a couple of her music videos—one with The Sugarcubes and one as a solo artist in all her artsy glory.

"Björk - Human Behavior (Official Music Video)," YouTube, youtu.be/KDbPYoaAiyc

"I Love to Love, - Björk (1976)" YouTube, youtu.be/rujxXO mYLUU

"Sucarcubes Birthday English," YouTube, youtu.be/noXY iNo5TOo

"Watch 17-Year-Old Björk Sing and Dance Her Heart Out" by Nina Corcoran, Nerdist, www.nerdist.com/watch-17-year-old -bjork-sing-and-dance-her-heart-out/

SELENA

Selena: The Queen of Tejano by Jill C. Wheeler (Abdo & Daughters, 1996)

To Selena, With Love by Chris Perez (Penguin Group, 2012)

Check out the music video of Selena performing "Bidi Bidi Bom Bom" (the song she and Chris wrote in the intro scene).

"Selena - Bidi Bidi Bom Bom," YouTube, youtu.be/RKGbjJarMeA

You can also watch the Selena movie, starring the now-famous Jennifer Lopez in her first big role.

Selena directed by Gregory Nava (1997)

FAWZIA KOOFI

I highly recommend this excellent autobiography, which Fawzia wrote as a series of letters to her daughters:

The Favored Daughter: One Woman's Fight to Lead Afghanistan into the Future by Fawzia Koofi (St. Martin's Griffin, 2013)

MINDY KALING

Mindy is a fantastic writer—both funny and personal.

> *Is Everyone Hanging Out without Me? (And Other Concerns)* by Mindy Kaling (Crown Archetype, 2011)
>
> *Why Not Me?* by Mindy Kaling (Three Rives Press, 2016)

I also thought this *Teen Vogue* interview was fantastic:

> "What Mindy Kaling Wishes She'd Known as a Teenager" by Lesley McKenzie, *Teen Vogue*, www.teenvogue.com/story/mindy-kaling-advice-for-teen-girls

Her show *The Mindy Project*, which she wrote and starred in, is also pretty fabulous.

JHAMAK GHIMIRE

There isn't a lot of material about Jhamak in English, but this wonderful collection of her writing has been translated from Nepali:

> *A Flower in the Midst of Thorns* by Jhamak Ghimire (Xlibris, 2012)

This article is also a good source of information:

> "Nepal's Prize-Winning Poet with Cerebral Palsy" by Thomas Bell, BBC News, www.bbc.com/news/world-south-asia-14762629

Want to see this amazing woman eat, brush her teeth, and write with her feet? Watch this short documentary. (The film is in Nepali, and unfortunately there are no subtitles, but it's still a great video to see Jhamak in action.)

> "Documentary of Jhamak Kumari Ghimire," YouTube, youtu.be/aRG8zXjqbvY

VENUS AND SERENA WILLIAMS

There are lots of great books about the Williams sisters. Here are two that I really enjoyed:

> *Venus and Serena Williams: Athletes* (Women of Achievement) by Anne M. Todd (Infobase Publishing, 2009)
>
> *Venus and Serena Williams: Tennis Champions* by Diane Bailey (The Rosen Publishing Group, 2010)

I was also amazed (and disturbed) by this video of the Williams sisters getting booed by fans at Indian Wells:

"Indian Wells Controversy," YouTube, youtu.be/TcUcTMdn4dE

BEYONCÉ

Here are a couple of good books on Beyoncé's life:

Beyoncé: A Life in Music by Mary Colson (Raintree, 2011)

Beyoncé (Hip-Hop Biographies) (Saddleback Educational Publishing, 2015)

And you absolutely have to watch the *Star Search* video of Beyoncé and her band, Girl's Tyme, to see the twelve-year-old singer strutting her stuff—it's inspiring!

"Star Search - Girls Tyme with Beyonce," YouTube, youtu.be /gWXPl18psZA

Beyoncé has a lot of amazing music videos in which she expresses her feelings on body image and being a woman and a feminist. This is one of my faves:

"Yours and Mine," YouTube, youtu.be/x4pPNxUzGvc

DANICA PATRICK

Here are a couple of good print sources on Danica and her racing career:

"Danica Patrick: From Go-Kart Racer to NASCAR Contender" by M. B. Roberts, *American Profile Weekly*, www.americanpro file.com/articles/danica-patrick-nascar

Danica Patrick: Racing's Trailblazer (*USA Today* Lifeline Biographies) by Karen Sirvaitis (Twenty-First Century Books, 2010)

And here's a fun ABC profile on Danica after she became the first woman to win the top pole position for the Daytona 500:

"Danica Patrick Wins Pole Position for Daytona 500," YouTube, youtu.be/aX2bymccfTE

Misty Copeland

Misty's autobiography is fabulous. Read it!

Life in Motion: An Unlikely Ballerina by Misty Copeland (Simon & Schuster, 2015)

You should also watch her powerful Under Armour ad that got so much attention.

"Misty Copeland - I WILL WHAT I WANT," YouTube, youtu.be /ZY0cdXr_1MA

And here's an amazing video of Misty dancing on the *Arsenio Hall Show* in 2014:

"Misty Copeland Defies Physics in a Stunning Dance Performance," YouTube, youtu.be/yw_LfOx-1-c

Sarah McNair-Landry

Here's another amazing woman that has no books written about her, but the online articles I read are really fun and interesting.

"Interview: 'Polar Adventurer Sarah McNair-Landry,'" Euronews, www.euronews.com/2014/07/01/interview-polar-adventurer -sarah-mcnair-landry

"Meet the Couple Who Just Spent 120 Days Traveling through the Arctic on a Dogsled" by Anubha Momin, *VICE*, www .vice.com/read/meet-the-couple-who-just-spent-120-days -traveling-the-arctic-on-dogsled-981

"ExWeb Interview with Sarah McNair-Landry: It Was Odd to Have to Worry about Finding Water" by Correne Coetzer, ExplorersWeb, www.explorersweb.com/polar/news.php?id=18498

And check out *Never Lose Sight*, the short film Sarah made in 2016.

Never Lose Sight by Sarah McNair-Landry, www.nfb.ca/film /never_lose_sight/

Nadia Nadim

Unbelievably there aren't any books about Nadia and her amazing story . . . yet. But there are some great articles. Here's a good one:

"After Escaping Afghanistan following Father's Execution, Sky
Blue FC Star Nadia Nadim Has Finally Found Life after Death"
by Wayne Coffey, *NY Daily News*, www.nydailynews.com
/sports/soccer/sky-blue-fc-star-nadia-nadim-finally-finds-life
-death-article-1.2181510

In this video from the Portland Thorns website, Nadia talks about going
to med school and her philanthropic work:

"Support Thorns FC Forward Nadia Nadim's From Street to
School Campaign," Portland Timbers website, www.timbers
.com/post/2016/09/28/support-thorns-fc-forward-nadia-nadims
-street-school-campaign

The Denmark-based group Nadia supports, From Street to School, gives
financial aid to homeless Afghan kids, helping them get an education and
stay off the streets. Visit the website to find out more. (FYI, the website
is in Danish!)

From Street to School website, www.FSTS.dk

ADELE

Adele: A Celebration of an Icon and Her Music by Sarah-Louise
James (Carlton, 2016)
Adele: The Biography by Marc Shapiro (St. Martin's Griffin, 2012)

And in case you need more proof of how cool Adele is, check her out
on Carpool Karaoke from *The Late Late Show with James Corden*. She
is the coolest!

"Adele Carpool Karaoke," YouTube, youtu.be/Nck6BZga7TQ

EMMA WATSON

Emma Watson by Dale-Marie Bryan (The Child's World, 2013)
Emma Watson: From Wizards to Wallflowers (Pop Culture Bios)
by Nadia Higgins (Lerner Publications Company, 2014)

The opening scene of Emma's chapter is based on her adorable first screen
test with Rupert Grint and Daniel Radcliffe. It's clear this nine-year-old
was meant to play Hermione Granger.

"Young Emma Watson, Daniel Radcliffe and Rupert Grint - Harry Potter," YouTube, youtu.be/3bNqQBIwUUo

This article focuses on the work Emma is doing for girls' rights around the world:

"Emma Watson on How Being Threatened for Speaking about Feminism Enraged and Motivated Her" by Joanna Robinson, *Vanity Fair*, www.vanityfair.com/hollywood/2015/03/emma -watson-feminism-threats-raging-heforshe

And if you'd like to learn more about the UN's HeForShe Campaign that Emma is a part of, visit this website:

HeForShe, www.heforshe.org/en

Hou Yifan

Yifan is another girl with no biographies, but this *Daily Mail* article was a fun read. I especially loved the glamour shots of the not-so-nerdy chess champ.

"Meet Yifan Hou—the Glamorous Women's World Chess Champion Who Is Changing the Face of the Notoriously Nerdy Game," *Daily Mail*, www.dailymail.co.uk/femail/article-2605502/Meet -Yifan-Hou-glamorous-Womens-World-Chess-Champion -changing-face-notoriously-nerdy-game.html

Lizzy Clark

Most of what I learned about Lizzy I found on her website and a few online articles.

Don't Play Me, Pay Me, www.dontplaymepayme.com
"Fame for Actress with Asperger [sic] Syndrome," BBC, www.bbc .co.uk/shropshire/content/articles/2008/09/16/aspergers_actress _feature.shtml

Bethany Mota

Here are some great books about Bethany, including her own book, that show how inspirational she is:

Bethany Mota (Real Bios) by Marie Morreale (Scholastic, 2016)

From Me to YouTube: The Unofficial Guide to Bethany Mota by Emily Klein (Scholastic, 2015)

Make Your Mind Up: My Guide to Finding Your Own Style, Life, and Motivation! by Bethany Mota (Gallery Books, 2017)

You'll surely enjoy watching Bethany's very first YouTube video. She's come a long way since then!

"First Video :) Mac and Sephora Haul," YouTube, youtu.be /h0wCoXVkjGA

TAVI GEVINSON

Fight Like A Girl: 50 Feminists Who Changed the World by Laura Barcella (Zest Books, 2016)

You can (and should) read Tavi's *Style Rookie* posts and interviews all collected into four awesome "yearbooks," starting with this one. The writing and layouts are cool, funny, and totally insightful for teens—I highly recommend them.

Rookie Yearbook One edited by Tavi Gevinson (Razorbill, 2014)

SIMONE BILES

You can learn more about Simone's inspiring life story from her memoir.

Courage to Soar: A Body in Motion, a Life in Balance by Simone Biles and Michelle Burford (Zondervan, 2016)

And check out this great article about Simone from *Time* magazine:

"Simone Biles Is Taking Her Sport to New Heights" by Alice Park, *Time*, time.com/4428013/simone-biles-gymnastics-usa

MALALA YOUSAFZAI

I Am Malala: How One Girl Stood Up for Education and Changed the World (Young Readers Edition) by Malala Yousafzai and Patricia McCormick (Little, Brown Books for Young Readers, 2016)

If you'd like to watch 16-year-old Malala giving her first speech at the United Nations in 2013, check out this powerful video:

"Girl Shot in Head by Taliban, Speaks at UN: Malala Yousafzai United Nations Speech 2013," YouTube, youtu.be /QRh_30C8l6Y

BINDI IRWIN

Bindi Irwin's Wild Life by Emily Klein (Scholastic, 2016)
Steve and Bindi Irwin (Conservation Heroes) by Amy Breguet (Chelsea House, 2011)

You can watch Bindi dance and pay tribute to her father during a *Dancing with the Stars* competition.

"Bindi Irwin Breaks Down during Emotional Tribute to Her Late Father, Steve Irwin," YouTube, youtu.be/DouVLDPPHGE

AMANDLA STENBERG

There are some fantastic interviews with Amandla, both in print and on video. Here are a few of my favorites, including one in which Beyoncé's sister, Solange, interviews Amandla:

"Amandla Stenberg and Gloria Steinem Talk Feminism," YouTube, youtu.be/SnMfnKT8Rvg

"Amandla Stenberg: 'I Don't Feel Afraid to Talk about Racism or Sexism or the Gender Binary" by Estelle Tang, *Elle*, www.elle .com/culture/q-and-a/a35917/amandla-stenberg-is-not-afraid/

"How Our February Cover Star Amandla Stenberg Learned to Love Her Blackness" by Solange Knowles, *Teen Vogue*, www.teenvogue .com/story/amandla-stenberg-interview-teen-vogue-february-2016

CHLOE KIM

There are no books about Chloe yet, but here is a great article:

"This Sixteen-Year-Old Girl Has Won Gold TWICE at the X Games" by Amanda Chan, *Teen Vogue*, www.teenvogue.com /story/chloe-kim-snowboarder-16-years-old-x-games

On this video you can watch Chloe tear up the half-pipe during her historic run, which was my inspiration for her opening scene. Check out those back-to-back 1080s!

"Chloe Kim's Historic Perfect Score - U.S. Snowboarding Grand Prix 2016," YouTube, youtu.be/BjJlFpwhERM

JAZZ JENNINGS

As with many of these girls and women, the best place to learn about them is when they write about themselves. Jazz's memoir is powerful and fun.

Being Jazz: My Life as a (Transgender) Teen by Jazz Jennings (New York: Crown Books for Young Readers, 2016)

You can also watch her reality TV show, *I Am Jazz*, on the TLC network.

ASHIMA SHIRAISHI

"This 15-Year-Old Girl Could Be the Best Rock Climber Ever" by Mandy Oaklander, *Time*, time.com/4352618/ashima-shiraishi -next-generation-leaders/

"A Conversation with Two of the Most Powerful Teens in Climbing" by Megan Michelson, *Outside*, www.outsideonline.com/2061271 /conversation-two-most-powerful-teens-climbing

It's super fun to watch Ashima climbing. Here are some great videos:

"Ashima Shiraishi Completes First Female Ascent of 24 Karats, 8C+ | EpicTV Climbing Daily, Ep. 141," YouTube, youtu.be /W-Ehw6LmFxA

"Ashima Shiraishi - World's Best Female Rock Climber?" YouTube, youtu.be/KKiqVsFAFjc

Here's a very funny video of Ashima teaching James Corden to rock climb on *The Late Late Show with James Corden*:

"Rock Climbing with Ashima Shiraishi," YouTube, youtu.be/ ZrYkQNzfMMA

Notes

Esther

1. Esther 4:16 (New American Standard Bible).
2. Eric A. Kimmel, *The Story of Esther: A Purim Tale* (New York: Holiday House, 2011), 4.
3. Rita Golden Gelman, *Queen Esther Saves Her People* (New York: Scholastic, Inc., 1998), 22.
4. Ibid., 31.
5. Ibid., 32.
6. "Purim How-To Guide," Chabad.org, accessed September 6, 2016, http://www.chabad.org/holidays/purim/article_cdo/aid/1362/jewish/Purim-How-To-Guide.htm.

Cleopatra

1. Susan Blackaby, *Cleopatra: Egypt's Last and Greatest Queen*, Sterling Biography (New York: Sterling Publishing Co., 2009), 2–5.
2. Stacy Schiff, *Cleopatra: A Life* (New York: Little, Brown and Company, 2010), 15–16.
3. Blackaby, *Cleopatra*, 23.
4. Schiff, *Cleopatra*, 40–44.
5. Blackaby, *Cleopatra*, 40.
6. Ibid., 30.
7. Ibid., 42–43.
8. Ibid., 46.
9. Ibid., 58–59.

10. Ibid., 113–115.

GRACE O'MALLEY

1. Barbara Sjoholm, *The Pirate Queen: In Search of Grace O'Malley and Other Legendary Women of the Sea* (Berkeley, CA: Seal Press, 2004), 4.
2. Ibid., xxiii.
3. Emily Arnold McCully, *The Pirate Queen* (New York: Putnam Juvenile, 1995), 5–6.
4. Ibid., 25–26.
5. Sjoholm, *Pirate Queen*, 33.
6. McCully, *Pirate Queen*, 9.

NAYA NUKI

1. Meriwether Lewis and William Clark, *The Journals of the Lewis and Clark Expedition: July 28–November 1, 1805*, vol. 5, ed. Gary E. Moulton (Lincoln, Nebraska: University of Nebraska Press, 1988), 221.

MARY WOLLSTONECRAFT SHELLEY

1. Martin Garrett, *Mary Shelley*, The British Library Writers' Lives (New York: Oxford University Press, 2002), 13.
2. Mary Wollstonecraft Shelley, *Frankenstein*, Barnes & Nobles Classic Series (Nero York Barnes & Noble, 2005), 37.
3. Ibid., 25–26.
4. Jane Blumberg, *Mary Shelley's Early Novels* (London: MacMillan Press, 1993), 94.
5. Garrett, 23–24.
6. John Lanzendorfer, "10 Monstrous Facts about *Frankenstein*," Mental_Floss, October 5, 2015, http://mentalfloss.com/article/69171/10-monstrous-facts-about-frankenstein.
7. Ibid.
8. Ibid.
9. Robert McCrum, "The 100 Best Novels: No. 8—*Frankenstein* by Mary Shelley (1818)," *The Guardian*, November 11, 2013, https://www.theguardian.com/books/2013/nov/11/100-best-novels-frankenstein-mary-shelley.
10. Lanzendorfer, "10 Monstrous Facts."

ADA BYRON LOVELACE

1. Laurie Wallmark, *Ada Byron Lovelace and the Thinking Machine* (Berkeley, CA: Creston Books, 2015), 2.
2. Sydney Padua, *The Thrilling Adventures of Lovelace and Babbage: The (Mostly) True Story of the First Computer* (New York: Pantheon Books, 2015), 14.
3. Ibid.
4. Ibid.
5. Wallmark, *Ada Byron Lovelace*, 29.

ANNIE OAKLEY

1. Stephanie Spinner, *Who Was Annie Oakley?* (New York: Grosset & Dunlap, 2002), 8.
2. Glenda Riley, *The Life and Legacy of Annie Oakley*, The Oklahoma Western Biographies (Norman, OK: University of Oklahoma Press, 1994), 6.
3. Shirl Kasper, *Annie Oakley* (Norman, OK: University of Oklahoma Press, 1992), 5.
4. Riley, *Life and Legacy*, 134.
5. Sue Macy, *Bulls-Eye: A Photobiography of Annie Oakley* (Des Moines, IA: National Geographic Children's Books, 2001), 19.
6. Brenda Haugen, *Annie Oakley: American Sharpshooter* (Minneapolis, MN: Compass Point Books, 2007), 40.
7. Spinner, *Who Was Annie Oakley?*, 62.
8. Ibid., 74.
9. Ibid., 105.

NELLIE BLY

1. Maria Popova, "What Girls Are Good For: 20-Year-Old Nellie Bly's 1885 Response to a Patronizing Chauvinist," *Brain Pickings* (blog), April 30, 2014, https://www.brainpickings.org/2014/04/30/nellie-bly-letter/.
2. Ibid.
3. Hannah Keyser, "The Story That Launched Nellie Bly's Famed Journalism Career," Mental_Floss.com, May 5, 2015, http://mentalfloss.com/article/63759/story-launched-nellie-blys-famed-journalism-career.
4. Bonnie Christensen, *The Daring Nellie Bly: America's Star Reporter* (New York: Alfred A. Knopf, 2003), 9.
5. Deborah Noyes, *Ten Days a Madwoman: The Daring Life and Turbulent Times of the Original "Girl" Reporter, Nellie Bly* (New York: Viking, 2016), 28.
6. Sylvia Branzei, *Rebel in a Dress: Adventurers* (Philadelphia: Running Press Kids, 2011), 69.
7. Christensen, *Daring Nellie Bly*, 17.
8. Noyes, *Ten Days*, 74.
9. Christensen, *Daring Nellie Bly*, 25.
10. Ibid., 26.
11. Noyes, *Ten Days*, 112.
12. Christensen, *Daring Nellie Bly*, 27.
13. Tekla Szymanski, "Women's History Month Profile: Nellie Bly—Undercover, Out and About," New York Women in Communications, March 25, 2010, http://www.nywici.org/features/blogs/aloud/womens-history-month-profile-nellie-bly---undercover-out-and-about.

ELEANOR ROOSEVELT

1. Russell Freedman, *Eleanor Roosevelt: Life of Discovery* (New York: Clarion Books, 1993), 23.
2. Ibid., 34.
3. Ibid., 63.

4. US House of Representatives, *Life and Ideals of Anna Eleanor Roosevelt* (Honolulu, HI: University Press of the Pacific, 2001), 30.
5. Allida Black et al., eds., "'My Day' Column (1935–1962)," Model Editions Partnership, 2006, https://www2.gwu.edu/~erpapers/mep/displaydoc.cfm?docid=erpo-myday.
6. Rachel Toor, *Eleanor Roosevelt: Diplomat and Humanitarian* (New York: Chelsea House Publishers, 1989), 65.
7. Doris Kearns Goodwin, *No Ordinary Time: Franklin and Eleanor Roosevelt, The Home Front in World War II* (New York: Simon & Schuster, 1994), 465.
8. Marc Peyser, *Hissing Cousins: The Lifelong Rivalry of Eleanor Roosevelt and Alice Roosevelt Longworth* (New York: Anchor Books, 2015), 275.

DORA THEWLIS

1. Julie McCaffrey, "The Baby Suffragette," *Daily Mirror*, last modified February 4, 2012, http://www.mirror.co.uk/news/uk-news/the-baby-suffragette-628607.
2. Ibid.
3. Karen Krizanovih, "Suffragette Timeline: The Long March to Votes for Women," *Telegraph*, 2015, http://www.telegraph.co.uk/film/suffragette/suffragette_timeline/.
4. "Woman Suffrage Timeline (1840–1920)," National Women's History Museum, accessed January 27, 2017, https://www.nwhm.org/education-resources/history/woman-suffrage-timeline.
5. Emmeline Pankhurst, *My Own Story: The Autobiography of Emmeline Parkhurst*, (London: Virago Limited, 1979), 38.
6. Ian Herbert, "Dora Thewlis: The Lost Suffragette," *Independent*, May 7, 2006, http://www.independent.co.uk/news/uk/politics/dora-thewlis-the-lost-suffragette-6101564.html.
7. McCaffrey, "Baby Suffragette."
8. Ibid.
9. Herbert, "Dora Thewlis."
10. McCaffrey, "Baby Suffragette."

JOSEPHINE BAKER

1. Peggy Caravantes, *The Many Faces of Josephine Baker: Dancer, Singer, Activist, Spy*, Women of Action (Chicago: Chicago Review Press, 2015), 4.
2. Patricia Hruby Powell, *Josephine: The Dazzling Life of Josephine Baker*, (San Francisco: Chronicle Books, 2014), 16.
3. Powell, *Josephine*, 29.
4. Caravantes, *Many Faces*, 9.
5. Powell, *Josephine*, 45.
6. Ibid., 58.
7. Ibid., 79.
8. Ibid., 68; Caravantes, *Many Faces*, 36.
9. Powell, *Josephine*, 96.
10. Caravantes, *Many Faces*, 80.

11. Jessica Goldstein, "March on Washington Had One Female Speaker: Josephine Baker," *Washington Post*, August 23, 2011, https://www.washingtonpost.com/lifestyle/style /march-on-washington-had-one-female-speaker-josephine-baker/2011/08/08/gIQA HqhBaJ_story.html.

GRACE MURRAY HOPPER

1. Andi Diehn, *Technology: Cool Women Who Code* (New York: Scholastic Press, 1998), 29.
2. Ibid., 23.
3. Rachel Swaby, *Headstrong: 52 Women Who Changed Science—and the World* (New York: Broadway Books, 2015), 203.
4. Ibid., 204.
5. Ibid.
6. Ibid.
7. Diehn, *Technology*, 45.
8. Kathleen Broome Williams, *Grace Hopper: Admiral of the Cyber Sea* (Annapolis, MD: Naval Institute Press, 2004), 175.
9. Swaby, *Headstrong*, 203.
10. Diehn, *Technology*, 46–47.
11. Mark Cantrell, "Amazing Grace: Rear Adm. Grace Hopper, USN, Was a Pioneer in Computer Science," *Military Officer* 12, no. 3 (March 2014): 52–55, 106.
12. Diehn, *Technology*, 39.

MARY LOU WILLIAMS

1. Linda Dahl, *Morning Glory: A Biography of Mary Lou Williams* (Berkeley, CA: University of California Press, 1999), 38.
2. Ibid., 17.
3. Ibid., 18.
4. Ibid., 23.
5. Ibid., 9.
6. Ibid., 26.
7. Ibid., 29.
8. Ibid., 44.
9. Max Jones, *Jazz Talking: Profiles, Interviews, and Other Riffs on Jazz Musicians* (Cambridge, MA: Da Capo Press, 2000), 201.
10. Dahl, *Morning Glory*, 32.
11. Ibid., 379.

BEVERLY CLEARY

1. Beverly Cleary, *A Girl from Yamhill: A Memoir* (New York: Morrow Junior Books, 1988), 105.
2. Ibid., 23.
3. Ibid., 71.

4. Mark Mancini, "12 Charming Tidbits about Beverly Cleary," Mental_Floss.com, April 12, 2016, http://mentalfloss.com/article/56708/12-charming-tidbits-about-beverly-cleary.

5. Cleary, *Girl from Yamhill*, 78.

6. Ibid., 76.

7. Melissa Jaeger-Miller, "Beverly Cleary Is Turning 100, but She Has Always Thought Like a Kid," as heard on *All Things Considered*, NPR, April 11, 2016, http://www.npr.org/2016/04/11/473558659/beverly-cleary-is-turning-100-but-she-has-always-thought-like-a-kid.

8. Cleary, *Girl from Yamhill*, 93.

9. Nora Krug, "Beverly Cleary on Turning 100: Kids Today 'Don't Have the Freedom' I Had," *Washington Post*, April 3, 2016, https://www.washingtonpost.com/entertainment/books/beverly-cleary-on-turning-100-kids-today-dont-have-the-freedom-i-had/2016/04/02/7a63e92c-e6d4-11e5-b0fd-073d5930a7b7_story.html.

10. Beverly Cleary, *My Own Two Feet: A Memoir* (New York: Avon Books, 1995), 320.

11. Ibid., 270.

12. Ibid., 321.

13. Ibid., 325.

14. Jaeger-Miller, "Beverly Cleary Is Turning."

RUTH BADER GINSBURG

1. "A Conversation with Justice Ruth Bader Ginsburg: Her Life as a Woman, a Jew, and a Judge," by Larry Josephson, *Only in America*, MP3 audio file, 15:10, September 2, 2004, http://www.onlyinamerica.cc/ginsburg.shtml.

2. James Roland, *Ruth Bader Ginsburg: Iconic Supreme Court Justice* (Minneapolis: Lerner Publications, 2016), 10.

3. Emma Hahn, *16 Extraordinary American Women* (Portland, ME: J. Weston Walch, 1996), 55.

4. Irin Carmon, "Ruth Bader Ginsburg on Marriage, Sexism and Pushups," MSNBC, February 17, 2015, http://www.msnbc.com/msnbc/ruth-bader-ginsburg-marriage-sexism-and-pushups.

5. Michelle Ruiz, "15 Things I Learned about Ruth Bader Ginsburg from *Notorious RBG*," *Vogue*, October 29, 2015, http://www.vogue.com/13366116/ruth-bader-ginsburg-notorious-rbg-book/.

6. Hahn, *16 Extraordinary*, 56.

7. "Conversation with Justice Ruth," 2:18.

8. Ibid., 4:07.

9. Roland, *Ruth Bader Ginsburg*, 19.

10. Ibid., 23.

11. Ibid., 26.

12. Ibid., 27–28.

13. Ibid., 37.

JULIE ANDREWS

1. Julie Andrews, *Home: A Memoir of My Early Years* (New York: Hyperion, 2008), 80. I imagined this scene after reading Julie's account of it in her excellent autobiography. It's definitely worth a read.
2. Ibid., 80.
3. Telisa Carter, "10 Things You Didn't Know about Julie Andrews," Fame10, September 30, 2016, www.fame10.com/entertainment/10-things-you-didnt-know-about-julie -andrews/.
4. Richard Stirling, *Julie Andrews: An Intimate Biography* (New York: St. Martins Press, 2009), 22.
5. Andrews, *Home*, 54.
6. Ibid., 85.
7. Irving Haberman, "The Theatre World Brings a New Musical and a Stage Success to Television This Week," *New York Times*, March 31, 1957.
8. Andrews, *Home*, 85.

WANGARI MAATHAI

1. Wangari Maathai, *Unbowed: A Memoir* (New York: Alfred A. Knopf, 2006), 46.
2. Franck Prévot, *Wangari Maathai: The Woman Who Planted Millions of Trees*, trans. Dominique Clément (Watertown, MA: Charlesbridge Publishing, 2015), 11.
3. Maathai, *Unbowed*, 39.
4. Ibid., 74.
5. Prévot, *Wangari Maathai*, 37.
6. Maathai, *Unbowed*, 125.
7. Prévot, *Wangari Maathai*, 42.
8. The Green Belt Movement home page, accessed January 27, 2017, http://www.green beltmovement.org.

ARETHA FRANKLIN

1. Tony Scherman, "The Man with the Million-Dollar Voice: The Mighty but Divided Soul of C. L. Franklin," *Believer*, July/August 2013, http://www.believermag.com/issues /201307/?read=article_scherman.
2. Silvia Anne Sheafer, *Aretha Franklin: Motown Superstar*, African-American Biographies (New York: Enslow Publishers, 1996), 21.
3. Gary Graff, "The Queen of Soul," *Orlando Sentinel*, October 5, 1992, accessed October 6, 2016, http://articles.orlandosentinel.com/1992-10-05/lifestyle/9210050403_1_queen -of-soul-aretha-soul-music.
4. David Ritz, *Respect: The Life of Aretha Franklin* (New York: Little, Brown and Company, 2014), 86.
5. Ibid., 48–63.
6. Joel Whitburn, *Top R&B/Hip-Hop Singles: 1942–2004* (Menomonee Falls, WI: Record Research, 2005), 215.
7. Ritz, *Respect*, 159.

8. *The 500 Greatest Albums of All Time*, ed. Joe Levy and editors at *Rolling Stone* (New York: Wenner, 2005), 83–178.

9. Gary Graff, "Aretha Franklin on Celebrating Six Decades as the Queen of Soul: 'Our Generation—The Artists Were Stronger,'" *Billboard*, March 25, 2016, http://www .billboard.com/articles/news/magazine-feature/7285247/aretha-franklin-celebrating -six-decades-as-the-queen-of-soul.

10. "That's Dr. Aretha Franklin to You," *Call and Post*, November 2, 2011, https://web .archive.org/web/20130521170445/http://www.callandpost.com/index.php/entertain ment/music/1329-thats-dr-aretha-franklin-to-you.

11. "100 Greatest Artists," *Rolling Stone*, December 2, 2010, http://www.rollingstone.com /music/lists/100-greatest-artists-of-all-time-19691231/aretha-franklin-20110420; "100 Greatest Singers of All Time," *Rolling Stone*, December 2, 2010, http://www.rollingstone .com/music/lists/100-greatest-singers-of-all-time-19691231?page=9.

HILLARY RODHAM CLINTON

1. Hillary Rodham Clinton, "Remarks at an Event Celebrating Amelia Earhart and the United States' Ties to Our Pacific Neighbors," (Benjamin Franklin State Dining Room, US Department of State, Washington, DC, March 20, 2012), https://votesmart.org /public-statement/677842/remarks-at-an-event-celebrating-amelia-earhart-and-the -united-states-ties-to-our-pacific-neighbors#.WPfNBRiZPLF.

2. Cynthia Levinson, *Hillary Rodham Clinton: Do All the Good You Can* (New York: HarperCollins, 2016), 10.

3. Dan Merica, "From Park Ridge to Washington: The Youth Minister who Mentored Hillary Clinton," CNN, April 25, 2014, http://www.cnn.com/2014/04/25/politics /clinton-methodist-minister/.

4. Levinson, *Hillary Rodham Clinton*, 16.

5. Merica, "From Park Ridge."

6. Carl Bernstein, *A Woman in Charge: The Life of Hillary Rodham Clinton* (New York: Alfred E. Knopf, 2007), 30.

7. Gail Sheehy, *Hillary's Choice* (New York: Random House, 1999), 26.

8. Hillary Clinton, "Hillary D. Rodham's 1969 Student Commencement Speech" (Wellesley College, Wellesley, MA, May 31, 1969), Wellesley College, http://www.wellesley.edu /events/commencement/archives/1969commencement/studentspeech.

9. Hillary Rodham Clinton, *Living History* (New York: Simon & Schuster, 2003), 69.

10. Bernstein, *Woman in Charge*, 130.

11. Jonah Winter and Raul Colón, *Hillary* (New York: Schwartz & Wade Books, 2016), 16.

12. Abigail Cutler, "Candidate Hillary," *Atlantic*, November 2006, http://www.theatlantic .com/magazine/archive/2006/11/candidate-hillary/305326/.

13. Joshua Green, "Take Two: Hillary's Choice," *Atlantic*, November 2006, http://www .theatlantic.com/magazine/archive/2006/11/take-two-hillarys-choice/305292/.

14. Winter and Colón, *Hillary*, 30.

15. Gayle Tzemach Lemmon, "The Hillary Doctrine," *Newsweek*, March 6, 2011, http:// www.newsweek.com/hillary-doctrine-66105.

16. CNN Politics, "2016 Election Results," CNN, accessed January 27, 2017, http://www
.cnn.com/election/results.

SHEILA SRI PRAKASH

1. "Ms. Sheila Sri Prakash-Architect and Urban Designer-Chennai-India - Speaker, IWC
2014," YouTube video, 6:05, February 2014, held at the Art of Living International
Center, Bangalore, India, posted by "artoflivingiwc," March 13, 2014, https://youtu.be
/WskgTcaty_Y. I expanded this scene from a description given by Prakash in this excellent
speech she gave to the 2014 International Women's Conference.
2. Ibid., 2:56.
3. Ibid., 3:56.
4. "Sheila Sri Prakash, Shilpa Architects, India," 361° Design Conference, presented by
Jasubhai Media Pvt. Ltd., accessed October 8, 2016, http://www.361degrees.net.in
/sheila_sri_prakash_2015.html.
5. Devyani Jayakar, "Sheila Sri Prakash and Responsible Architecture," *Inside Outside
Magazine* (January 2014): 50–53.

ARLEN SIU BERMÚDEZ

1. Selucha, "Grupo Pancasán - Maria Rural," *Patria es humanidad* (blog), March 8, 2012,
http://selucha.tumblr.com/post/18972540794/panca-mariarural.
2. Carlos Agaton, "Arlen Siu Bermúdez," *Agaton* (blog), February 8, 2014, http://carlos
agaton.blogspot.com/2014/02/arlen-siu-bermudez.html.
3. "Nicaragua: The Somoza Era, 1936–74," Country-Data.com, December 1993, http://www
.country-data.com/cgi-bin/query/r-9212.html; "1972: Earthquake Wreaks Devastation in
Nicaragua," On This Day: 1950–2005, BBC News, accessed September 15, 2016, http://
news.bbc.co.uk/onthisday/hi/dates/stories/december/23/newsid_2540000/2540045.stm.
4. Hortensia Hernandez, "Arlen Siu Bermúdez," *Heroinas* (blog), August 14, 2016, http://
www.heroinas.net/2016/08/arlen-siu-bermudez.html.
5. Héctor Perla Jr., "Sandinistas," Encyclopedia.com, accessed January 27, 2017, http://www
.encyclopedia.com/history/latin-america-and-caribbean/nicaragua-history/sandinistas.

BJÖRK

1. Ian Gittins, Bjö*rk: There's More to Life Than This* (New York: Thunder's Mouth Press,
2002), 11–13. This scene is inspired by the account in Ian Gittins's fascinating Björk
discography. It is both an in-depth biography and a fascinating description and history
of each song she recorded.
2. Ibid., 6.
3. Ibid., 11.
4. Ibid., 10.
5. David Fricke, "The Sugarcubes: The Coolest Band in the World," *Rolling Stone*,
July 14, 1988, http://www.rollingstone.com/music/features/the-coolest-band-in-the
-world-19880714.
6. Ibid.
7. Gittins, *Björk*, 35.

8. "Björk Bio," *Rolling Stone*, accessed October 8, 2016, http://www.rollingstone.com /music/artists/bjork/biography.
9. "Artists/Björk," *Billboard*, accessed January 27, 2017, http://www.billboard.com /artist/286810/bj-rk/chart; David Robert, *Guinness Book of British Hit Singles and Albums*, 17th ed. (London: Guinness World Records, Ltd., 2004), 60.
10. Bernadette McNulty, "Björk at Manchester International Festival, Review," *Telegraph*, July 1, 2011, http://www.telegraph.co.uk/culture/music/rockandpopreviews/8611370 /Bjork-at-Manchester-International-Festival-review.html.
11. Linda Sharkey, "Björk's Infamous Swan Dress Now Honoured at Moma Museum— Almost 15 Years Later," *Independent*, March 16, 2015, http://www.independent.co.uk /life-style/fashion/features/bjork-s-infamous-swan-dress-is-now-honoured-at-moma -museum-almost-15-years-later-10110915.html.
12. Thomas Bartlett, "All Hail the Ice Queen," *Salon*, September 6, 2003, http://www .salon.com/2003/09/06/Bjork_2/.

SELENA

1. Chris Perez, *To Selena, With Love* (New York: Penguin Group, 2012), 227–228.
2. Bill Hewitt, "Before Her Time," *People*, April 17, 1995, http://people.com/archive /cover-story-before-her-time-vol-43-no-15/.
3. Ibid.
4. Jill C. Wheeler, *Selena: The Queen of Tejano* (Edina, MN: Abdo & Daughters, 1996), 4.
5. Ibid., 13.
6. Jessiac Lucia Roiz, "'Selena Live!' Celebrates 23 Years; Watch Throwback Speech of 'Queen of Tejano' Winning Grammy," *Latin Times*, May 5, 2016, http://www.latintimes .com/selena-live-celebrates-23-years-watch-throwback-speech-queen-tejano-winning -grammy-383866.
7. "Past Tejano Music Awards Winners," Tejano Music Awards, accessed November 15, 2016, http://www.tejanomusicawards.com/past-award-winners.
8. Roiz, "Selena Live!"
9. Katherine Seligman, "Latin Pop Singer's Slaying Stuns Fans," *San Francisco Chronicle*, April 1, 1995, http://www.sfgate.com/news/article/Latin-pop-singer-s-slaying-stuns -fans-3148358.php.
10. María Celeste Arrarás, *Selena's Secret: The Revealing Story Behind Her Tragic Death* (New York: Simon & Schuster, 1997), 51.
11. Seligman, "Latin Pop Singer's Slaying."
12. Wheeler, *Selena*, 17.

FAWZIA KOOFI

1. Fawzia Koofi, *The Favored Daughter: One Woman's Fight to Lead Afghanistan into the Future* (New York: St. Martin's Press, 2012), 12–13. Although this isn't a direct quote from Fawzia's mother, I wrote the scene based on Fawzia's description in her autobiography, as described to her by her mother.
2. Ibid., 43.

3. Ashley Fantz, "In Afghanistan, a Mother Bravely Campaigns for President," CNN, June 19, 2012, http://www.cnn.com/2012/06/17/world/fawzia-koofi-afghanistan-president/.

4. Koofi, *The Favored Daughter*, 51.

5. Ibid., 41.

6. Fantz, "In Afghanistan, a Mother."

8. Koofi, *The Favored Daughter*, vi.

7. "Women and Girls in Afghanistan," Razia's Ray of Hope Foundation, accessed November 16, 2016, https://raziasrayofhope.org/women-and-girls-in-afghanistan.html.

9. "A Historical Timeline of Afghanistan," PBS NewsHour, May 4, 2011, http://www .pbs.org/newshour/updates/asia-jan-june11-timeline-afghanistan/.

MINDY KALING

1. Mindy Kaling, *Is Everyone Hanging Out without Me? (And Other Concerns)* (New York: Crown Archetype, 2011), 38. This is another scene where Mindy didn't give me the exact dialogue she and Mavis had during this encounter, except her mom's. I had to imagine it based on the description in her excellent, hysterical memoir.

2. Ibid., 20.

3. Ibid., 31.

4. Ibid., 89.

5. Ibid., 87.

6. Lesley McKenzie, "What Mindy Kaling Wishes She'd Known as a Teenager," *Teen Vogue*, February 10, 2014, http://www.teenvogue.com/story/mindy-kaling-advice-for-teen-girls.

7. Jada Yuan, "The New New Girl: Mindy Kaling Promotes Herself out of *The Office* and into *The Mindy Project*," Vulture, September 9, 2012, http://www.vulture.com/2012/09 /mindy-kaling-mindy-project.html.

JHAMAK GHIMIRE

1. Jhamak Ghimire, *A Flower in the Midst of Thorns*, ed. Govinda Raj Bhattarai, trans. Nagendra Sharma (Del Valle, TX: Hasta Gautam "Mridul," 2012), 8.

2. Ibid., 3.

3. Ibid., 17.

4. Ibid., 22.

5. Ibid., 107.

6. Ibid., 110.

7. Ibid., 108.

8. Ibid., xxxvii.

VENUS AND SERENA WILLIAMS

1. Diane Bailey, *Venus and Serena Williams: Tennis Champions*, Sports Families (New York: The Rosen Publishing Group, 2010), 7–9. Venus and Serena's dad really did get beat up by the gangs, he really did pay them for protection while they played, and he really did yell "Duck!" whenever there was shooting. I found those details in many different accounts, including Diane Bailey's book.

2. "'We'd Skin You Alive': Venus Williams Ends Fifteen-Yr Boycott of 'Racist' Indian Wells," RT, March 3, 2016, www.rt.com/usa/334442-venus-williams-racism-boycott/.

3. Bailey, *Venus and Serena Williams*, 29.

4. Marcin Bryszak, "Sabine Lisicki Sets Record for Fastest Serve in Women's Tennis—but Loses," *Guardian*, July 30, 2014, https://www.theguardian.com/sport/2014/jul/30/sabine-lisicki-record-fastest-serve-women-tennis-stanford.

5. Bailey, *Venus and Serena Williams*, 21.

6. Kurt Badenhausen, "Serena Williams Tops Sharapova as the World's Highest-Paid Female Athlete," *Forbes*, June 6, 2016, http://www.forbes.com/sites/kurtbadenhausen/2016/06/06/serena-tops-sharapova-as-the-worlds-highest-paid-female-athlete/#1b9055764f79.

7. "Most Tennis Grand Slam Titles Winners (Men and Women)," totalSPORTEK, July 9, 2016, http://www.totalsportek.com/tennis/grand-slam-titles-winners-mens-women/.

8. Harvey Araton, "Williams Sisters Leave an Impact That's Unmatched," *New York Times*, August 27, 2015, http://www.nytimes.com/2015/08/31/sports/tennis/venus-and-serena-williams-have-a-lasting-impact.html?_r=0.

9. Charlotte Hall, "Tennis Making Strides toward Promoting Diversity on Professional Tours," *Red & Black*, April 24, 2014, www.redandblack.com/sports/column-tennis-making-strides-toward-promoting-diversity-on-professional-tours/article_6fb4816c-ea9a-11e4-8b91-f353e6b2d37a.html.

BEYONCÉ

1. "Star Search - Girl's Tyme with Beyonce," YouTube video, 0:04, 1993, posted by "ntim-8stranger," January 1, 2010, https://youtu.be/gWXPl18psZA. Check out twelve-year-old Beyoncé belting it out in this amazing *Star Search* performance.

2. Mary Colson, *Beyoncé: A Life in Music*, Culture in Action (Chicago, IL: Raintree, 2011), 7; Rachel McRady, "Beyonce Shows Childhood Footage Losing *Star Search* in 'Flawless' Music Video," *US Weekly*, December 18, 2013, http://www.usmagazine.com/entertainment/news/beyonce-childhood-footage-losing-star-search-flawless-music-video-20131812. I created this scene after reading several accounts of the contest, including Beyoncé's own memory of it, and after watching the YouTube video cited above.

3. "Greatest Trios of All Time: Destiny's Child," *Billboard*, accessed October 27, 2016, https://web.archive.org/web/20080430084937/http://www.billboard.com/bbcom/greatesttrios/2006/destinys_child.jsp.

4. Zack O'Malley Greenburg, "Beyonce's Net Worth: $265 Million in 2016," *Forbes*, June 1, 2016, www.forbes.com/sites/zackomalleygreenburg/2016/06/01/beyonces-net-worth-265-million-in-2016/#3c0fa199689d.

5. Suzanne Hodges and Lorraine Bracco, "New Again: Destiny's Child," *Interview*, January 30, 2013, http://www.interviewmagazine.com/music/new-again-destinys-child/#_.

6. "Beyoncé Is Sasha Fierce," Oprah.com, accessed October 27, 2016, http://www.oprah.com/oprahshow/beyonces-alter-ego.

DANICA PATRICK

1. Karen Sirvaitis, *Danica Patrick: Racing's Trailblazer*, USA Today Lifeline Biographies (Minneapolis, MN: Twenty-First Century Books, 2010), 12.
2. M. B. Roberts, "Danica Patrick: From Go-Kart Racer to NASCAR Contender," *American Profile Weekly*, February 8, 2014, http://americanprofile.com/articles/danica-patrick -nascar/.
3. Sirvaitis, *Danica Patrick*, 6.
4. Ibid., 5.
5. Ibid., 6–9.
6. Ibid., 10.
7. Sirvaitis, *Danica Patrick*, 90.
8. Roberts, "Danica Patrick."
9. "Danica," the Official Website of Danica Patrick, accessed October 9, 2016, http://www .danicapatrick.com/danica.
10. Ibid.

MISTY COPELAND

1. Misty Copeland, *Life in Motion: An Unlikely Ballerina* (New York: Simon & Schuster, 2015), 32–33. This whole scene, including the inner and outer dialogue, was inspired from the actual event Misty wrote about in this excellent autobiography.
2. Ibid., 20.
3. Ibid., 21.
4. "'This Week' Sunday Spotlight: Misty Copeland," YouTube video, 1:10, posted by "ABC News," April 6, 2014, https://youtu.be/KD1SWt8-GhA.
5. Allison Adato, "Solo in the City," *Los Angeles Times*, December 5, 1999, http://articles .latimes.com/1999/dec/05/magazine/tm-40787/2.
6. "Misty Copeland—I WILL WHAT I WANT," YouTube video, 0:02, posted by "Under Armour," July 30, 2014, https://youtu.be/ZY0cdXr_1MA.
7. "Misty Under Armour Ad Goes Viral," the Official Website of Misty Copeland, accessed October 4, 2016, http://mistycopeland.com/misty-under-armour-ad-goes-viral/.
8. "Native Icon: Misty Copeland," YouTube video, 3:20, posted by "NewYorkNatives," January 30, 2015, https://youtu.be/U5hwuC7z7Ys.
9. Ibid., 2:05.

SARAH McNAIR-LANDRY

1. Anubha Momin, "Meet the Couple Who Just Spent 120 Days Traveling through the Arctic on a Dogsled," *VICE*, June 8, 2015, http://www.vice.com/read/meet-the-couple -who-just-spent-120-days-traveling-the-arctic-on-dogsled-981.
2. Correne Coetzer, "ExWeb Interview with Sarah McNair-Landry: It Was Odd to Have to Worry about Finding Water," ExplorersWeb, July 17, 2009, http://www.explorersweb .com/polar/news.php?id=18498.

3. Correne Coetzer, "Sarah McNair-Landry and Erik Boomer to Circumnavigate Baffin Island: ExWeb Interview," ExplorersWeb, January 29, 2015, http://www.explorers web.com/polar/news.php?url=circumnavigate-baffin-island_1422533388.

4. "Interview: 'Polar Adventurer Sarah McNair-Landry,'" Euronews, last modified January 7, 2014, http://www.euronews.com/2014/07/01/interview-polar-adventurer -sarah-mcnair-landry.

5. Coetzer, "ExWeb Interview with Sarah."

6. "Interview: Polar Adventurer Sarah."

7. Ibid.

NADIA NADIM

1. Wayne Coffey, "After Escaping Afghanistan following Father's Execution, Sky Blue FC Star Nadia Nadim Has Finally Found Life after Death," *NY Daily News*, April 11, 2015, http://www.nydailynews.com/sports/soccer/sky-blue-fc-star-nadia-nadim-finally-finds -life-death-article-1.2181510.

2. Ibid.

3. Howard Megdal, "Years after Fleeing the Taliban, a Player Hopes to Lift a U.S. Women's League," *New York Times*, April 8, 2015, http://www.nytimes.com/2015/04/09/sports /soccer/womens-soccer-league-star-is-happy-to-be-an-ambassador.html?_r=0.

4. Ibid.

5. Coffey, "After Escaping Afghanistan."

6. "Nadia Nadim," Timbers, accessed January 30, 2017, http://www.timbers.com/players /nadia-nadim.

7. ThornsFC.com Staff, "Blood, Sweat, and Roses: Thorns All Access—Nadia Nadim," Timbers, September 27, 2016, http://www.timbers.com/post/2016/09/27/blood-sweat -and-roses-thorns-all-access-nadia-nadim.

8. Ibid.

9. Ibid.

10. Ibid.

11. "2016 NWSL Attendance," *Soccer Stadium Digest*, accessed January 30, 2017, http:// soccerstadiumdigest.com/2016-nwsl-attendance/.

ADELE

1. Marc Shapiro, *Adele: The Biography* (New York: St. Martin's Griffin, 2012), 19.

2. Biography.com Editors, "Adele Biography," Biography.com, last modified February 13, 2017, http://www.biography.com/people/adele-20694679.

3. Shapiro, Adele, 23.

4. Ibid., 24.

5. Ibid., 31.

6. Ibid., 32.

7. Ibid., 38.

8. Ibid.

9. Ibid., 82.

10. Chuck Arnold and Tiffany McGee, "Picks and Pans Review: Adele," *People* 69, no. 24 (June 23, 2008): 19, http://www.people.com/archive/picks-and-pans-review-adele-vol -69-no-24/.

11. Sarah-Louise James, *Adele: A Celebration of an Icon and Her Music* (New York: Sterling, 2012), 157.

12. Ibid., 153.

13. Guinness World Records News, "Adele Scoops Triple World Record Success in New *Guinness World Records* 2012 Edition," Guinness World Records, September 14, 2011, http://www.guinnessworldrecords.com/news/2011/9/adele-scoops-triple-world-record -success-in-new-guinness-world-records.

14. Liz Jones, "Adele: 'I Have All the Say; I Have Power over Everything I Do,'" *Daily Mail*, February 13, 2009, http://www.dailymail.co.uk/home/you/article-1135182/Adele- I-say-I-power-I-do.html.

15. Pink, "Adele: Singer," The World's 100 Most Influential People: 2012, *Time*, April 18, 2012, http://content.time.com/time/specials/packages/article/0,28804,21119 75_2111976_2111950,00.html.

EMMA WATSON

1. Christopher Rosen, "Let's Remember the First Time Harry and Ron Met Hermione," *Entertainment Weekly*, July 23, 2015, http://www.ew.com/article/2015/07/23/emma -watson-hermione-harry-potter. This scene is based on Emma's adorable first screen test with Rupert Grint and Daniel Radcliffe! She has incredible poise for a nine-year-old. She is Hermione, entirely.

2. Dale-Marie Bryan, *Emma Watson* (Mankato, MN: The Child's World, 2013), 20.

3. Ibid., 8.

4. Rosen, "Let's Remember the First."

5. "Harry Potter," Box Office Mojo, accessed January 14, 2017, http://www.boxofficemojo .com/franchises/chart/?id=harrypotter.htm; Melissa Unger, "Top 10 Highest Grossing Movie Franchises Worldwide," Screen Rant, July 25, 2015, http://screenrant.com /top-10-highest-grossing-movie-franchises-worldwide/.

6. "Emma Watson: Reviews from Philosopher Stone Era," Emma-Watson.net, accessed October 7, 2016, http://emma-watson.net/emma/review_ps.php.

7. Ella Alexander, "All About Emma," *Vogue*, June 15, 2011, http://www.vogue.co.uk /article/emma-watson-on-style-fashion-and-james-franco.

8. Laura Woods, "Harry Potter Cast Showdown: Emma Watson Net Worth Vs. Daniel Radcliffe Net Worth and More," GOBankingRates.com, March 31, 2016, https://www .gobankingrates.com/personal-finance/harry-potter-cast-showdown-emma-watson -net-worth-vs-daniel-radcliffe-net-worth/.

9. Joanna Robinson, "Emma Watson on How Being Threatened for Speaking about Feminism Enraged and Motivated Her," *Vanity Fair*, March 8, 2015, http://www .vanityfair.com/hollywood/2015/03/emma-watson-feminism-threats-raging-heforshe.

10. Nadia Higgins, *Emma Watson: From Wizards to Wallflowers*, Pop Culture Bios (Minneapolis: Lerner Publications Company, 2014), 19.

11. Ibid., 27.

Hou Yifan

1. Peter Foster, "Hou Yifan—Talented Chess Champion Next Door," *Chess News Blog*, January 30, 2011, http://www.chessblog.com/2011/01/hou-yifan-talented-chess-champion-next.html.
2. Chess24 Staff, "Hou Yifan Takes On the Financial Markets," Chess24, August 22, 2016, https://chess24.com/en/read/news/hou-yifan-takes-on-the-financial-markets.
3. Foster, "Hou Yifan—Talented Chess Champion."
4. Ibid.
5. Ibid.
6. "Meet Yifan Hou—the Glamorous Women's World Chess Champion Who Is Changing the Face of the Notoriously Nerdy Game," *Daily Mail*, April 15, 2014, http://www.dailymail.co.uk/femail/article-2605502/Meet-Yifan-Hou-glamorous-Womens-World-Chess-Champion-changing-face-notoriously-nerdy-game.html.
7. Ibid.
8. Foster, "Hou Yifan—Talented Chess Champion."

Lizzy Clark

1. "Fame for Actress with Asperger [sic] Syndrome," BBC Shropshire, last updated November 19, 2009, http://www.bbc.co.uk/shropshire/content/articles/2008/09/16/aspergers_actress_feature.shtml.
2. Ibid.
3. Dresden Shumaker, "11 Famous People with Autism," Babble, accessed January 14, 2017, https://www.babble.com/entertainment/famous-people-with-autism-2/.
4. Amelia Hill, "Mentally Disabled Actors Are Victims of Modern 'Blacking-Up,' Says Campaigner," *Observer*, November 14, 2009, https://www.theguardian.com/society/2009/nov/15/disabled-actors-television-campaign.
5. "Fame for Actress with Asperger."
6. Chris Curtis, "BBC1/ITV1 Boosted by Xmas Dramas," *Broadcast*, December 22, 2008, http://www.broadcastnow.co.uk/news/multi-platform/news/bbc1/itv1-boosted-by-xmas-dramas/1955939.article.
7. Bernadette McNulty, "Dustbin Baby," *Telegraph*, December 19, 2008, http://www.telegraph.co.uk/culture/tvandradio/3851819/Dustbin-Baby.html.
8. Elizabeth Wagmeister, "Able-Bodied Actors Play 95% of Disabled Characters in Top 10 TV Shows, Says New Study," *Variety*, July 13, 2016, http://variety.com/2016/tv/news/disabled-actors-television-study-1201813686/.
9. Hill, "Mentally Disabled Actors."
10. Ibid.

Bethany Mota

1. Bethany Mota, "First Video :) Mac and Sephora Haul," YouTube video, 0:00–0:03, posted by Bethany Mota, June 12, 2009, https://youtu.be/h0wCoXVkjGA.
2. Ibid., 0:26–0:40.

3. Ibid,. 0:00–5:14. To get a feeling for how Bethany felt during her first-ever video, I watched it. It's amazing to see Bethany at the start of her career—to see how far she's come—but how endearing she was from the very beginning.

4. Marie Morreale, *Bethany Mota*, Real Bios (New York: Scholastic, 2016), 8.

5. Ibid., 10.

6. Ibid., 8.

7. Ibid., 9.

8. Ibid.,12.

9. Ibid., 19–20.

10. Ibid., 35.

11. Ibid.

12. Ibid., 23.

13. "Bethany Mota Meets Ellen," YouTube video, 3:00, posted by "TheEllenShow," April 7, 2015, https://youtu.be/y38QOASwSpc.

14. Clare O'Connor, "2014's Most Googled Fashion Designer: YouTube Teen Bethany Mota Beats Kate Spade, Valentino," *Forbes*, December 16, 2014, http://www.forbes.com/sites /clareoconnor/2014/12/16/2014s-most-googled-fashion-designer-youtube-teen-bethany -mota-beats-kate-spade-valentino/#c0993b.

15. Morreale, *Bethany Mota*, 27.

Tavi Gevinson

1. Lizzie Widdicombe, "Tavi Says: Fashion Dictates from a Fourteen-Year-Old," *New Yorker*, September 20, 2010, http://www.newyorker.com/magazine/2010/09/20/tavi-says.

2. Ibid.

3. Ibid.

4. Laura Barcella, *Fight Like a Girl: 50 Feminists Who Changed the World* (San Francisco: Zest Books, 2016), 190.

5. Nicole Dieker, "18 Things You Didn't Know about Tavi Gevinson," *SparkLife* (blog), SparkNotes, January 28, 2015, http://community.sparknotes.com/2015/01/28/18 -things-you-didnt-know-about-tavi-gevinson.

6. Tavi Gevinson, "One Zero Zero," *Style Rookie* (blog), September 24, 2008, http://www .thestylerookie.com/2008/09/one-zero-zero.html.

7. Barcella, *Fight Like a Girl*, 189.

8. Dieker, "18 Things You Didn't Know."

9. Tavi Gevinson, "Dreams," *Style Rookie* (blog), December 18, 2008, http://www .thestylerookie.com/2008/12/dreams.html.

Simone Biles

1. Tom Leonard, "Awesome Triumph: How the 4ft 8in Smiling Girl Who's Set the Olympics Alight Overcame an Appalling Childhood," *Daily Mail*, August 12, 2016, http:// www.dailymail.co.uk/news/article-3738356/Awesome-triumph-4ft-8in-smiling-girl-s -set-Olympics-alight-overcame-appalling-childhood.html. There's no written account of exactly what was said during Simone's first field trip to the gymnastics class, but

she and her parents have talked about how she copied the routine of the girls she saw practicing there. And the teacher did send home a note begging Simone's mother to sign her up for gymnastics classes, which she did. You can read about the event in many news articles, including this one.

2. Ibid.

3. Sam Escobar, "13 Fun Facts That Will Make You Love Simone Biles Even More," *Good Housekeeping*, August 11, 2016, http://www.goodhousekeeping.com/life/inspirational -stories/news/g3779/who-is-simone-biles/.

4. Ibid.

5. Leonard, "Awesome Triumph."

6. Alice Park, "Simone Biles Is Taking Her Sport to New Heights," *Time*, July 28, 2016, http://time.com/4428013/simone-biles-gymnastics-usa/.

7. Leonard, "Awesome Triumph."

8. Janice Rodden, "Having ADHD and Taking Medicine for It Is Nothing to Be Ashamed Of," *ADHD News Feed* (blog), *ADDitude*, accessed October 12, 2016, http://www .additudemag.com/adhdblogs/19/12149.html.

9. "CDC Growth Charts: United States," Centers for Disease Control and Prevention, accessed January 14, 2017, https://www.cdc.gov/growthcharts/data/set2/chart-08.pdf.

10. "Inspiring Quotes from Female Olympic Athletes," Ellevate, accessed October 12, 2016, https://www.ellevatenetwork.com/articles/7590-inspiring-quotes-from-female-olympic -athletes.

MALALA YOUSAFZAI

1. Christina Ng, "Malala Yousafzai Describes Moment She Was Shot Point-Blank by Taliban," ABC News, October 5, 2013, http://abcnews.go.com/International/malala -yousafzai-describes-moment-shot-point-blank-taliban/story?id=20459542. Malala has given many accounts of the shooting, but this one is quite gripping.

2. Heidi Dore, "Girl Who Was Shot by Taliban Says 'Going to School Is Very Precious,'" *Daily Express*, October 7, 2013, http://www.express.co.uk/news/uk/434859/Girl-who -was-shot-by-Taliban-says-going-to-school-is-very-precious.

3. Sonia van Gilder Cooke, "Pakistani Heroine: How Malala Yousafzai Emerged from Anonymity," *Time*, October 23, 2012, http://world.time.com/2012/10/23/pakistani -heroine-how-malala-yousafzai-emerged-from-anonymity/.

4. Dinah Brown, *Who Is Malala Yousafzai?* Who Was . . . ? (New York: Grosset & Dunlap, 2015), 65.

5. "Girls' Education," Malala Fund, accessed November 23, 2016, https://www.malala. org/girls-education; Ewan Watt, "10 Reasons Why Children Don't Go to School," Theirworld, November 26, 2014, http://www.theirworld.org/news/10-reasons-why -children-don-8217-t-go-to-school; Ash, "10 Nations that Don't Allow Girls to Go School," *Tour de STFU* (blog), accessed November 23, 2016, http://www.tourdestfu .com/2016/02/10-nations-that-dont-allow-girls-to-go.html.

6. "Malala Yousafzai's Speech at the Youth Takeover of the United Nations," Theirworld, accessed October 23, 2016, https://theirworld.org/explainers/malala-yousafzais-speech -at-the-youth-takeover-of-the-united-nations.

7. Alexandra Topping, "Malala Yousafzai Accepts Nobel Peace Prize with Attack on Arms Spending," *Guardian*, December 10, 2014, https://www.theguardian.com/world/2014/dec/10/malala-yousafzia-nobel-peace-prize-attack.

Bindi Irwin

1. Steve Irwin, "Trapping Crocodiles," The Crocodile Hunter, accessed September 29, 2016, http://www.crocodilehunter.com.au/crocodile_hunter/trapping.html.
2. Amy Breguet, *Steve and Bindi Irwin*, Conservation Heroes (New York: Chelsea House, 2011), 9.
3. Tammy Gagne, *Bindi Sue Irwin*, Randy's Corner: Day by Day with . . . (Hockessin, DE: Mitchell Lane Publishers, 2013), 13.
4. Dennis Passa, "Irwin Remembered for His 'Zest for Life,'" *Washington Post*, September 19, 2006, http://www.washingtonpost.com/wp-dyn/content/article/2006/09/19/AR2006091900695.html.
5. Gagne, *Bindi Sue Irwin*, 20.
6. "Bindi Tops TV Poll," *Sydney Morning Herald*, December 18, 2006, http://www.smh.com.au/news/tv--radio/bindi-tops-tv-poll/2006/12/18/1166290447686.html.
7. Breguet, *Steve and Bindi Irwin*, 75.

Amandla Stenberg

1. Jevon Phillips, "*Hunger Games*' Star on *Columbiana* and Life on the Set," *Los Angeles Times* blog, September 23, 2011, http://latimesblogs.latimes.com/movies/2011/09/hunger-games-colombiana-amandla-stenberg-connection.html.
2. Todd Brown, "Columbiana Review," *ScreenAnarchy* (blog), August 5, 2011, http://screenanarchy.com/2011/08/colombiana-review.html.
3. Karen Springen, "Hungry for More about the Hunger Games? A Q&A with Amandla Stenberg (aka Rue)," *Publishers Weekly*, January 19, 2012, http://www.publishersweekly.com/pw/by-topic/childrens/childrens-book-news/article/50236-hungry-for-more-about-the-hunger-games-a-q-a-with-amandla-stenberg-aka-rue.html.
4. "Biography," Amandla Stenberg, accessed October 27, 2016, www.amandlastenberg.com/biography.html.
5. "*The Hunger Games*," Box Office Mojo, last modified September 15, 2016, http://www.boxofficemojo.com/franchises/chart/?view=main&id=hungergames.htm&p=.htm.
6. Solange Knowles, "How Our February Cover Star Amandla Stenberg Learned to Love Her Blackness," *Teen Vogue*, January 7, 2016, http://www.teenvogue.com/story/amandla-stenberg-interview-teen-vogue-february-2016.
7. Ibid.
8. "Amandla Stenberg and Gloria Steinem Talk Feminism," YouTube video, 4:23, August 10, 2016, posted by "Teen Vogue," https://youtu.be/SnMfnKT8Rvg.
9. Lotte Jeffs, "Cover Star Amandla Stenberg Is Born to Rule," *Elle* UK, August 10, 2016, http://www.elleuk.com/life-and-culture/culture/longform/a31407/coverstar-amandla-stenberg-speaks-out-on-race-gender-and-sexuality/.

10. Caroline Ryder, "Amandla Stenberg: The New Agenda," *Dazed*, Autumn 2015, http://www.dazeddigital.com/artsandculture/article/25798/1/amandla-stenberg-the-new-agenda.

11. "The 30 Most Influential Teens of 2015," *Time*, October 27, 2015, http://time.com/4081618/most-influential-teens-2015/; "The 30 Most Influential Teens of 2016," Time magazine website, October 19, 2016, http://time.com/4532104/most-influential-teens-2016/.

12. Knowles, "How Our February."

CHLOE KIM

1. "Chloe Kim's Historic Perfect Score - U.S. Snowboarding Grand Prix 2016," 0:59, February 6, 2016, posted by "USSANetwork," https://youtu.be/BjJlFpwhERM.

2. Ibid., 1:00.

3. Ibid., 1:10.

4. Ibid., 1:23.

5. Audrey Cleo Yap, "16-Year-Old Snowboarding Champion Chloe Kim Is Just a Regular Teenager," NBC News, May 23, 2016, http://www.nbcnews.com/news/asian-america/16-year-old-snowboarding-champion-chloe-kim-just-normal-teenager-n575411.

6. "Chloe Kim," XGames, accessed August 30, 2016, http://xgames.espn.com/xgames/athletes/3088782/chloe-kim.

7. "Chloe Kim's Back to Back 1080s: U.S. Snowboarding Grand Prix 2016 Park City," *TransWorld SNOWboarding*, February 8, 2016, http://snowboarding.transworld.net/videos/chloe-kims-back-to-back-1080s-u-s-snowboarding-grand-prix-2016-park-city/#z7R6h0hGO2OJCfTb.99.

8. "Snowboarding Athletes: Chloe Kim," US Snowboarding, accessed August 30, 2016, http://ussnowboarding.com/athletes/chloe-kim.

9. Yap, "16-Year-Old Snowboarding."

JAZZ JENNINGS

1. Jazz Jennings, *Being Jazz: My Life as a (Transgender) Teen* (New York: Crown Books for Young Readers, 2016), 24–25.

2. Ibid., 1.

3. Jamie Tabberer, "15 Things You Need to Know about Trans Teen Trailblazer Jazz Jennings," GayStarNews, November 19, 2015, http://www.gaystarnews.com/article/15-things-you-need-to-know-about-trans-teen-trailblazer-jazz-jennings/#gs.L0Gz0o8.

4. James Poniewozik, "Review: An Extraordinary, Ordinary Girlhood in TLC's *I Am Jazz*," *Time*, July 15, 2015, http://time.com/3957689/review-i-am-jazz-tlc-transgender/.

5. Paul J. Weber, "What's at Stake in the Latest Legal Battle over Bathroom Rights for Transgender Students," *Los Angeles Times*, August 14, 2016, http://www.latimes.com/nation/nationnow/la-na-transgender-issues-20160813-snap-story.html.

6. Jennings, *Being Jazz*, 6.

7. Ibid., 138.

8. Weber, "What's at Stake."

9. Jennings, *Being Jazz*, 138.

10. "Transgender Youth at Risk for Depression, Suicide," Harvard School of Public Health, accessed November 23, 2016, https://www.hsph.harvard.edu/news/hsph-in-the-news /transgender-youth-at-risk-for-depression-suicide/.

11. Jennings, *Being Jazz*, 117–118.

12. Tabberer, "15 Things You Need to Know."

13. Jennings, *Being Jazz*, 122.

14. Poniewozik, "Review: An Extraordinary."

Ashima Shiraishi

1. I had to imagine this scene of Ashima's first climb, as there are no detailed accounts. But I started rock climbing when I was a young girl, like Ashima, so I drew on my own memories of early climbs and imagined what it might have been like to climb in Central Park!

2. Joanna Walters, "Reaching New Heights: Girl Ascends to Rock-Climbing Royalty—at Only 13," *Guardian*, March 22, 2015, https://www.theguardian.com/world/2015 /mar/22/rock-climbing-ashima-shiraishi-breaking-record-spain.

3. Elizabeth Weil, "Ashima's Most Daring Climb," ESPN, November 11, 2015, http:// www.espn.com/espn/feature/story/_/id/14098651/ashima-shiraishi-become-best -female-climber-world-just-14.

4. Megan Michelson, "A Conversation with Two of the Most Powerful Teens in Climbing," *Outside*, March 15, 2016, http://www.outsideonline.com/2061271/conversation-two -most-powerful-teens-climbing.

5. Ibid.

6. Mandy Oaklander, "This 15-Year-Old Girl Could Be the Best Rock Climber Ever," *Time*, June 3, 2016, http://time.com/4352618/ashima-shiraishi-next-generation-leaders/.

7. Andrew Bisharat, "14 Year Old Achieves Hardest Boulder Climb Ever Done by a Woman," *Beyond the Edge* (blog), March 22, 2016, http://adventureblog.nationalgeographic. com/2016/03/22/14-year-old-ashima-shiraishi-climbs-hardest-boulder-problem-ever -done-by-a-woman/.

8. Ibid.